EXPERIENCING TCHAIKOVSKY

The Listener's Companion
Gregg Akkerman, Series Editor

Titles in **The Listener's Companion** provide readers with a deeper understanding of key musical genres and the work of major artists and composers. Aimed at nonspecialists, each volume explains in clear and accessible language how to listen to works from particular artists, composers, and genres. Looking at both the context in which the music first appeared and has since been heard, authors explore with readers the environments in which key musical works were written and performed.

EXPERIENCING TCHAIKOVSKY

A Listener's Companion

David Schroeder

ROWMAN & LITTLEFIELD
Lanham • Boulder • New York • London

Published by Rowman & Littlefield
A wholly owned subsidiary of The Rowman & Littlefield Publishing Group,
Inc.
4501 Forbes Boulevard, Suite 200, Lanham, Maryland 20706
www.rowman.com

Unit A, Whitacre Mews, 26-34 Stannary Street, London SE11 4AB

British Library Cataloguing in Publication Information Available

Library of Congress Cataloging-in-Publication Data

Schroeder, David P., 1946–
Experiencing Tchaikovsky : a listener's companion / David Schroeder.
pages cm. – (Listener's companion)
Includes bibliographical references and index.
ISBN 978-1-4422-3299-0 (cloth : alk. paper) – ISBN 978-1-4422-3300-3 (ebook)
1. Tchaikovsky, Peter Ilich, 1840–1893–Criticism and interpretation. I. Title.
ML410.C4S37 2015
780.92–dc23
2014039082

Printed in the United States of America

CONTENTS

SERIES EDITOR'S FOREWORD

The goal of the Listener's Companion series is to give readers a deeper understanding of pivotal musical genres and the creative work of their iconic practitioners. Contributors meet this objective in a manner that does not require extensive music training or any sort of elitist shoulder-rubbing. Authors of the series are asked to situate readers in the listening environments in which the music under consideration has been or still can be heard. Within these environments, authors examine the historical context in which this music appeared, exploring compositional character and societal elements of the work. Positioned in real or imagined environments of the music's creation, performance, and reception, readers can experience a deeper enjoyment and appreciation of the work. Authors, often drawing on their own expertise as performers and scholars, are like tour guides, walking readers through major musical genres and the achievements of artists within those genres, replaying the music for them, if you will, as a *lived* listening experience.

In a moment of pompous irony, the title character of the television show *Frasier* mentions how he and his brother Niles, as uneducated youths, "thought the *1812 Overture* was great music," to which Niles dryly replies, "Were we ever that young?" Facetious as the quip is, it accurately reflects how often youthful enjoyment serves as a barometer for what society ultimately decides is "good music." More than 130 years after Tchaikovsky composed the *1812*, I gathered with a few thousand fellow Americans to watch and hear the piece performed at an outdoor concert featuring the San Diego Symphony, complete with cannon shots and fireworks. With me were two young children, eight and ten, respectively, witnessing their first live performance of classical music. Through them I experienced the wonder and power of Tchaikovsky's composition in ways that had grown clouded by years of academic bluster and musicological pontificating. For me, the *1812* is now beyond criticism. It exists in the realm of the eternal and little can be said by any contemporary to deflate its lofty position there. For all practical purposes, the work, along with the most popular symphonic music of the nineteenth century from Beethoven, Brahms, Berlioz, and Wagner, among others, has *transcended* its time of composition. And yet none of that mattered to my two companions. They brought no prejudgments or expectations. They cared not at all if the conductor imposed his own concept of tempo in the introduction or if a few of the string players deviated from the bowing patterns of the concertmaster. They held no grudge about performances from previous years, made no comparisons to orchestras in larger cities. Instead they listened, completely open to the experience of the moment, judging it entirely on what was placed in front of them. How I envied them their liberation and baggage-free interpretation.

Not surprisingly, the attention of these young music enthusiasts wavered now and then (kicking feet, poking each other), but by the bombastic finale their eyes—and imaginations—had filled with the glorious fury and spectacle. As the last note rang out, their faces became illuminated with smiles of satisfaction and delight. I already saw them in my mind's eye telling school friends the following Monday all about the concert ("With real cannons!") and in coming years recalling this performance with exuberance. They may not recall Tchaikovsky's name, but I suspect the *feeling* they received from the music will linger well into their adulthood. And all because of a musical work that the composer himself labeled "unsuitable for symphony concerts." Sometimes "good music" happens regardless of what the composer, or television characters, think.

Pyotr Ilich Tchaikovsky (1840–1893) is the best-known Russian composer of the romantic era, and his life and creative output are more than acknowledged by music enthusiasts around the world. For this reason alone, he is an ideal topic for the Listener's Companion series. Tchaikovsky was the first Russian composer to achieve a truly international impact on the world stage. He also formed a direct connection to

American art music by guesting as the conductor for the debut performance at Carnegie Hall in 1891. Besides his beloved *1812*, Tchaikovsky is responsible for some of the most varied and highly regarded works of his era, including *Romeo and Juliet*, *Swan Lake*, and *The Nutcracker* (from which the *Nutcracker Suite* is extracted).

In casting for an author to explore Tchaikovsky's work in the series, I was thrilled to learn of David Schroeder's interest. After writing *Our Schubert* for Scarecrow Press, Schroeder accepted the task of writing *Experiencing Mozart: A Listener's Companion* and delivered a manuscript that quickly became the model for the series. In addition, Schroeder's previous works on Haydn and Mozart round out a catalog of excellent writing. As series editor, I greedily looked forward to reading drafts of *Experiencing Tchaikovsky: A Listener's Companion* and am more than pleased to see the final version of this remarkable work now available to all.

Gregg Akkerman

LIST OF ABBREVIATIONS

Throughout the book I cite quotations of letters from a number of English biographies or collections of letters, and for the purposes of citation I use the following abbreviations (full entries can be found in the Selected Reading section).

B1 David Brown, *Tchaikovsky*, vol. 1

B2 Brown, *Tchaikovsky*, vol. 2

B3 Brown, *Tchaikovsky*, vol. 3

B4 Brown, *Tchaikovsky*, vol. 4

BF Catherine Drinker Bowen and Barbara von Meck, *"Beloved Friend": The Story of Tchaikowsky and Nadejda von Meck*

LD Alexander Poznansky, *Tchaikovsky's Last Days: A Documentary Study*

LL Modeste Tchaikovsky, *The Life and Letters of Peter Ilich Tchaikovsky*

SH Dmitri Shostakovich et al., *Russian Symphony: Thoughts about Tchaikovsky*

SR Victor I. Seroff, *Rachmaninoff*

TM Edward Garden and Nigel Gotteri, *"To My Best Friend": Correspondence between Tchaikovsky and Nadezhda von Meck*

WB Roland John Wiley, *Tchaikovsky's Ballets*

WT Wiley, *Tchaikovsky*

Citations are not otherwise used, but all sources of information appear in the Selected Reading section.

TIMELINE

1840 Born in Kamsko-Votkinsk, Vyatka province, on 7 May to Ilya Petrovich Tchaikovsky and Alexandra Andreyevna Tchaikovskaya. Older siblings include Zinaida (half sister from his father's first marriage) and Nikolay

1841 Birth of sister Alexandra (Sasha)

1843 Birth of brother Ippolit

1848 Family leaves Votkinsk, visits Moscow and St. Petersburg

1849 Family moves to Alapaevsk

1850 Twin brothers Modest and Anatoly born; Pyotr starts in preparatory division of the School of Jurisprudence in St. Petersburg

1852 Parents settle in St. Petersburg; Pyotr now in main division of the School of Jurisprudence

1854 His mother dies of cholera

1855 Starts piano lessons with Rudolf Kündinger

1859 Graduates from School of Jurisprudence; enters civil service in the Ministry of Justice

1861 Takes a course in music theory through the Russian Musical Society in St. Petersburg

1862 Enrolls in the newly established St. Petersburg Conservatory

1863 Leaves the Ministry of Justice; starts studying with Anton Rubinstein

1864 Composes overture *The Storm*

1865 Public performance of his Characteristic Dances; graduates from the Conservatory

1866 Settles in Moscow; begins teaching at Moscow Conservatory, founded by Nikolay Rubinstein (Anton's brother); writes First Symphony

1867 Starts opera *The Voevoda*; meets Hector Berlioz in Moscow

1868 Finishes *The Voevoda* and composes *Fatum*; affair with Désirée Artôt

1869 Composes *Romeo and Juliet* and the opera *Undine*

1870 Begins opera *The Oprichnik*

1871 Composes First String Quartet

1872 Finishes *The Oprichnik*; composes Second Symphony; spends more time as music critic

1873 Composes *The Tempest*; spends summer in Europe

1874 Composes opera *Vakula the Smith*, Second String Quartet, First Piano Concerto

1875 Piano Concerto receives first performance in Boston; composes Third Symphony and starts on *Swan Lake*; meets Camille Saint-Saëns

1876 Composes Third String Quartet, *Francesca da Rimini*, and *Variations on a Rococo Theme*; beginning of correspondence with Nadezhda von Meck

1877 Begins Fourth Symphony and *Eugene Onegin*; *Swan Lake* performed; marries Antonina Milyukova; travels in Europe to avoid her

1878 Finishes Fourth Symphony and *Eugene Onegin*; composes Violin Concerto; tries unsuccessfully to divorce Antonina

1879 Composes opera *The Maid of Orleans*, First Suite, Second Piano Concerto; travels in Europe and spends time at Kamenka

1880 Composes *Capriccio Italien*, Serenade for Strings, *1812 Overture*

1881 Nikolay Rubinstein dies

1882 Composes Piano Trio and the opera *Mazepa*

1883 Completes *Mazepa* and writes Second Suite

1884 Composes Third Suite; complains about health

1885 Revises *Vakula* as *Cherevichki*; composes *Manfred* Symphony; starts opera *The Enchantress*

1886 Health issues become worse

1887 Conducts his own *Cherevichki*; writes *Mozartiana* and *Pezzo capriccioso*; continues conducting outside of Russia

1888 Takes a home in Frolovskoe; composes Fifth Symphony and *Hamlet* Overture; given an annuity by Tsar Alexander III

1889 Composes *The Sleeping Beauty*

1890 Composes opera *The Queen of Spades*; correspondence with Nadezhda von Meck ends

1891 Tour of the United States, conducting in New York (Carnegie Hall), Baltimore, and Philadelphia; also visits Niagara Falls; begins Symphony in E flat and *Iolanta*

1892 More conducting in Russia and Europe; completes *Iolanta* and *The Nutcracker*; settles into rural home at Klin

1893 Composes Sixth Symphony; travels to England and receives honorary doctorate at Cambridge University, conducting there and in London; conducts Sixth Symphony in St. Petersburg on 16 October and dies just over a week later, on 25 October

INTRODUCTION

Few composers remain as much loved by twenty-first-century audiences as Pyotr Ilich Tchaikovsky, despite the attempts of some commentators to convince us that we should long ago have left his nineteenth-century presumed sentimentalism behind. Thankfully audiences often have more sense than critics, but just in case we remain susceptible to the naysayers, one of the main objectives of this book is to show how Tchaikovsky's musical voice can have as much genuine resonance for us as it did when he lived a century and a half ago. In fact, some of the architects of modernism in music, including Igor Stravinsky (who at times claimed music had nothing to do with feelings), Sergey Prokofiev, and Dmitri Shostakovich, had the greatest possible respect for him. Stravinsky regarded Tchaikovsky as nothing short of a hero, and the homage he paid will be described in chapter 9.

In order to write a book about a composer, in this case Tchaikovsky, I need to be able to pinpoint the reasons for my enthusiasm. The answer for me is remarkably simple: the drama in his music stirs me viscerally, I respond with delight to much of the music being so memorable, and I embrace the ways it speaks to the soul. It may surprise some that in looking back on the great musical legacy of the past, Tchaikovsky admired one composer above all others, not a recent contemporary, but one who preceded him by a full century: Mozart. Having written two books on Mozart—one in this Listener's Companion series—I can easily identify with his passion for Mozart's music. In curious ways I can relate to him on other levels as well, and one of these involves my own heritage. Tchaikovsky spent many of his happiest times on extended visits to Kamenka, with his sister Alexandra (Sasha) and her family on her husband's estate in rural Ukraine; both of my parents grew up in similar rustic settings not far from there. The Russian Revolution in 1917 changed everything for my family, and may have for Tchaikovsky, if he had lived to a ripe old age instead of dying at fifty-three. I have another vague connection with Tchaikovsky, who, just before he died in 1893, received an honorary doctorate from Cambridge University, at a ceremony celebrating the fiftieth anniversary of the Cambridge University Musical Society (CUMS); as a graduate student at Cambridge from 1974 to 1977, I sang in the CUMS choir. Had I arrived there a few years earlier, I could have been one of the student extras in the Russian film *Tchaikovsky*, which in a later scene shows the actor portraying him with King's College Chapel in the background (my college), and students wildly cheering as he enters the Senate House for the conferring of his degree.

As a composer Tchaikovsky almost always wrote in such a way that his works had personal significance for him, even when taking his subject matter from literary sources, as in operas and symphonic poems. If a work did not mean something to him he doubted it would mean anything to listeners either, although rarely does he spell that out for us. Instead, it's left to us to intuit the significance, and more often than not the nature of the music will give the hints we need. A listener's companion to his music can take pleasure in the sound itself, but more importantly it can probe where the composer may be leading us. In some ways this will be highly speculative, but in a sense he invites this kind of speculation. There are of course dangers in attempting to make direct links between the composer's life and his music, and to the extent that I do this, I try as much as possible to follow the cues he gives. This can be a little like walking a tightrope, since part of the problem lies in what we actually know about his life. Letters, for example, do not always offer a reliable source of information, and in fact only in the past couple of decades have researchers even had access to the full range of his letters, since many had been suppressed by Soviet authorities. The connections that can be established between his life and works will not necessarily be things that all listeners can relate to, and therefore we need to find association on different levels, involving emotions, ideas, or experiences that can apply more broadly—that we can share with him.

By now a number of excellent biographies of Tchaikovsky exist, although even among these significant disagreements can be found on some of the most basic aspects of his life. Two of the more contentious issues concern how he died and his homosexuality. A number of theories abound about his death: Was it suicide from drinking unpurified water that led to cholera, was he induced by outside forces to commit suicide, was it for personal reasons, or was drinking the water simply a careless mistake? Depending on which explanation one takes, the interpretations of certain works, especially his final symphony, can vary drastically.

The matter of his homosexuality can be even more contentious. For over half the time since he died, Russia was part of the Soviet Union, and while his iconic status never wavered during those decades, the Soviets completely suppressed all thought of him being a homosexual. Even today, with his letters to his brother Modest now available that leave no question of him being gay, some reluctance to acknowledge this in Russia (and elsewhere) still exists. In other parts of Europe and North America the opposite stance occasionally has been taken to the extreme, especially in the now prevalent type of analysis that seeks to reveal the meaning of works by gay composers as being distinctly gay. His homosexuality no doubt had a bearing on many of his works, but probably not in the overt ways that some have tried to show. Part of the discussion must also include how restrictive Russian society was about homosexuality during his time, and here too opinion varies tremendously. For Tchaikovsky this raises questions about whether his attempts to become integrated into heterosexual society resulted from the fear of consequences if he did not, or if he had other personal reasons unrelated to laws or social standards. This book in no way attempts to be a biography, but these issues will necessarily be touched on, hopefully in the most balanced possible way, since the exploration of many of his works cannot proceed without addressing such matters.

One of the most fascinating aspects of Tchaikovsky's biography concerns his relationship with Nadezhda von Meck, the wealthy widow of one of the builders of Russia's railway system, and in some ways she can be a cue for us in how we might respond to his music. She reacted profoundly to it, and for thirteen years carried on a vibrant correspondence with him, not only about his music but also on very personal matters; the two of them never actually met in person. This correspondence provided a spiritual lifeline to her, and he valued it deeply as well, considering her to be his best friend. She also provided the financial wherewithal that freed him from teaching at the Moscow Conservatory and allowed him to get on with the business of being a full-time composer. At her urging he sometimes explained works to her, such as the Fourth Symphony, but we would be mistaken to take such explanations as apt programmatic guides to his works. The correspondence was highly personal, not intended to be published, and things he said to her should not necessarily be construed as useful for the rest of us, since he could easily have shaped his responses to suit her in particular. Oxford University Press at one time intended to publish the full correspondence in English in three volumes, but only the first of these (1876–1878) ever came out, in a volume not readily accessible to the public. Some of the best biographies, by David Brown, Roland John Wiley, and Alexander Poznansky, cite these letters extensively, and of course they make for absolutely fascinating reading. Another one of the biographical mysteries concerns why the correspondence ended when it did, a few years before he died.

I take the position with this type of listener's companion that it's more useful to look at a few works in detail than to consider a large number superficially. I prefer to believe that promptings about certain ones will provide some basis for thinking about other similar kinds of works. I make exceptions to this approach: in the case of ballet I examine all three, with most emphasis on *Swan Lake*, which gets its own chapter. Also, I give *Eugene Onegin* a full chapter, and no space at all to some of his other operas; my selections may not be the usual ones, focusing on *Cherevichki* and *Iolanta*. In some cases I have left out entire genres, such as songs, solo piano pieces, and choral works. Some of these have had a very limited life outside of Russia, and therefore seem less appropriate for this type of book. My exclusions in no way pass judgment on quality. All the works I include are readily available on DVD or CD, or in many cases online, on YouTube or other sources. For those interested in scores, the urtext edition (the *Complete Collected Works*, published by Mazgiz in Moscow during the Soviet era) can be accessed online on IMSLP (it's easiest to search by individual works). I direct this book to interested listeners and students, and as much as possible avoid technical musical terms. When I do use these terms I explain them immediately, and fuller definitions can be found in the glossary.

When writing about a Russian composer, one inevitably must deal with the issues of spelling and Russian or English forms of names. Since the Russian language does not use the alphabet most of us are accustomed to, instead using the Cyrillic alphabet, there can be widely divergent ways of transliterating words into English. My choices may not be entirely consistent, but generally I try to use the spellings already most familiar to us, taking *The New Grove Dictionary of Music and Musicians* as a general but not exclusive guide. When words end with either "y" or "i" (or even "ii" or "ij"), I usually opt for "y." For some names I give the English instead of the Russian version, so I prefer *Eugene Onegin* over *Evgeny Onegin*. For the composer's name, though, I stay closer to the Russian Pyotr instead of Peter. As for the spelling of his surname, here are some of the available options: Čajkovskij, Chaikovskii, Tschaikovsky, Tchaikowsky, and the familiar one that I use, Tchaikovsky. As for his patronymic, the added middle name for Russians that indicates lineage through the father's side, I use the simplest English form of it: Ilich. Dates can also be confusing, since during the time in question the Russian calendar was twelve days behind the Western. All dates given in this book conform to the Western calendar.

As with the other books in this series, each chapter has a "you were there" section, which projects the listener into an actual performance situation. One of the reasons I have opted to write a second book in the series, aside from my love of the composer's music, is the enjoyment I received from setting up these performances in my book on Mozart. With a composer who lived a century and a half ago, some of the same types of setups can hold, where the performance can be either from the composer's time or something more recent. Obviously I did not attend the ones from the nineteenth century, so a certain amount of fiction comes into play as I base the description on documentation from the time. The more recent ones also indulge in some fiction as I create a cast of characters representing you the listener, who attend all of these actual performances, and I put thoughts in their heads that could very well come from novels. I can only hope that readers will enjoy these characters in the way I did in creating them.

I would like to thank my friend Natalia Pavlovskaia, a graduate, like Tchaikovsky, of the St. Petersburg (Leningrad when she attended) Conservatory and an outstanding pianist, for her insights about the Conservatory and especially about studying there during the Soviet era. I also thank my wife, Linda, a much finer musician than myself, for reading and critiquing the manuscript; as with all my books, I dedicate this one to her.

SYMPHONIC POEMS, SHAKESPEARE, AND MUSIC WITH MEANING

During the middle of the nineteenth century virtually no Russian could seriously consider a career as a professional composer. The one person who did succeed, Mikhail Glinka (1804–1857), did so against all odds. As a career option the possibility existed in central or southern Europe, especially in Italy and Germany, and some composers from Europe, such as Giovanni Paisiello and John Field, spent parts of their careers as court composers in Russia's highly sophisticated capital, St. Petersburg. Any Russian wishing to have an advanced education in music had to leave the country to get it, as Glinka did, and not until 1859 did Russia have a school of music, when Anton Rubinstein (who studied in Germany) established the Russian Musical Society in St. Petersburg, with classes in music under the auspices of this performance society. European musical influences predominated in Russia, because of both visitors and the education received by Russians abroad, despite the rich folk music traditions at home. Some objected to this cultural westernization of Russia, most notably the so-called Mighty Five (Cui, Borodin, Balakirev, Musorgsky, and Rimsky-Korsakov), who preached the virtues of avoiding the trappings of traditional European music and replacing this with an appreciation of Russian folk music. Each had great musical talent, but with the necessity of other professions to make ends meet (Borodin, for example, had a career as a professor of chemistry), they had to treat music as an extra-professional passion. Aside from the practicality of composition not existing as a possible career, musicians garnered little respect, and it could be embarrassing to admit to being one.

Pyotr Ilich Tchaikovsky showed precociousness in music as a child, but even his artistically inclined mother, by far the greatest influence on him until she died during his fourteenth year, could not imagine her sensitive son taking music too seriously. His family enrolled the twelve-year-old Pyotr, born in 1840, in the School of Jurisprudence in St. Petersburg, and there he stayed until he graduated in 1859, taking a position in the Ministry of Justice as a civil servant following that. He worked hard, but his heart was not in it, and his love of music led him to the classes offered by the Musical Society, where he took a course in music theory in 1861. A year later he entered the newly founded St. Petersburg Conservatory, and finally in 1863 he abandoned active service in the Ministry of Justice. He now did what he loved, but as a twenty-three-year-old man, his professional prospects looked fairly bleak, since the career he aspired to did not exist at home. Fluent in French and competent in German, Italian, and English, he could have contemplated moving abroad, but as much as he loved to travel, he could not imagine living somewhere other than Russia.

He distinguished himself as a student at the Conservatory, especially in theory and composition, and also achieved a high although not virtuoso level as a pianist, graduating in 1865. Fortunately Anton Rubinstein's brother, Nikolay, started a conservatory in Moscow in 1866, and with a recommendation from Anton, he offered Tchaikovsky a position at the new school teaching theory and composition. The two Rubinstein brothers, in fact two of the finest pianists in all of Europe and formidable composers as well, dominated the musical scene in Russia's two leading cities, and with egos to match their talent, they could be very difficult as mentors or bosses. Tchaikovsky took a room in Nikolay's house, and thus began the roller-coaster ride of admiring Nikolay's great talent but at the same time trying to survive the often deprecatory treatment his employer dished out. During his time as a student and now as a professor with an exceptionally heavy teaching load, Tchaikovsky's desire to succeed as a composer mostly had to be put on hold during the teaching terms and saved for summer vacations. His earliest efforts showed promise, but in his mid-twenties he did not emerge as a rising star. He no doubt found a certain amount of consolation in the good life with his male friends his own age.

His early compositions revealed the range in both vocal and instrumental music necessary for a composer at this time (unless he happened to be Verdi or Wagner), but gradually a trend emerged that would define his career in a distinctive way, and would carry through until he died in 1893. This happened in both vocal and instrumental writing, but success came first on the instrumental side. He had no interest in writing music purely for its own sake, but as a person with a complex and deep-rooted sense of the power of emotions, he determined that his music had to be meaningful both to himself and anyone listening to it, and needed to achieve this with an accessible intelligibility. As well as exploring the emotions it would also be dramatic, and he could clearly see the need for this within himself. Not least of all because of his homosexuality he saw himself to a certain extent in conflict with the world around him, although possibly not as much as some biographers would have us believe. In many respects his music became not only a means of survival through escape, but more importantly a way of coming to terms with conflict, perhaps finding resolution, and if not that, then at least of seeing the issues and finding ways of coping. He was exceptionally well read, in both Russian literature and that of other countries, and in great literary works he could see others trying to come to terms with conflict, struggling as profoundly as he felt he was to tame his own demons. Here a common bond existed between himself and his favorite authors, not necessarily on the specific issues, but more in the efforts to address them.

Embracing literature could very well be an artistic as well as personal means to an end, and in fact the two could easily merge. The two best ways of getting there with music involved opera or song, where texts could actually be set to music, or by writing programmatic instrumental music, where the music could represent the essence of the conflict in literary works. Opera had the potential to be more dramatic than song, but had the disadvantage of being on a very large scale; it took a huge amount of time to write a single opera, which may or may not succeed. Young composers seldom achieved great things with early operas, but one could not hope to reach a high standard without experience. Despite the obstacles, he plunged into his first opera, *Voevoda*, in 1867, and despite it being a relative failure, the act of writing it gave him much-needed experience. In the case of opera it would take him the better part of a decade to profit fully from the experience, but he never doubted he could do something with it, both to satisfy his own needs and to produce works worthy of the medium.

Programmatic music had been a mainstay of the nineteenth century, at least since Beethoven's Sixth Symphony, *The Pastoral*, but actually long before that, as numerous eighteenth-century composers also embraced it. Many had followed suit, including Hector Berlioz, Felix Mendelssohn, Robert Schumann, Franz Liszt, and Camille Saint-Saëns, among the most outstanding, either devising their own programmes, which could be highly personal, or using notable literary works, by the likes of Shakespeare, Byron, and Goethe. During 1867 Berlioz visited Moscow, where Tchaikovsky met him, but for the inclination to launch into this area himself, Tchaikovsky did not need to meet one of the foremost practitioners of this type of composition. A year later he wrote his own distinctly programmatic work, the symphonic poem *Fatum* (Fate), and while it may not have been a complete success, he discovered something that could work admirably well for him. In this case he could write a work of a distinctly personal nature, its drama in all likelihood relating to his own life, and present it as a work that could be moving for all listeners.

If *Fatum* had a programme, Tchaikovsky carefully concealed it, suggesting it may very well have been autobiographical, as his friend and colleague at the Moscow Conservatory Nikolay Kashkin suspected. During the time that he wrote this work, between September and December of 1868, his relationship with the Belgian singer Désirée Artôt had grown to the point that he contemplated the possibility of marrying her. He met her in the spring of that year when she came to Moscow with an Italian opera company to perform, and when the company returned in September, his interest in her intensified considerably, first because of her fine voice, and then the personal attraction, which appeared to be mutual. Their brief affair, which ended in February of 1869 when he discovered she had married the Spanish baritone Mariano Padilla y Ramos, had a striking effect on him, as he discovered that despite being a homosexual he could be both spiritually and physically attracted to a woman (at the same time he did not hesitate to have relationships with men). Even during the fall of 1868, though, when all continued to go well with them, he no doubt had premonitions of how hopeless this type of relationship was for him—that his attraction to her and his wish to join conventional society would probably not be enough to change him.

I have no basis aside from the date of composition and the apogee of the relationship to suggest the two are related, but it does appear to be plausible. Here we have one of the most momentous episodes of his life to date, a liaison with the potential to put him on the track he hoped to be on, but still shrouded with all the doubts that perpetually haunted him. That he should write the work at this point that would more than any other define his direction as a composer does not seem coincidental—a work that could be of the deepest conceivable meaning to himself and therefore fire his musical imagination in the best possible way. He had not had this opportunity in any previous work, so this one stood very much as a learning experience, in which he could grapple with the musical language needed for this type of expression, including formal structure (or lack of it), themes, and tonality. That he did not entirely succeed should not surprise us, although the work is better than some have suggested. He learned much from it, and only a year later he wrote another symphonic poem that would lift him into the highest echelons of composition, based on Shakespeare's *Romeo and Juliet*, a work that first defined him as a great composer and remains firmly fixed in the repertory. I will make the case that the affair with Mlle Artôt not only had a bearing on that work, but on other later ones as well, including his first piano concerto.

The one-word title *Fatum* proved confusing, especially to the conductor of the first performance, Nikolay Rubinstein, who felt the audience would wish to have something more definite, and at the suggestion of someone else, Tchaikovsky agreed to add a verse by the poet Batyushkov as a programme: "You know that grey-haired Melchizedek, bidding farewell of life, declared: 'Man was born a slave, he goes to his grave a slave—and death will scarcely tell him why he traversed this sorrowful vale of tears, why he suffered, endured, wept, and vanished'" (B1 165). Since this had little to do with his own situation at the time, being a young man, Tchaikovsky may have thrown it out as a smoke screen, diverting any attention away from himself. If he intended it as a ruse, it did not work, since critics pounced on the disconnect between the verse and the music. He learned his lesson, and for his next symphonic poem he used one of the greatest of all literary works, one that allowed him to provide music with passion that plumbed the depths of the tragic story and also allowed him to see himself in it, probing personal matters by way of a literary masterpiece.

ROMEO AND JULIET: FANTASIA OVERTURE

As appealing as this subject turned out to be for Tchaikovsky, the idea of writing a symphonic poem representing the drama of Shakespeare's *Romeo and Juliet* did not come from him, but instead from one of the members of the Mighty Five with whom he was on very good terms, Mily Alexeyevich Balakirev. As their correspondence unfolded, Tchaikovsky led Balakirev to believe that his inspiration had run dry, and that he needed suggestions about how to proceed. Balakirev leapt into his role as mentor with relish, holding back little on how he thought the work should develop, including formal structure as well as the thematic representation of characters and dramatic situations. A symphonic poem representing a play will not necessarily attempt a linear narrative, but instead may focus on the primary characters and overall dramatic thrust, thematically fashioning these into a musical work with its own form. For at least a century the primary form for embodying drama in instrumental music had been sonata form, perfected by Haydn in his symphonic first movements, and used by every symphonist since. Balakirev believed sonata form would give this work the musical and dramatic cohesion it needed, and Tchaikovsky agreed, applying it in a way that yields clearly identifiable sections. He starts with an introduction and follows that with an exposition incorporating two contrasting themes providing the basis of the conflict; then comes a working out of the discord in a development, next a recapitulation that shows the results of the antagonism, and in conclusion a coda (or epilogue) with a final comment on the tragedy.

A purely instrumental work, with no words, will focus on the dramatic essence of the play and reveal the emotions, which can best be expressed in music. That essence in this play proved fairly easy to define—as the destruction of the beauty of young love by the animosity of two feuding clans. Aside from Romeo and Juliet, only one other character needed representation in the music, and that's Friar Lawrence, who plays a significant role as a facilitator of the love that bridges the clans. Other major characters, including the Nurse, find themselves on one side or the other of the Capulets and Montagues, and in musical terms can all be lumped together under the general notion of conflict. Even Romeo and Juliet need not be portrayed separately since together they embody love, the force that stands against destruction. In a letter to Balakirev Tchaikovsky outlined the plan: "A large portion of what you advised me to do has been carried out as you instructed. In the first place, the scheme is yours: the introduction depicting the friar, the struggle (allegro), and love (second subject)" (B1 182). He even followed the suggested key scheme, using B minor for the first subject depicting conflict, and the very remote key of D flat for love. After finishing it and hearing the first performance conducted by Nikolay Rubinstein in Moscow, he took it through further major revisions before it became the work we now know, especially the introduction, which in the revision starts with a chorale-like passage, and the coda, which became a funeral march for the two dead lovers.

After completing much of the composition, the composer sent Balakirev, who was breathing down his neck, a letter with the main themes written out. Balakirev had promised not to critique it, but he simply could not help himself, and he did not always have complimentary things to say. The love theme, though, he found delightful: "I play it often. . . . Here is tenderness and the sweetness of love. . . . When I play [this theme] then I imagine you are lying naked in your bath and that the Artôt-Padilla herself is washing your tummy with hot lather from scented soap" (B1 184). This is a very curious (and comical) comment for him to make, getting at the sensuality of it, which he described as "a passionate physical languor." Even more curious is that he should refer specifically to Désirée, now Mme Artôt-Padilla, almost a year after the affair had ended, still projecting the now married singer into a physical love scene with the composer. Surely he would not have brought her into the equation if Tchaikovsky had not given him some reason for doing so, and it could very well be that in his own conception of the work, moving from the tragedy of the two young lovers to his own circumstances, Tchaikovsky drew some type of parallel—however vague—in his discussions with Balakirev. Tchaikovsky could have looked on his affair with Désirée as love doomed by the hand of fate—between a heterosexual woman and a homosexual man, with the inner conflict of their respective sexual orientations and the outer conflict of a society that both behaviorally and legally expected heterosexuality. It may seem an exaggeration to compare that to the fate of Romeo and Juliet, but probably not for this composer. In any event, he could portray the destruction of love by warring positions with a sense of personal empathy.

As Tchaikovsky had informed Balakirev, the work begins with an introduction that depicts Friar Lawrence, although it may do more than that, following the play itself, which starts with a prologue. Like earlier symphonic introductions, this one moves relatively slowly, *andante*, and commences with half-note chords in clarinets and bassoons that give it a chorale-like feeling, immediately steering the tone in the direction of religion. The melody line of the chords can be thought of as the friar's theme, and it will recur later at crucial points when the voice of the friar needs to be heard amid the tumult. Representing religion, detached from the secular world of strife, the friar plays a special role, not only as the one who marries the lovers and devises a solution for them to be reunited after Romeo has been banished, but as one who wishes peace between the Capulets and Montagues, seeing the marriage as a way to achieve that. His plan to reunite them fails since Romeo's servant sees Juliet under the influence of the sleeping potion, feigning death to avoid marriage to Paris, and imagining her actually to be dead he rushes to Romeo with the news, getting there faster than the messenger from the friar, who would reveal the plot (oh, if they had only had email!). The friar's desire for peace comes from Christian conviction, and the chorale-like chords give that sense along with a possible premonition of death, so much a part of the chorale tradition. For Tchaikovsky the friar became little more than "a solitary soul, with spiritual aspirations for heaven," and the music of the intro emphasizes that as it continues, with rising half-note figures in doubled flutes followed by rising rolled chords in the harp. Nothing could be more heavenly than these chords in the harp, but perhaps they denote an element of hope as well, if only that the reuniting will happen in a better place than their calamitous Verona torn by hatred and discord.

The intro transitions to the exposition with a quickening of the pace, first an *accelerando* and then *allegro*, and ends with chords alternating between winds and strings, as though to allow dueling forces to be heard in conflict. That strife breaks through as the exposition begins, the full orchestra giving a distinctive rhythm that along with the theme in the first violins represents the conflict of the feuding families in the key of B minor. Conflict becomes the background against which all else unfolds, and here the music parallels the play, which after the prologue immediately launches into fighting that leaves young men injured and provokes the wrath of the Prince of Verona. This first subject of the exposition continues at length, starting at a *forte* level and *allegro giusto* (fast in a fixed way after the more variable ending of the intro) and adding more destabilization as it proceeds, with syncopations and increased volume to *fortissimo*, and even some fugato writing, a type of counterpoint that pits two parts against each other without the full complexity of a fugue. Against a flurry of rapid motion in the strings, the winds at times give quick punctuated chords off the beat, occasionally delayed to the point that they take us by surprise. Near the end of this subject those chords in the winds fall on the beat, suggesting a temporary end to the strife, and a return to *piano* allows a transition to the extreme contrast of the new theme.

The new theme, a melody marked *dolce* (sweetly) and *espressivo*, could not be more different than the uproar that has just ended, and the instrumentation, clarinet and violas in unison, underlines the expressiveness of the love theme—as does the new key of D flat. He follows the melody with richly harmonized chords in the strings that provide a sense of musical growth, as though the love itself grows—just as it does in the play, from Romeo and Juliet's first playful meeting at the festivities at her house, through the balcony scene of tender exchanges, to the explosion of unrestrained passion before the friar marries them. These peaks appear to be highlighted in the music: the second statement of the melody, much higher and in a new key, follows a rapidly rising flourish in the flutes and oboes. This time growth occurs in the melody itself, since instead of giving it only as a single eight-bar phrase as he did the first time, Tchaikovsky now extends it over most of the remainder of the section (thirty-one bars), developing it in the most beautifully organic way, showing his melodic and harmonic skills at their most loving (including erotic) best. The section ends with the chords heard after the first statement of the melody, extended longer than before and supporting fragments of the melody.

After the presentation of the tension that forms the background and the passionate love in the foreground, these forces collide in the development section. It starts with material from the conflict subject followed by a brief interjection from the friar, and when a glimmer of the love theme emerges, it does so against syncopations that destabilize. Shortly after that the friar's theme from the intro comes in, as though to protest the conflict, with all three of the main forces of the drama now interacting, which they continue to do. This becomes especially poignant when conflict dominates every voice in the orchestra except for one, the trumpet, which in counterpoint raises the lone voice of sanity against the raucous strife. After eight bars of trying, the friar's voice succumbs to the assault and drops out. At that point the love theme in the piccolo makes a brief two-bar stand against the violence, and it too cannot withstand the forcefulness of the strife, emphasized by the punctuated chords on offbeats heard in the exposition, more syncopation, and the return of the conflict music at louder levels. Late in the development the love theme returns, underscoring the fact that the love of Romeo and Juliet cannot be quelled, in fact now resounding in as many as six voices, both in winds and strings, but no longer with a straightforward accompaniment. Until the end of the development we hear the love melody set against fairly rapid triplets in almost all of the winds, putting it on edge; this love must sustain itself against the most terrible odds, provoked by the quarrel in which Romeo kills the Capulet Tybalt, who has killed Romeo's dear friend and kinsman Mercutio (with Romeo trying to stop their dueling). The music does not represent these events specifically, nor the banishment; Juliet taking the sleeping potion; Romeo drinking poison, believing her dead; or Juliet stabbing herself when she awakens to be with her dead husband; but these can be implied in the counterpoint embodying their deep love and the conflict.

The recapitulation begins with a variant of the love theme, still recognizable as such, but changed—not as the loss of love but in what it must overcome against external forces; those forces are represented in an accompanying variant of the triplets heard at the end of the development. Reversing the order of the exposition, with love now coming first, we hear it for only a fraction of the time we did in the exposition, and it gives way to some of the destabilizing forces, such as syncopations. Conflict returns with a vengeance, as does the friar's voice, which proves ineffectual against the violence, as all of these rapidly alternate or interact in counterpoint. It appears that love has been defeated, and a violent outburst of conflict comes near the end of the recap, which winds down in the lowest registers of the bassoons, cellos, and basses.

That type of low writing often indicates that the worst has happened, and here it clearly has, supported by a drum roll, with the death of one of the most beautiful portrayals of love in all of literature. Tchaikovsky may have recalled here the ignominious death of his own affair with Désirée after her marriage (which she did not bother to tell him about), and the role of fate in leading to that outcome.

The overture ends with a funeral march, driven by a rhythmic figure in the timpani, with the melody a fragmented variant of the love theme, which eventually simply dies out. The love of course has not actually died, and in a final moment of brilliance Tchaikovsky combines the actual love theme with a variant of the friar's theme and the rising rolled harp chords heard in the intro, although he sets these against syncopations in the winds reminiscent of the conflict from the development. A sense of transcendence now overcomes the violence, augmented by the rising figure associated with the harp chords from the intro, as the lovers reunite in a better world, and the feuding families have finally given up their grievances with each other; it took not a marriage but their deaths to accomplish that. Yet the final chords do not convince us that all is well: the rhythmic figure associated with conflict leads off the final four bars, and until the last chord the next five occur only on offbeats. He ends very much as Shakespeare does in the play, in a sense musically giving the Prince the final words: "A glooming peace this morning with it brings; / The sun for sorrow will not show his head: / Go hence, to have more talk of these sad things; / Some shall be pardon'd and some punish'd: / For never was a story of more woe / Than this of Juliet and her Romeo."

Audiences did not recognize the brilliant success of Tchaikovsky's achievement with this overture fantasia immediately, but over the years and to the present they have. In a number of works that followed, he stayed with the idea of specific programmes, including two more on plays by Shakespeare—*The Tempest* in 1873 and *Hamlet* much later, in 1888. Others also borrowed from great literary works, such as his fantasia on *Francesca da Rimini* (1876) based on a portion of Dante's *Inferno*, to be noted in chapter 9 because of Alfred Hitchcock's inclusion of it in one of his films, and the *Manfred* Symphony, derived from Byron. Even before *Fatum* he had as a student written *The Storm*, an overture to the play by Alexander Nikolayevich Ostrovsky, and he also thought of his first symphony (*Winter Daydreams*) programmatically. A case can be made for each of his symphonies after that also being programmatic, although in no other instance did he specify a source. There can be no doubt that something autobiographical stirred him in each of these cases, associations that he could bring out in ways that make them accessible and meaningful to all in his audience. The symphonic poem resulted in his earliest success and, along with opera and ballet, shaped the composer he became.

FESTIVAL OVERTURE, 1812

It's the Fourth of July 2013 in Boston, Massachusetts, and your city was the focus of international attention just a few months earlier, when terrorists' bombs went off near the end of the Boston Marathon. Things have almost returned to normal, and nothing can bring out the spirit of the city like the Independence Day celebrations at the Charles River Esplanade, with the Boston Pops Orchestra performing as it has done for decades. You knew this year would be special because of what the city has been through, and to find a spot on the lawn in front of the Hatch Shell, which looks, appropriately for Boston, like a giant clam-shell, you knew you would need to arrive very early for the 7:00 p.m. concert, since hundreds of thousands are expected and this space can accommodate only a fraction of that number. The overflow will line the side of the Charles River, also a good spot to see the fireworks, but you happily have your place in the middle of the band-shell lawn. No city celebrates the Fourth with as much verve as Boston, and of course the Pops Orchestra, founded by the legendary Arthur Fiedler, adds a unique touch. This year the concert, conducted by Keith Lockhart, will include performers either from or with a strong connection to Boston, such as Susan Tedeschi, Howie Day, Ellis Hall, and Ayla Brown.

At seven o'clock on this hot, ninety-degree evening the hosts for the concert, Lisa Hughes and Jonathan Elias, from television station WBZ, introduce the proceedings; this includes a special announcement about Tchaikovsky's *1812 Overture*, which will come in a couple of hours. This happens to be the fortieth anniversary of its performance at Fourth of July celebrations in Boston. In 1973, concerned about declining at-tendance, Fiedler had a discussion with the philanthropist David Mugar about how to get it back on track, and aside from covering the cost of the pyrotechnics show, Mugar persuaded Fiedler to perform the *1812 Overture*, which, with its cannon fire and bells at the end, would also work well with fireworks.

Thus started the tradition of performing this work for every Fourth of July concert in Boston, and it caught on in other cities as well, so much so that you are not entirely certain Tchaikovsky didn't write it for this American celebration. Near the beginning the hosts interview General Scott Rice of the Massachusetts Guard, who, expressing how happy he and his unit are to serve their country, also notes how they enjoy "firing off howitzers and giving that punch to the *1812 Overture*."

By nine o'clock the sky has darkened, and when the hosts announce that the next work to be performed is the *1812 Overture*, you are surprised to see not only the orchestra on the huge stage but a large chorus as well, in fact the Tanglewood Festival Chorus. Tchaikovsky did not write a choral part for the work; this was added by the Hartford-born conductor Igor Buketoff, the son of a Russian Orthodox priest, at the request of Eugene Ormandy for the Philadelphia Orchestra, and considering some of the other anachronisms in the work (noted below), why not throw in a chorus as well. Tchaikovsky himself had nothing but disdain for this piece, written for a commission that did not appeal to him, and having put it together as a kind of hotchpotch of anthems, folk music, and his own previously unknown music, he probably would not have minded. He had been given a choice between writing an overture for an important upcoming exhibition, an overture for the tsar's silver jubilee, or a cantata with Orthodox tunes for the Cathedral of Christ the Savior in St. Petersburg, which was being built to commemorate the Russian victory over the French in 1812. He considered it an annoyance, opting for an overture to mark the consecration of the cathedral, and wrote to Nadezhda von Meck that it "will be very loud and noisy," and that he wrote it "with no warm feeling of love, and therefore there will probably be no artistic merits in it." Many critics have agreed with his assessment, but we should not always take what he wrote to her at face value. Even though he visited the United States about a decade after writing it in 1880, he most clearly did not write it for America.

The actual historical events of 1812 in Russia do not paint a pretty picture, and while technically the French won, they ultimately lost because of the harshness of the onset of Russia's winter (which the Nazis would also discover at the siege of Leningrad over a century later).

Napoleon's forces defeated the Russians at Borodino near Moscow in September, with enormous loss of life and injuries, and from there they moved on to Moscow, taking it with little resistance. The Russians had retreated, burning much of the city as they left, leaving no food or supplies behind. During the winter the French themselves had to retreat, faced with starvation, diseases, freezing temperatures, and skirmishes with Russian forces. Eventually Napoleon himself abandoned his army, which had been reduced to a small fraction of its original size. More so than Tsar Alexander's army, the harshness of Russia itself had defeated the French, which played no small role in the downfall of Napoleon and the reshaping of Europe at the Congress of Vienna in 1814.

In this overture the music follows a narrative scheme more closely than it had in *Romeo and Juliet*, representing the events of Napoleon's invasion, the actions of the Russians, and the collapse of the French forces. When the roughly half-million French forces with cannons and other artillery crossed the Niemen River en route to Moscow, the small, ragtag Russian army could do nothing to stop them, so the Russian Orthodox patriarch asked people to pray for God's intervention and an end to conflict. The people responded en masse, and the overture begins with their prayer, the Orthodox chant "Save Us, O Lord," scored in six-part harmony by Tchaikovsky for two solo violas and four solo cellos. This provided an obvious place for Buketoff to add a chorus, singing the prayer a capella, but for this Boston performance the chorus doubles the strings; the prayer for liberty makes the beginning of this overture seem especially apt for Independence Day in the United States. More of the orchestra comes in, leading to a *crescendo* and then loud music of conflict as the French forces advance. The music identifies them with fragments of "La Marseillaise," the French national anthem, although anachronistically, since this famous anthem—perhaps the most memorable of all anthems—had not yet been written in 1812. At the first hint of recognition the audience at the Esplanade cheers, unaware that this music represents the enemy.

As more music of conflict ensues, "La Marseillaise" becomes increasingly persistent, with tiny fragments morphing into actual phrases, representing the French taking everything in their path, wielding ferocious strength. With the Russian army incapable of stopping them, the tsar pleads with peasants and other ordinary Russians to join the fight.

As they consider his request, we hear, after some music borrowed from his own unsuccessful early opera *Voevoda*, a Russian folk song, "U vorot" (At the gate, at my gate), with its distinctive folk rhythms, and a text making clear to all that this conflict will affect them directly. The nature of this folk song makes it unsuitable for a choral setting, and the conflict between the folk song, "La Marseillaise," and military music of necessity unfolds in instrumental counterpoint. As this conflict develops, with Russians joining the battle to the strains of "U vorot," the lead appears to move back and forth as one side takes the upper hand over the other and then back again. Late in this conflict we hear cannons fire, scored to sound on offbeats, but with the difficulty of firing howitzers at precise timing, it's enough just to hear the cannons. Clearly we cannot have howitzers on the stage, so for the Esplanade the Massachusetts Guard under General Rice has them some distance away on the bank of the Charles River, with a video link to conductor Lockhart. On his cue some Guard members load the weapons while others fire them, and two others signal when the blasts will happen; a two-way video link has brought the picture of the cannons firing back to the Esplanade, on two large screens set on either side of the stage. The Guard members doing the firing have found themselves in the unlikely situation of being musicians, and they try their best to look the part. The orchestral writing then seems to get stuck on a descending figure, and slows down, as though Moscow burns; an icy wind blows across the landscape, and nature steps in to beleaguer the French.

That slowing down leads to a momentous outburst of the original hymn from the beginning, at a *largo* tempo, sung by the chorus to the accompaniment of the full orchestra. Rescue has come, not from Russian might, but from the intervention of God, and this heralds the time for celebration, not only with a *fortissimo* orchestra but with chimes also at full volume, presumably of the bells of churches all over the nation. Tchaikovsky did not add more cannons at this point, but the Boston performance does, augmenting the crashing of the cymbal and other percussion, and during this final section of the overture the fireworks start as well. For the final rejoicing of the Russians at their deliverance, Tchaikovsky adds the Russian national anthem, not the Soviet one that Americans would likely recognize or even one that existed in 1812, but instead the tsarist anthem of his own time. Some may find it a little ironic that the premier musical work used to celebrate the Fourth of July is in fact the commemoration of a Russian victory over a long-standing American ally, but no one should be distressed by this, since early in the nineteenth century Russia and America regarded each other as friends. Tchaikovsky was absolutely right about the noise, and he probably would not have objected to the fireworks; at the end Lockhart shakes hands with the concertmaster while the crowd goes crazy.

2

A LITTLE HELP FROM MY FRIENDS

Concertos

By the age of thirty-five, in 1875, Tchaikovsky had tried his hand at most types of instrumental and vocal composition, and certain patterns of success had started to emerge, especially with orchestral music. His third symphony came that year, and three of his earlier symphonic poems, *Fatum* (1868), *Romeo and Juliet* (1869), and *The Tempest* (1873), defined him as a composer. In two of these he could combine literary subjects with matters of personal or autobiographical interest, and regardless of whether audiences heard that connection or not, it allowed him to pour himself into his works in ways that made them essential to his own sense of well-being. By giving them personal significance he made them dramatically and emotionally appealing to listeners as well. At this point one type of instrumental composition remained unexplored, one with even more potential for drama than symphonies or symphonic poems: the concerto. Tchaikovsky played the piano—at a very high level, but surrounded at the conservatory by virtuosos, he claimed not to be a pianist; future leading Russian composers would be virtuosos, such as Rachmaninoff and Prokofiev, but Tchaikovsky made no such claim about himself and did not appear on stage playing the piano. To write a piano concerto at the highest possible virtuoso level, he would need some help from a virtuoso who could tell him what was playable, and with the violin or cello he would need even more help, being even less familiar with the possibilities on those instruments. He therefore set out writing concertos for these instruments assuming he could get that advice later, as with his first piano concerto, or he could work collaboratively with a string player, as he did for his Violin Concerto.

Where the impulse came from to write a piano concerto—the first of his concertos—we do not know, aside from the likely wish to show his ability at that type of composition and the potential he could see in it for creating something even more dramatic than his prior orchestral works. While working on it in the late fall of 1874, a comment that he made about the Fourth Concerto by Henry Litolff, one of his favorite composers at the time, about the opposition of the piano and orchestra, got at that dramatic potential: here he felt the piano "was not playing a preeminent role, but would wrestle with its mighty competitor" (WT 88). Of course he would want his own concerto to be played by the best pianist in Moscow, his boss Nikolay Rubinstein, as he told his brother Anatoly, but he had concerns about this since the composition did not always flow smoothly, especially the solo piano part, and Rubinstein's opinion could be brutal. He finally did play it for Rubinstein, and his account to Nadezhda von Meck three years later of what happened deserves to be cited in full. We should keep in mind that at that point in 1878 he hoped to leave his position at the Conservatory, and making Rubinstein seem like an ogre would, he believed, strengthen his case with her. This account may not be entirely accurate, but based on Nikolay Kashkin's later confirmation, it came fairly close to the truth:

> In December 1874 I wrote the [First] Piano Concerto. As I am not a pianist, I had to refer to a virtuoso, a specialist who could tell me what might, technically, be unplayable, unrewarding, ineffective, etc. Just for this external side of my work I needed a critic who was severe but at the same time well disposed towards me. . . . I must state the fact that some inner voice protested against the choice of Rubinstein as a judge of this mechanical aspect of my composition. I knew that he wouldn't be able to miss the opportunity for *a bit of petty tyranny*. Still, not only is he the number one pianist in Moscow, but he really is an outstanding player, and, as I had already known that he would be deeply offended to learn that I had left him out, I suggested that he should hear the concerto through and comment on the piano part. This was Christmas Eve, 1874. That evening we had both been invited to a Christmas party at Albrecht's, and N[ikolai]

G[rigor'evich] suggested that we should find ourselves a place in one of the classrooms of the Conservatoire before the party. This we did. I turned up with my manuscript and then NG and Hubert joined me . . .

I played through the first movement. Not a single word, not a single comment! If only you knew how foolish and intolerable is the position of a man who offers his friend food which he has prepared himself, and the friend then eats it in silence! Go on, say something, even if it's a kindly insult, but for goodness' sake show some interest, even if you can't manage praise. Rubinstein was preparing his thunderbolts. . . . But the main thing was that I didn't need a verdict on the artistic aspect. I needed comments from the angle of the virtuoso piano technique. R[ubinstein]'s eloquent silence had considerable significance. It was as if he was saying to me: "How can I talk about details, my friend, when the very essence of the thing is offensive to me!" I summoned up the patience to play to the end. Again silence. I stood up and asked: "Well?" Then a torrent of words poured forth from NG's lips, quiet at first, then more and more in the style of Jupiter the Thunderer. It transpired that my concerto was no good, that it was impossible to play, that some passages were hackneyed, awkward, and clumsy beyond redemption, that as a composition it was bad and banal, that I had pilfered this bit from here and that from there, that there were only two or three pages which would do, and that the rest would have to be either discarded or completely reworked. "Here, for example, what's this supposed to be?" (he caricatures the passage concerned). . . . I can't convey to you the most significant thing, i.e. the *tone* in which it was all said. In a word, any outsider who happened to come into the room would have thought that I was a talentless imbecile, a clueless hack who had come to importune a distinguished musician with his trash. . . .

I was not only astonished by this scene but insulted by it. I am no longer a small boy trying his hand as a composer. I don't need lessons from anybody, especially expressed in so acerbic and hostile a manner. I need friendly advice and always will—but there was no friendly comment here. It was a sweeping and decisive censure, expressed in such a way that it cut me to the quick. I left the room in silence and went upstairs. I was speechless with anger and agitation. Rubinstein came up shortly afterwards, and, seeing my distraught state, took me to a room some distance away. Once again he told me that my concerto was impossible, pointed out innumerable passages requiring radical alteration, and said that, if I were to alter the concerto in accordance with his demands by such-and-such a date, he would do me the honour of including my piece in one of his concerts. "I won't alter a single note," I replied, "and I shall have it printed exactly as it is at the moment." And that's what I did. (TM 150–152)

Well, not quite. Tchaikovsky did receive advice from other pianists, and the published version we know incorporates these revisions. After this meltdown, the last thing he wanted was for Rubinstein to perform it, and in fact the premiere took place not in Russia or even in Europe, but in Boston, Massachusetts, played by the distinguished German pianist Hans von Bülow, who suggested some of the changes. Tchaikovsky first heard a live performance with his former pupil Sergey Ivanovich Taneyev as the pianist, conducted by none other than Rubinstein, a performance that completely satisfied the composer. Not long after, Rubinstein added it to his own repertory, and despite his biting critique championed the work as long as he lived.

In the previous chapter I suggested that this concerto, along with *Fatum* and *Romeo and Juliet*, may have an association with Désirée Artôt, the woman Tchaikovsky loved late in 1868, and this may even have something to do with his choice to write a piano concerto. He wrote the first of the symphonic poems during their affair and the second immediately afterward, so their connections seem plausible; a work coming five or six years later appears less so, but Tchaikovsky seems to have built the association into the music itself with a type of musical identification tag. David Brown first noted the possibility of this in his magisterial four-volume biography of Tchaikovsky, although he treats it with great caution, avoiding committing himself to the idea by presenting it as a kind of extended footnote. Perhaps I should not leap into this at the deep end, but the possibility seems too good to pass up. After the works he had already completed there can be no doubt that he would wish this one to have personal significance as well, and bringing Désirée into it in fact helps to make the work more intelligible, involving formal considerations as well as themes and tonal treatment. It also helps to make sense of the relationship between the piano and orchestra, setting up the piano as a necessary part of the dramatic equation. Returning to this relationship a number of years after the fact similarly need not be troubling; the importance of the affair cannot be underestimated, and by 1874 he had had time to reflect on it and put it into the perspective of the way his life continued to unfold.

By way of musical tags or ciphers Tchaikovsky identifies both himself and Désirée in this concerto. His method for doing this was already well established in musical practice, and would continue to be used in the twentieth century. Composers can do this by playing a kind of game of musical anagrams, using the letters of the notes of the musical scale as the identifiers in order to spell a name (or at least partially spell it). That may seem very limited, with only seven notes (A, B, C, D, E, F, and G), but when we bring in the usages from other languages, especially German but also French, the list gets longer. For example, Germans identify some notes with flats separately, so in their nomenclature B flat is B, meaning the note B must be something else, and it becomes H; similarly E flat = Es, and A flat = As. Since Es sounds like S, S can be the note E flat. These add nicely to the options, so the composer BACH could spell his name in musical notation as B flat, A, C, B, as he in fact did. With his short surname he could spell it out completely in notation. A composer with a longer name has to settle for using only some letters/notes as the name tag.

One composer used something very similar to what Tchaikovsky did in this concerto, fusing the musical anagram of his name with that of a woman he loved, and that was Robert Schumann in his solo piano work *Carnaval*. Midway through this set of character pieces he throws in some cryptic notations, not actually to be performed, and the second of these, which he calls the *Lettres dansantes*, gives it most clearly: A.S.C.H. – S.C.H.A. What do these mean? The notes that can be extracted from his last name are SCHumAnn, the second part of his equation, musically giving E flat, C, B, A. When scrambling these he comes up with the anagram ASCH, which happens to be the name of the town, Asch, where his fellow student and lover at the time, Estrella, hailed from. He saw this not as a coincidence but as a matter of great significance. These four notes in their respective orders become motifs that run throughout some of the pieces that make up the larger work, and while it may seem a coldly calculated way of generating motifs, in fact it works admirably, not suffering musically in the slightest. Just before the *Lettres dansantes* he gives some other unperformed variants in long notes under the heading "Sphinxes": E flat, C, B, A = Es, C, H, A; A flat, C, B = As, C, H; and A, E flat, C, B = A, Es, C, H. After Tchaikovsky Alban Berg would do similar things with his name and that of his presumed mistress (probably more of a muse), Hannah Fuchs, in his *Lyric Suite*, and again in his *Chamber Concerto*, using the names of his closest colleagues, Arnold Schönberg and Anton Webern, along with his own.

Obviously, in Russian, with its Cyrillic script, this game will not work. Using, though, the usual central European spelling of his name during his time, Peter Tschaikovsky, but excluding Schumann's S/Es, as Brown does, we have pEtEr tsCHAikovsky, which yields the notes E, C, B, A. This contour of descending notes happens, perhaps not so coincidentally, to be the first four notes of the first movement, played by the horns. As for Désirée, Brown gives a couple of options: we can add French notation to the mix, with a long version spelling out her full first name as D Es SI RE E = D, E flat, B, D, E, along with the first letter of her surname, A; or there can be a short version, as Dés[irée] A[rtôt] = D flat, A, where the "és" after the D adds the flat. This becomes the basis for one of the later themes in the first movement, along with a B flat, giving a three-note contour, and also defines the theme of the second movement. Once established, these motifs do not have to be stated starting on the exact notes but can come in any transposition, and similarly, they can be inverted, so that the contour instead of the exact sequence defines them. Invoking these tags yields a fascinating dramatic and emotional unfolding of the work, allowing us a kind of secret programme. We can also simply ignore that and enjoy the music on its own, but I will opt for the former, to see where it may lead.

FIRST PIANO CONCERTO

It's 13 April 1958, and as a member of the U.S. legation in the U.S.S.R. during the height of the Cold War, you have come to the Bolshoy Salle of the Moscow Conservatory to hear the American pianist who has made it to the final eight and has caused a great stir at the first Tchaikovsky Competition. No non-Soviet entrant has ever previously won a music competition in the Soviet Union, and you have little reason to think that will change this time, considering the prestige this event has garnered. A number of Americans have entered the competition. Because of your duties at the embassy you have had some involvement with securing their visas and other details facilitating their entry and stay in the U.S.S.R., and all the Russians you have spoken with have talked with great excitement about this event. Some have joked with you about the prospects of a twenty-three-year-old Texan against the very finest young Russian pianists with the rigors of their conservatory educations, selected from among the many thousands who could have been chosen. You agree the task is daunting if not intimidating, knowing that many of the best pianists in the world hail from this country, from Anton Rubinstein, who founded the St. Petersburg Conservatory, to his brother Nikolay, who did the same in Moscow; the greats who left after the revolution, such as Sergey Rachmaninoff, Vladimir Horowitz, and Josef Lhevinne; and the next generation of masters, including Emil Gilels and Sviatoslav Richter, both members of the Tchaikovsky Competition jury (with Gilels as head).

This young Texan, Van Cliburn, had already quieted the critics in the first stages of the competition, performing solo works of his own choice and other mandatory pieces. These performances were open to the public, and after he played, the public embraced him completely and rapturously, suspecting that he may actually have Russian blood in him; perhaps "Van" was simply an abbreviation of Vanya or Vanushka. A genealogical search turned up nothing of the sort, but musical heritage made up for that. The skeptics in Moscow doubted that anyone who studied only with his mother until the age of seventeen—especially a mother with a name like Rildia Bee—could be up to much, but they failed to notice that Rildia Bee had herself studied with the legendary Arthur Friedheim, from St. Petersburg and initially a pupil of the Conservatory's founder, Anton Rubinstein. Finding Rubinstein's teaching too disorganized, he left the country in search of a better teacher (since no better teacher existed in Russia), and Franz Liszt, the greatest pianist of the entire nineteenth century, accepted him. From Friedheim, Rildia Bee learned the great romantic tradition of pianism, with equal emphasis on technique and creative individuality, and had circumstances for women in Texas been different early in the twentieth century, she may have had an outstanding career as a performer.

By the time Van Cliburn arrived at the Juilliard School of Music in New York at the age of seventeen, he had been taught exceptionally well, and after his audition with Rosina Lhevinne, she readily made room for him despite having a full class. In fact, no one could have instilled the great tradition of Russian musicianship in him more effectively than Rosina Lhevinne, and theirs quickly became the ideal teacher/student relationship. She had herself won the gold medal when graduating from the Moscow Conservatory (as Rosina Bessie), and seemed destined for a brilliant career. She married Josef Lhevinne, and the two of them frequently performed as duo pianists, but after someone commented that he liked her playing better than his, she dropped out of performing completely, devoting herself exclusively to the promotion of his career. They emigrated to the United States, where he took a position at the fledgling Juilliard School, but he spent much time on the road, and she stepped in as teacher during his absences. He died unexpectedly in 1944, and the school without hesitation made her professor of music; during her long career there she became perhaps the finest piano teacher of the twentieth century. Her own background included close friendships with the likes of Rachmaninoff, whose Third Piano Concerto Cliburn also played for the competition, and with the sound of the master's playing in her ears, she could teach this work as no one living in the Soviet Union could. The same held true for Tchaikovsky's Piano Concerto, since she still lived the tradition from which it came in the nineteenth century, understanding the passion in it as it came from the source.

Ironically, the American from Texas as a musician turned out to be more Russian than the Russians, and with his brilliant technique to match his understanding of the emotional quality of the works he played, it's no surprise that Moscow audiences embraced him as they did. On that evening the Bolshoy Salle could not have been more packed, with all fifteen hundred seats taken, and other enthusiasts standing wherever they could. Behind the orchestra now tuning hung the large medallion-shaped photograph of Tchaikovsky, as though he would be personally overseeing the performance. The front of the stage appeared to be a sea of flowers. When Cliburn made his entrance the audience erupted in clapping, cheering, and foot-stomping, greeting him as no American audience had to this date, breaking down all the barriers between Russians and Americans as no diplomatic forays could possibly have succeeded in doing. Conductor Kirill Kondrashin came out behind Cliburn, and this being a competition, he insisted on decorum, rapping his baton on the podium to silence the outburst.

FIRST MOVEMENT

With the audience silent, Kondrashin raised his baton and conducted a bar and a half before the entrance of the orchestra, since Tchaikovsky wrote the score with a bar and a half of rests before we hear any music. Some will find this curious—that the composer writes silence before the work starts—but since he has written the rests, we must take them to be part of the work itself, there for some reason. We could perhaps think of this written silence as something to make us more conscious of the music when it enters, or another possibility that some have suggested is to compare it to a painting with a frame, the silence being the frame in time before the tonal colors hit the ear. The opening few bars here have become perhaps the most famous of any concerto ever written, so distinctive and overwhelming that they even lend themselves to comical caricature. Some may remember Victor Borge's gag on this: with the first three chords in the piano coming in after five bars, each chord considerably higher than the one before, Borge falls off the piano bench at the treble end as he reaches for the third chord.

Not only does the entrance of the piano set this concerto apart, but so does the way the orchestra precedes it. After the opening rests you hear only the horns in unison, playing a descending pattern of four notes, which just happen to be the four notes that can be extracted (in transposition) from Tchaikovsky's name: F, D flat, C, B flat (from E, C, B, A); this seems unlikely to be a coincidence. He immediately follows this with a loud chord in the full orchestra on B-flat minor, the key of the work, setting up a great contrast between his name motif and the hammering orchestral response to it. Two more times you hear the name motto in the horns, each time answered by a chord, but each time harmonically changed, suggesting a progression of sorts. After the third time instead of one chord he gives six, and in fact it has now progressed to the relative major (D flat); on the D-flat chord the piano barges in with its upward-flowing rolled chords, using the same chord as the orchestra.

In spelling out his name here, with a dismissive crash after each statement, you can rightly assume that some message may be embedded, and for that Beethoven can add some clues. The rhythm of the motto, three eighth notes followed by a quarter note, has something in common with the opening of Beethoven's Fifth Symphony; in both cases a rest precedes the three notes, and the fourth note falls at the beginning of the next bar, although Beethoven holds his fourth note much longer. Tchaikovsky clearly did not want his fourth note to go on so long, because of the way he cuts it off with the big chords in full orchestra, now perhaps reminiscent of Beethoven's jarring and equally dismissive chords in the middle of the first movement of the *Eroica*, or the one at the very beginning of the fourth movement of the Ninth, which tells us (even with a singer's words later on) to attune ourselves to something new. We all know Beethoven's opening motto in the Fifth as his fate motif, and Tchaikovsky may very well be doing the same, putting himself right at the center of the pointing of the finger of fate. Fate was central to his previous symphonic poems, one even given the name "Fate" or *Fatum*, so it should not surprise us to encounter it again, pointing directly at the composer himself.

The voice of fate, like the "mighty competitor" he referred to in the letter to his brother, comes in the orchestra—a powerful force, like an unsympathetic Greek god with the might of the whole universe behind it, that must be reckoned with. In response, the piano, Tchaikovsky's own instrument, and now very much the individual trying to cope with a weighty thrust, does not shrink back but musters its own potent energy, driving upward assertively, in the same direction as the harp in *Romeo and Juliet*, now with profane resolve instead of otherworldliness. As the piano continues its chords for the next twenty bars it does so against an orchestra that has backed off somewhat, having taken the name motif as the basis for a more extended and entirely memorable melody. Any concern we may have had about a four-note musical cell derived from a name not being able to generate good music now dissipates as Tchaikovsky transforms the cell into his melodic best, even more effectively than Schumann had in *Carnaval*. What seemed at first would be jarring conflict, like the second movement of Beethoven's Fourth Piano Concerto, ceases to be that as the orchestra stays in a lyrical mode with its melody, making the piano's response seem like an overreaction. Together the orchestra and piano carve out an introduction to the movement. The piano may think the orchestra has been playing possum with its melody, since the next time the piano enters, it does so imitating the orchestra's melody with an aggressive dotted rhythm, and then launches into an extended cadenza, ending that with an off-key paraphrasing of how the orchestra started. Tension remains in the air for much of the remainder of the intro, finally lapsing into apparent exhaustion for both.

In a structure close enough to sonata form to call it that, the piano begins the exposition, now setting out with a jaunty little tune based on a Ukrainian folk song that Tchaikovsky had heard performed by blind beggar musicians at a market near Kamenka, the town near Kiev where his sister Alexandra (Sasha) lived with her husband, Lev Davïdov, and family, at whose estate he periodically took residence. Up to this point in his life he regarded Kamenka as a refuge from the anxieties of Moscow, an idyllic spot in the country with the charms of a beautiful landscape and simple peasant folk, and most of all the joy of being surrounded by a loving family. This tune may very well tie those things together as it provides a striking contrast with the earlier fate motif and tension associated with personal struggles. Not surprisingly, for a substantial amount of time the piano takes this theme either by itself or with only the most limited harmonic backing from the orchestra, emphasizing the piano's association with the individual, now as a voice of contentment. Eventually the orchestra picks up the melody as well, as the piano's part becomes more exuberantly florid, suggesting for the moment that all is well with the world in this happy environment. This cannot last forever, and something more torrid, mostly for the piano by itself, becomes a transition leading to the second theme group of the exposition.

At the first break in the rapid solo piano pattern, still an extension of the folk song, a group of wind instruments interjects three gently stated chords, and repeats this insertion two more times before the piano briefly drops out. For these interjections the oboe provides a three-note motif (the third time it goes to the clarinet), using the motto (sometimes transposed or inverted) that comes from Désirée's name: D flat, A [B flat]; as the clarinet extends it into a melody Tchaikovsky emphasizes its character with the marking *molto espressivo*. After an eight-bar phrase of this the piano immediately takes it up as a solo, now *dolce e molto espressivo* (sweetly and very expressively), although this gives way fairly soon to the second theme of this group. The piano for its short solo has had no difficulty taking and expanding the Désirée motto, with complete affection, not only not in any way resisting but as though it wishes to make this theme its own. For him she represented a number of things that seemed highly desirable, especially considering his homosexuality and how that put him at odds with conventional society. He had very strong feelings about her and may have even desired her sexually, which could have put him on a path toward normalcy as far as society was concerned. This may have been foreign to him, just as she was (being Belgian), but the possible transformative nature of marriage with her could have solved some of his most persistent problems. Perhaps it seemed too good to be possible, but that did not stop his wistfulness about it, something that simply would not go away, as his urge to get married a few years later amply illustrated.

The exposition quickly returns to her motif, and continues for some time to elaborate it at length, although the more it does, the more ornamental and perhaps extraneous the piano's part becomes. After the piano continues in this vein by itself, the winds introduce a new fate theme, this time a triplet leading to a longer note, making it more like Beethoven's, and the piano cannot avoid this, combining her motif with the triplet pattern for much of the remainder of the exposition. Even before the exposition ends the pipe dream seems in a certain amount of jeopardy. The forces of the drama have been established in the exposition, but the nature of the conflict seems anything but clear. Home (Russia/Ukraine), simplicity, family, attraction to women, and fitting into society all seem desirable, but there may be bumps in the road, including hypocrisy from the outside and being true to himself on the inside. The drama will play out as the work continues.

To begin the development section the piano drops out and the orchestra quickly iterates all the previous themes, not only compatibly but even seeming to fuse some of them together, such as the Tchaikovsky and Désirée mottos. This may seem too good to be true, and the entry of the trumpets with a dotted rhythm disturbs the peace, forcing out the themes and ushering in rapid descending passages. A loud chord in the full orchestra takes the orchestra out as the piano starts into a long cadenza, first with the same descending passages as the orchestra just had. The piano recovers from this, with a *dolce* inversion of the Désirée motto that leads into actual counterpoint between her motto and Tchaikovsky's in the left hand and right hand, respectively, for the moment interacting compatibly. That changes when four loud and somewhat dissonant chords in the orchestra nullify this compatibility, with the same jarring effect of the chords from the beginning of the movement. After this the themes become more fragmented, and two more noisy chords bring the development to a close. If dramatic clarity had been lacking at the end of the exposition, it's fairly nonexistent at the end of the development.

By itself the piano begins the recapitulation, using passage-work it had played in the exposition, and as this continues for some time, other motifs appear in the orchestra, especially Désirée's. When the piano drops out we get a stronger dose of her motif and its melodic extension, first in the oboe, ruffled though by persistent syncopations in the strings. The return of the piano banishes the syncopations as it joins in on the melody with pianistic embellishment, and a dominant pedal on F suggests an imminent conclusion, although another abrasive chord seems to negate that. The extended dominant pedal finally resolves, not to the tonic (B minor), but deceptively to G flat (vi instead of i), adding a new wrinkle in that deception in music suggests a false element in the drama. In fact, Tchaikovsky reinforces this twist with metric instability and the triplet figure that revives the presence of fate. This becomes very agitated with a series of loud chords that now come not only from the orchestra but the piano as well, setting off another very long piano cadenza still in the deceptive area of G flat. The piano now mulls over prior themes, especially Désirée's, at one point descending into the lowest register of the instrument and oscillating on a couple of notes, as though it has lost its bearings, with nothing musically intelligible to say. After more mulling the orchestra finally rescues the piano, although the extension of that rescue seems tenuous as orchestra and soloist proceed in an uneasy partnership. The uneasiness takes on more tension, and loud chords return and continue until the end of the movement. Earlier these kinds of chords were somewhat ominous, as dismissals or cutoffs, and as the movement ends the deluge of these chords leaves things very unsettled.

SECOND MOVEMENT

The first movement ended with eight *fortissimo* chords in the home key of B minor, and like a distant echo of this the second movement starts with eight very quiet chords in the strings, muted and *pizzicato*, in the relative major key of D flat, with the expression marking *andantino semplice*. After four bars the simple chords continue, but now with a *dolcissimo* melody in the flutes, clearly derived from Désirée's motif in the prior movement. The eight-bar melody, though, has two distinctive halves, the first from her motif and the second from the Tchaikovsky motif, reversing the descending contour so it now moves upward. Piano and orchestra participate equally in the presentation of this, and after the orchestra drops out, a solo cello beautifully picks up the melody, accompanied by the piano. The cello hands it over to a solo oboe, so for the first part of this glorious movement, the mottos of Désirée and Tchaikovsky coexist in delicious harmony.

A new fast section (*allegro vivace assai*) changes this, at first for solo piano, with a fun-loving atmosphere, and this transitions to a waltz—and not just any waltz but one based on a tune well known to Tchaikovsky, since Désirée often included this chansonnette on her recital programs. It has the title "Il faut s'amuser, danser et rire" (One must have fun, dance, and laugh), and its inclusion creates a three-part form in the movement, ABA, in which the waltz (B) disrupts the flowing beauty of the melody in the first part. Clearly the music does have fun, especially the piano, which indulges in rhythmic bounce and quick passage-work, although midway through its extended cadenza another loud and somewhat dissonant chord seems to try to dampen the fun. It succeeds, although not immediately, as the rapid passages continue until the arrival of an almost recitative-like statement (*quasi andante*), which heralds the return of the part-one melody and the return of that section.

In other three-part movements of this type, especially in slow movements, Tchaikovsky would sometimes follow a procedure that Mozart and Schubert had occasionally used, where the beautiful melody of the first part suggests nostalgia, the boisterous second part destroys the atmosphere, and after that destruction, attempts to recover the beauty of the first part fail. In this case he alters the melody ornamentally and changes the accompaniment, but he does not change it fundamentally until the last roughly eight bars. Here, as the clarinet gives fragmented statements of the Désirée motif, the piano plays rising rolled chords not unlike the ones heard at the beginning of the first movement, only now in diminution—on eighth notes instead of quarter notes, in fact integrating her motif into the rising pattern. At the beginning of the work those chords seemed to suggest a defiance of fate, but now they imply a tacit acceptance of the motto they accompany. Far from rejecting her, the music does not give up on what she stands for, and even the jaunty, fun-loving middle section did not dislodge anything; perhaps he could have fun and a normal relationship in conventional society.

THIRD MOVEMENT

With such an intensive drama unfolding in the first two movements, without any definitive resolution of the issues, we expect the third movement to weigh in and bring the drama to a suitable conclusion. This could go in any one of a number of directions, and we should also be prepared for a possible element of surprise. As far as the mottos go, Désirée's has been front and center in the first two movements, invoking not so much the person as what she represented to Tchaikovsky, finding a larger picture going well beyond the composer's own personal situation into areas that could be of great concern to anyone. The surprise now comes in the fact that the third movement makes no reference to her at all, instead taking the conclusion in a very different direction. We expect finales to be energetic, and this one, at *allegro con fuoco* (fast, with fire), very clearly is that. The fire takes us back to Tchaikovsky himself as he reaffirms his own zest for life.

In each of the previous movements he has either invoked musical anagrams or quoted other songs or folk dances, and once again he uses a quotation as the first theme of the third movement. As in the first movement he returns to a Ukrainian folk song, even more prominently now since it comes as the first theme, and it plays a major role throughout the entire finale. The folk song in question could be "Viydi, viydi Ivanku" (Come, come Ivanku), and if that's correct, aside from its vibrant and life-affirming character, it may be the composer sending a message to himself as he turns the tables from where this drama has been heading. Perhaps we could think of it as "come, come Pyotr, pull yourself together and be true to yourself." The fact that he again uses a Ukrainian folk song returns him to the joys of home (Tchaikovsky would have made little distinction between Ukraine and Russia, especially because of his refuge at Sasha's Kamenka), to the landscapes he loved, the diversity of his homeland, and simplicity as well. When the theme comes, after four short bars of introduction from the orchestra, the piano plays it unaccompanied, and then with accompaniment: the individual and group share it equally.

After a rousing extension of this theme by the full orchestra and a brief piano cadenza with lots of upward motion, before the piano drops out the violins introduce a new theme, a melody every bit as appealing as ones from prior movements, which may in fact point to the dramatic conclusion in that it fuses important elements together. It contains a rhythmic figure (short-short-long) familiar from folk music, including the first theme of the movement, tying it directly to the beginning despite being much more lyrical in tone. We heard something vaguely similar much earlier in the work, near the beginning of the first movement as the melodic extension of the Tchaikovsky motto, and this new melody in the finale now appears to bring together two of the most important threads in the work—the composer himself and his sense of home, or perhaps of being true to himself. Needless to say, this melody will recur significantly later in the movement.

Another passage of note comes about one-third of the way through, and that's a rising dotted rhythm figure, in fact the same dotted rhythm used by the piano near the beginning of the first movement, as a somewhat defiant response to the apparent fate reference that led off the entire work. Now we hear it first in the woodwinds, but it soon gets passed around to everyone at some length, including the piano. Later in the movement the rising dotted figure and the first theme will come together in counterpoint, not in any combative way but in a spirit of accord, suggesting that the earlier struggle against fate has been resolved as the individual has been reconciled with his environment. When after a late piano cadenza the full orchestra and piano come together on the fusion theme, *molto meno mosso* (much slower) and *fortissimo*, we know the final resolution has been reached, and the work can end in a rousing manner. We can, as I have suggested, take the piece as a complex working of human issues of great importance to the composer and applicable to anyone listening, or we can simply enjoy its sound, musical elaborations, and virtuosity as one of the most brilliant piano concertos in the repertory.

At the end of Cliburn's performance the audience could not be restrained as they clapped, stamped their feet, and shouted, "First prize, first prize!" The aging Alexander Goldenweiser, one of Russia's foremost piano teachers, could be heard calling him a genius. The jury's chair, Gilels, had made up his mind, even though six contestants remained, and had to make an exception to competition rules in allowing

Cliburn to return to the stage for a second bow. Even the orchestra stood up to acknowledge him. The jury agreed he should win first prize, but this was the Soviet Union, where only Soviets won. Gilels took the matter directly to Premier Nikita Khrushchev, who asked, "Is he the best?" Receiving an affirmative answer, he told them to give him the prize. Not only did this assure Cliburn of a brilliant career, but on returning to New York he received a ticker tape parade on Broadway, an honor never previously bestowed on a classical musician. Carnegie Hall quickly arranged for him to play the works from the competition there, and at Cliburn's insistence, Kondrashin came to conduct the concertos, with all involved cutting through the red tape to allow a Soviet conductor to work in the United States.

A few years later, Cliburn made his triumphant return to the U.S.S.R. to play concerts around the country, again with Kondrashin conducting, and the ovations if anything were even more fanatical than in 1958. Young women not only threw flowers, but gave him family keepsakes of great personal value to themselves. When students could not get into concerts, he played the entire program as dress rehearsals at no charge to them. When he played at the Moscow Conservatory, Khrushchev himself attended, and Cliburn, speaking in Russian, dedicated the concert to the much esteemed but now deceased Goldenweiser, adding an encore of Chopin's Fantasy in F Minor for Khrushchev. That concert in 1962 was filmed, and is available as a DVD (*Van Cliburn in Moscow*, vol. 1). While diplomatic forays were failing miserably, with Khrushchev pounding his shoe on his desk at the United Nations, nuclear tensions escalating, the United States trying to catch up after Sputnik, the shooting down of a U.S. spy plane, and numerous other conflicts, an unassuming young American from Texas won the hearts of the Russians, and at least for a moment melted the ice of the Cold War. It appeared that musicians could accomplish what politicians could not.

VIOLIN CONCERTO

Tchaikovsky's Violin Concerto, written in March 1878, could not be more different from the First Piano Concerto with all its drama and tension. It seems a fair assumption that the Violin Concerto is about

love, considering its tone and the time he wrote it, as well as the character of its melodic writing. At least one notable American composer with
the same Russian connection that Van Cliburn had seems to agree with
that. In writing his music for the original *Star Wars* trilogy, perhaps
most evident in *The Empire Strikes Back*, John Williams used Wagner-
like leitmotifs to identify characters, ideas, or emotions, and for some of
these he wrote motifs that sound very similar to well-known classical
themes. The Darth Vader theme, for example, sounds similar to the
second-movement funeral march from Chopin's Piano Sonata in B-flat
Minor, death being an appropriate association for this character. Even
more striking is the love theme for Han Solo and Princess Leia, initially
heard when these two first kiss, and in this case his motif comes remarkably close to the first theme of the first movement of Tchaikovsky's
Violin Concerto, introduced by the solo violin after five introductory
bars. How fitting that Williams should borrow this for his love theme,
when Tchaikovsky appears to be thinking of it that way himself. Later in
the film, during the roughly five-minute scene when Lando carbon-
freezes Han, the three most important motifs interact rapidly to create
a music drama, involving Luke (the *Star Wars* theme), Vader, and the
love between Han and Leia. In fact, Williams's Tchaikovsky-like music
rescued a very icy-sounding love pledge from the partners. Like Cliburn, Williams studied the piano at Juilliard under Rosina Lhevinne.

Tchaikovsky wrote only one violin concerto, but this was not the first
time he wrote for the combination of solo violin and orchestra. The first
came in the work immediately following the First Piano Concerto, the
Sérénade mélancolique (1875), a moderately slow piece filled with emotion that allowed him to explore the kind of feeling this instrument
could evoke. With the Valse-Scherzo written just before the concerto
he could enjoy a lighter side, but perhaps most significant is the way he
treated the solo violin in his ballet *Swan Lake* (1876), to be discussed in
chapter 4, using it especially in parts of the *pas de deux* when the love
between Siegfried and Adele (the transformed swan) solidifies. Again in
The Sleeping Beauty the solo violin stands out. Early in 1878, just after
completing the Fourth Symphony and the opera *Eugene Onegin*, and
also just following the rapid demise of his marriage to Antonina Milyukova, he fled Russia to Clarens, Switzerland, first living with his brother
Modest, and then joined by the violinist Yosif Yosifovich Kotek. Kotek
had emerged as a first-rate violinist, a graduate of the Moscow Conser-

vatory, later a student of Joseph Joachim in Germany, and an on-again-off-again lover of Tchaikovsky. Despite having written for this instrument previously, Tchaikovsky needed guidance on what a violinist could achieve, and for this he depended heavily on Kotek. Unlike Leopold Auer, the great Hungarian violinist working in Russia, who initially took a dim view of the work (although he later, as with Rubinstein and the piano concerto, added it to his repertory), Kotek gave him all the support he needed, and, no doubt, love and confidence as well. Kotek's world also included women, and Tchaikovsky, barely free of his own misguided marriage, had difficulty dealing with that. If this concerto stands as a love ode to Kotek, elements of tension that finally come in the finale may evoke strains in the relationship, as well as the composer's own insecurities, ambivalence about Russia, and personal demons.

The opening orchestral introduction of the first movement gives little foretaste of the theme to come in the solo violin, and if this theme represents love, in a moderate tempo after the opening *allegro*, Tchaikovsky underlies that possibility with the designation *dolce*. After the opening statement and elaboration, it comes a second time, amplified with chords for the soloist instead of just single notes. When the second theme arrives, *con molt' espressione* (with much expression), it has figures in common with the first melody, and in no way changes the warm tone so far permeating the movement. He follows sonata form in this movement, ending the exposition with a closing orchestral section that gives a more rousing presentation of the opening theme. Unlike the typical treatment of sonata form he gives no dramatic conflict in the exposition, but at the beginning of the development there appears to be a breakdown of the previous sense of affectionate accord as neither of the earlier themes returns, and a feeling of uncertainty, wandering, and even aimlessness creeps in. The development overcomes this with the return of the first theme in the solo violin, and the recapitulation presents no further problems as it brings the movement to a close.

The short second movement, a canzonetta instead of a larger aria, sings with wistful grace, giving a feeling of nostalgia for something of great beauty—maybe a past desire that cannot be recovered. Introductory hymnlike writing in the winds sets the tone, perhaps establishing a type of Russian religious atmosphere, before the ravishing *molto espressivo* violin melody enters. The richness of the melody does not abate, and when the violin drops out near the end, the same hymnlike strains

from the beginning return, finally fading into fragmentation and reduced in volume. With such a short movement, Tchaikovsky has linked
it together with the finale, with no break between the two, marked
attacca subito (sudden attack) for the beginning of the third movement.
With that attack, which turns out to be a real attack with a loud and
jolting chord, we get our first sense of possible discord in the work.
Because of the brevity of the second movement, we may be inclined to
hear it as the first section of a three-part ABA form, as was true of the
First Piano Concerto, but in this case the finale acts as the disruptive B
section, which of course does not allow the nostalgia previously heard to
return.

Unlike what often happens in those types of three-part forms, where
the B section may be ominous, the finale here behaves anything but
ominously; in fact, it is exuberant in the extreme as an opening introduction leads into the rhythmically buoyant theme in much the same
way as happened at the beginning of the first movement. The rhythmic
theme here has something of the atmosphere of a folk dance, undoubtedly Russian, bringing in a reminder of the simplicity and appeal of the
Russian countryside, as happened as well in the First Piano Concerto.
The Russian folk character becomes even more pronounced with the
second theme, with a simpler rhythmic folk-dance theme accompanied
in the cellos by open fifths that seem to suggest the drone of a bagpipe,
giving a double reminder of home.

When the violin drops out of this rondo finale, a new section begins,
with a motif introduced in the oboe and then taken up by other winds
and finally the solo violin, which has a striking resemblance to a key
passage from Lensky's act-two aria in *Eugene Onegin*, to be described
in chapter 5, which Tchaikovsky had just finished a few months earlier.
In that aria Lensky, about to fight a duel with his friend Onegin and
convinced he will die—which he does—speculates on what might have
been for him as a poet and a lover, and on how he will be remembered,
especially by his fiancée, Olga. The aria mixes nostalgia for the happy
time of love, for his poetic voice, which will now be silenced, and the
role of fate in overtaking his life, making love impossible and closing the
book on his poetic inspiration. Tchaikovsky could identify with these
sentiments exactly, as love for him could never be a reality, his inspiration often teetered on the brink of collapse, and fate always played its
superior hand, blocking the possibility of love. In this movement the

exuberant first movement returns, as does the bagpipe-accompanied folk-dance theme, but so does the Lensky fate motif, casting its shadow over all else in an irrevocable way. When the first theme returns to bring the work to an end, it does so as a formality, ending the form as it needs to end, but this may be something of a ruse, leaving fate to have the real final word, as was true in so many other works before and after. Some have complained about his treatment of form—or the lack of it—in this work, but for Tchaikovsky form always came second to what he had to say, which in the Violin Concerto he said in the most beautiful possible way, yielding one of the most wonderful concertos in the violin repertory.

Tchaikovsky wrote other concertos or concerto-like works, both at this time and later in his career, adding the cello to piano and violin. His major work for cello, if we can call it that, *Variations on a Rococo Theme* (1876), came only a year after the First Piano Concerto, and was one of his various concessions to eighteenth-century music, although, as the name suggests, with less substance than his various homages to Mozart, such as his *Mozartiana* suite, to be discussed in the next chapter. He returned to the cello just over a decade later with the *Pezzo capriccioso* (1887), a shorter but more substantial work that once again addresses the issue of fate. After what ultimately proved to be a brilliant success for the piano, he did not give up on writing concertos for that instrument, but never managed to find again what he had with the First. He wrote his Second in 1880, with mixed success, and a Third in the year he died, 1893, which in fact he did not complete. Similarly, he did not complete the Andante and Finale, which his former student and friend Taneyev orchestrated. One other concerted work for piano, the Concert Fantasia (1884), has little of the inspiration found in his First. In the end he wrote two extraordinary concertos, one for piano and one for violin, both relatively early in his career, and we are fortunate to have them in the repertory.

3

FOR THE LOVE OF MOZART
Chamber Music, Suites, and Serenades

Early in 1878 Tchaikovsky tried to persuade his newest best friend, Nadezhda von Meck, that she, like him, should love the music of Mozart. He had his work cut out for him on this, since she, his now faithful and diligent correspondent, had nothing but contempt for the composer he considered his idol. She did not mince words about this: "How sorry I am, my dear friend, that I cannot develop a taste for Mozart . . . I love depth, power, grandeur—consequently I can't love anything superficial, objective, wishy-washy, or insignificant. Those qualities can only be attractive in the most superficial connections and neither they nor their works impress me" (TM 233). Those of us who love Mozart may shudder at her dismissal, and if Tchaikovsky took offense, he tried not to show it; in fact, some of his arguments to dissuade her may make us cringe just about as much. He made a stronger case in trying to emulate Mozart in some of his own music, most notably in his chamber music—especially the string quartets—and certain orchestral works, such as the four suites. If his comments about Mozart evoke a certain amount of embarrassment, we perhaps need to ask if some of these works, and especially the most obvious homage, such as the Suite No. 4 (*Mozartiana*), do the same.

Of course we need to remember when this discussion took place, and the general lack of interest not only in Mozart but in just about any music from the eighteenth century at that time. Mendelssohn had brought about a revival of some of J. S. Bach's music, but the full-scale revival of Bach would not come during the nineteenth century. As for Mozart, audiences late in the nineteenth century knew only a few of his works well, such as *Don Giovanni* and the Piano Concerto in D Minor, since these appealed to demonic or unworldly sentiments from the time, but his chamber music, symphonies, concertos, and other operas had all but disappeared, not to come alive again until well into the twentieth century. With the music of Berlioz, Wagner, Verdi, Brahms, Liszt, and the like dominating the period, it should not surprise us that Mozart would be out of fashion, considered by many—such as Mrs. von Meck—to be trivial, thin, too happy, and forced by necessity that may preclude inspiration. Liszt had written transcriptions of Mozart's works, recasting them in a nineteenth-century aura, but Tchaikovsky would be among the first to wish to bring back the spirit of the eighteenth century in some of his own music. It appears not to have been by chance that the phenomenon of "neoclassicism" in music had its greatest resonance in Russia, with giants such as Stravinsky and Prokofiev picking up where Tchaikovsky left off. He forged a new direction with his love of Mozart, and considering the lack of knowledge about and accessibility to the music of Mozart, his own misjudgments can surely be forgiven.

In defense of Mozart, Tchaikovsky wrote at great length, probably occasionally adjusting his arguments in deference to his patron. Here are some of his main points:

> I don't just like Mozart—I idolize him. For me, *Don Giovanni* is the best opera ever written. . . . It is true that Mozart spread himself too thinly and often wrote not from inspiration but from necessity. But, if you read Otto Jahn's beautifully written biography of him, you will see that he could not help it. . . . But take Mozart's operas, two or three of his symphonies, his Requiem, the six quartets dedicated to Haydn, and G minor String Quintet. Surely in all these you can't deny that there is great charm? True, Mozart is not as profoundly arresting as Beethoven; his range is not as wide. Just as in his life he was to the very end a carefree child, so his music lacks the deep personal sadness which is felt so powerfully and mightily in Beethoven. Yet this did not prevent him from creating an impersonally tragic character, the most powerful, the most amazing human type ever portrayed in music. I refer to *Donna Anna* in *Don Giovanni.* . . .

In Mozart's chamber music it is the charm, the purity of texture, and the wonderful beauty of the part-writing which is captivating, but sometimes one comes upon things which bring tears to the eyes. Take the Adagio of the G minor Quintet. Nobody has ever expressed so beautifully in music the feeling of resigned and hopeless grief.

Do read *Otto Jahn's* weighty but interesting book on Mozart. You will see what a wonderful, pure, infinitely good and angelically chaste person Mozart was. He personified the ideal of the great artist who creates through the instinctive impulse of his genius. . . . And how easy it was for him to write! He never made rough drafts. The power of his genius was so great that all his compositions were written directly in full score. He worked them out in his head down to the smallest details. . . .

Everyone loved Mozart, he had the most wonderful, jolly, and even temperament. He was not a bit proud. Whenever he met Haydn he would declare his love and admiration for him in the most sincere and warm terms. The purity of his soul was untarnished . . . and I think that all this can be heard in his music, which is by its very nature conciliating, enlightening, and tender.

I could talk till kingdom come about this radiant genius for whom I have a sort of religious devotion . . . but I have never wanted so much to convert anyone to Mozart as I do you. . . . Through its [*Don Giovanni's*] medium I penetrated that region of artistic beauty where only the greatest geniuses dwell. Up till then I had known only Italian opera. It is thanks to Mozart that I dedicated my life to music. He triggered my musical potential and made me love music more than anything else in all the world. . . . If, some day, when you've listened, say, to the Andante of the G minor Quintet, you write to me and say you have been *moved*, I'll be delighted. (TM 219–222)

Much of this rings true, and shows the genuine depth of his debt to Mozart. He singles out Donna Anna, whose suffering he could probably relate to Tatiana's in *Eugene Onegin*, and he may therefore have thought of her as the most special character in *Don Giovanni*, if not as the character with the most deeply felt emotions in all of opera. He also took special delight in the part writing of the chamber music, and more than once commented on the moving aura of the Andante of the Quintet in G Minor, even contradicting himself in saying no music had ever captured grief as profoundly as this, just after saying Mozart could not compare favorably to Beethoven in this respect. The comment on Beethoven may have been for the benefit of Mrs. von Meck, who held him far above Mozart; the remark about the Andante probably comes closer to what he actually thought. With that Andante we have the ideal Tchaikovsky set for himself in the slow movements of his own chamber works, and his admiration for Mozart's part writing would be infused into his other movements; all of this came together in his String Quartet No. 1. At the same time, he had the highest respect for Beethoven, and his next two quartets come much closer to Beethoven's conception, especially in the later quartets.

At the same time, Tchaikovsky spouted lots of nonsense about Mozart, and much of this can be attributed directly to the biography he so admired by Otto Jahn. Relatively few biographies of Mozart appeared in the nineteenth century, and the massive one by Jahn in the middle of the century tried to make the mostly unknown Mozart palatable to the mindset of that century. Biographical distortions of Mozart started with the earliest efforts, for example the one by Georg Nissen, Mozart's widow's second husband, a biography presumed to be authoritative because of her involvement with it. That proved anything but true as the two of them crafted an image of Mozart they wished to leave for posterity, turning Mozart into the embodiment of goodness, purity, childlike simplicity, and spirituality. To come up with this, they had to excise portions of his letters with scatological language, crude sexual references, or arguments with his father, as well as things like scatological texts to canons. Similarly, the notion that Mozart could write without making drafts has long since been dispelled, especially when working on complex counterpoint in string quartets; we know that ignorance of drafts does not preclude their existence. These false impressions of Mozart can certainly not be blamed on Tchaikovsky, who found himself at the mercy of a well-meaning nineteenth-century writer who nevertheless had an axe to grind.

Where Tchaikovsky got things right about Mozart, his impressions came directly from the music, and here his judgments proved sound for the most part, giving him something he could transfer to his own operas and especially to his chamber music. At the same time, of course, his sensibilities belonged to his own century, and his perception of the best of the eighteenth century could not help but be modified by the times. Clearly he was not the first composer of his century to admire aspects of the previous century, and the extent that this turns up in these composers' music can be interesting. Berlioz, for example, considered Gluck to be the greatest of all previous composers of opera, but we see little of that influence in his own music; Wagner thought very much the same, and here we find even less (for Wagner this may have been more philosophical than musical). A composer such as Beethoven with a foot in both centuries may have seen himself transcending his predecessors, but that did not prevent him from acknowledging that he could never achieve what Mozart had with piano concertos. He dismissed operas such as *Don Giovanni* as being morally repugnant, and attempted to take the high road with his own *Fidelio*. A peculiar notion emerged at one time because of these thoughts about transcending the past—that some sort of progressive continuum exists in the history of music, fueled by extremists or megalomaniacs like Wagner, with successive generations advancing beyond previous ones. Our century can look back at Mozart and accept that no such qualitative advancement exists—that no real "progress" beyond Mozart has ever occurred, and Tchaikovsky may have been among the first to realize this.

A perhaps more generous view of the past has come from Franz Liszt, the master of the piano transcription, whose transcriptions of Schubert's songs were a clear act of homage to a composer he loved dearly. Similarly, his transcriptions of opera extend back to the eighteenth century, certainly to Handel, but importantly to Mozart, whose *Don Giovanni* he animates in a nineteenth-century spirit with his *Reminiscences of Don Juan*, extrapolating a few key sections of the opera to achieve this. To our ears these reinterpretations may seem a little humorous in being over the top, but we can be fairly certain that Liszt never thought of them in this way, as the term "reminiscence" had a distinctive nineteenth-century meaning, in an entirely positive sense. As his reminiscences moved closer to the present, through Meyerbeer, Rossini, Donizetti, Bellini, and Verdi, they took on a different significance, now more a transference of medium than of time, allowing his listeners to experience similar emotions from a new perspective, perhaps the way Musorgsky walks us through a gallery of Victor Hartmann's paintings with his *Pictures at an Exhibition*. Liszt takes this right to the present and Tchaikovsky himself, with his *Polonaise from Eugene Onegin*, a tour de force presenting not only the opening of the opera's third act as a piece of virtuosity for the piano, but his musical thoughts on the music that leads to the high point of fate in the opera. The next step invoking the eighteenth century would be neoclassicism, and Tchaikovsky can perhaps be thought of with one foot reminiscent of Liszt and the other setting in motion the direction in which Stravinsky and Prokofiev would move. Just as Liszt conceived of his reminiscences with respect, we need to keep this in mind with Tchaikovsky's *Mozartiana*; if we find this embarrassing, perhaps the problem lies more with the modern listener than the nineteenth-century composer.

By the time Tchaikovsky wrote his First String Quartet in 1871, the first quartet by any notable Russian composer, the medium had been around for well over a century and had gone through some notable transformations. During the nineteenth century a number of lesser-known composers, including Reicha, Gyrowetz, and a few others, wrote numerous quartets, but the composers we know best, such as Mendelssohn, Schumann, Smetana, Franck, and Brahms, wrote very few, in some cases no more than one. Only with Tchaikovsky's contemporary Dvořák would the quartet come back into its own with multiple works, and it would be a mainstay of some later composers, such as Shostakovich. The issue for many of the mid-century composers undoubtedly lay in what had been done with quartets by the four earlier giants of the medium: Haydn (who can be credited with inventing it), Mozart, Beethoven, and Schubert. Similar types of writing existed before Haydn, but he not only turned it into the exchange among four equals that it ultimately became, but gave that musical exchange social significance intended for an intimate setting, not unlike the novel, which originated around the same time. Mozart could not help but learn from Haydn, whose debt he acknowledged, but he consciously turned it into something very different, with a greater emphasis on the sound itself, which results from complex contrapuntal and motivic writing, the beauty of themes, and the richness of harmony in the interaction of the voices. Beethoven and Schubert both learned from their predecessors, but ultimately went in yet new directions, in their later quartets going beyond the sound itself into expressiveness that can be deeply personal. Beethoven especially made his last five quartets personal in the extreme, exceptionally complex works that almost dare us to try to comprehend his own complexity. Occasionally he gives us verbal clues, such as writing, "Muss es sein? Es muss sein" (Must it be? It must be) in the score for motifs in Op. 135, or instead of an expression marking for the slow movement in Op. 132 writing, "Dankgesang eines Genesenen an die Gottheit, in der lydischen Tonart" (Song of thanksgiving of one recovered from an illness, in the Lydian mode).

These four composers more than any others defined the essence of the string quartet, and with their works, which for the most part Tchaikovsky knew well, he had a dizzying array of possible influences. In his comments Mozart stands out as his model, but in his three quartets features from all four can be heard; the actual sound often has less to do with Mozart than with Schubert or Beethoven. Despite the sound, Mozart remains the central influence, and this may have more to do with an aesthetic approach than technique, since he did not make the quartet personal as Schubert and Beethoven ultimately did, but stayed more with the sound world that Mozart preferred. The string quartet may be intimate, but Tchaikovsky had symphonic music and to some extent opera into which he could pour himself, and for him the quartet became more of a purely musical challenge. What appealed to him appeared to be taking himself out of the equation, and engaging with the fundamentals of composition on the level of form, motivic working, counterpoint, tonality, themes, and harmony. Just as with Mozart this did not have to result in works devoid of feeling, but the expressiveness could be something other than his own tortured self, objectifying emotions in commonly shared experiences. But most of all, as Mozart had done in his G Minor Quintet, he could concentrate on the sound itself, exploring what could be audibly achievable in a small, tightly knit ensemble. He perhaps saw this as a rite of passage for a serious composer, as Mendelssohn, Brahms, and others had, and as his own colleague Borodin soon would. In its origins the quartet had been distinctly Viennese, but with the sound he hoped to create, perhaps he could steer that toward something more Russian. That possibility of nationalism in quartets would become the norm with Dvořák, Smetana, Gade, Grieg, Borodin, and most of all in the next century, Bartók.

STRING QUARTET NO. I

It's Friday, 27 April 2012, and you have come to the Weill Recital Hall on the third floor of Carnegie Hall in New York to hear a concert by the outstanding Czech string quartet the Pavel Haas Quartet, currently on an American tour. This beautifully decorated auditorium, with a seating capacity of only 268 and excellent acoustics helped by the partially rounded ceiling and blue drapes on the wall, is ideal for the intimacy of a quartet concert. This one begins with Tchaikovsky's String Quartet No. 1 in D Major, Op. 11, continues with Shostakovich's Quartet No. 7 in F-sharp Minor, and concludes with Smetana's Quartet No. 1 in E Minor ("From My Life"). The members of the quartet, Veronika Jarusková and Eva Karova (violin), Pavel Niki (viola), and Peter Jarusek (cello), came together about a decade ago in Prague, and now have been touted as one of the finest young quartets in the world. You cannot help but notice the name they have chosen for their ensemble, in recognition of the noted Jewish Czech composer Pavel Haas, who, after internment at Terezín (called Theresienstadt by the Nazis), was murdered by the Nazis at Auschwitz in 1944. This concert is being broadcast live on radio station WQXR, with distribution to affiliated NPR stations; it remains available online as *Carnegie Hall Live: Pavel Haas Quartet*. They enter to the warm applause of the audience, seating themselves with the first violin on the left, the second violin beside her, then the cellist, and the violist on the right.

With the first notes of this quartet, Tchaikovsky establishes his own distinctive voice in his first attempt at this most difficult of all types of composition; if he thought of this as a rite of passage for a serious composer, he certainly passed with flying colors. A number of things strike you in the first bar. Instead of four voices you hear six, since the viola and cello are playing double stops, immediately giving a fuller texture to the sound. Instead of something fast this one begins *moderato*, and unlike some fairly aggressive openings (e.g., Schubert's *Death and the Maiden* quartet in D minor), this one, in D major, has a gentle lilt, marked *piano* (quietly) and *dolce* (sweetly). That lilt has a peculiar character since tied notes thwart the 9/8 meter, with a pattern of quarter note, dotted quarter, quarter note, and two eighth notes emerging in the first bar, leaving no clear sense of meter but at the same time not sounding distorted or especially unstable. This unusual metric figure will persist throughout the movement, so despite its avoidance of the beat it takes on a normalcy by being persistent. Also in the first few bars no particular melody emerges, as if to give equality to all the voices. Under Haydn's guidance that sense of equality, or potential equality at any given moment, became the guiding principle of the string quartet, and Mozart, despite his obsequious recognition in a dedicatory letter of what Haydn had done, soon surpassed the master with his group of six dedicated to Haydn. Throughout this quartet you hear shades that could at different times be associated with any one of the four greats working in Vienna from 1750 to 1828, but never does that take away from this being uniquely Tchaikovsky.

The first movement follows the classical sonata form to a tee, with the roughly equal dimensions of the exposition, development, and recapitulation, and also with its traditional treatment of tonality, avoiding the kind of tonal adventures already characterizing his early tone poems and symphonies. With this quartet he went out of his way to make it a real quartet in the mode of his hero Mozart, taking it away from the more personalized expression of a work such as *Romeo and Juliet,* and aside from the form, it places special emphasis on the treatment of the interrelationship of the four voices. Almost never do you hear the first violin as a soloist with the other voices as accompaniment, and in the few instances where that happens, a high level of motivic or contrapuntal activity carries on in the accompaniment, always returning to the principle of equality. Any voice can carry the melody, and like Mozart (and Schubert), Tchaikovsky often gives it to the viola; at times it passes quickly from one voice to another, or all voices carry it in unison. When the recap arrives in the first movement, he accepts the tenet sometimes apparent in Mozart and more frequently in Schubert that there can be no direct repetition, since much has happened in the development to change the original theme or motif, and straight repetition would dodge the issue. We can easily get caught up in the charm of an initial theme, but subsequent dramatic activity precludes the possibility of it sounding just as it did before.

Even though Tchaikovsky went out of his way to write a type of "pure" or "absolute" music here, devoid of extramusical associations, that did not prevent him from giving the work a distinctly Russian tone, and that happens most notably in the second movement. To Mrs. von Meck he more than once mentioned Mozart's slow movement in the Quintet in G Minor, asking if it had moved her, and some parallels can be drawn with that movement and this one marked *andante cantabile* (singable). Some commentators have described Mozart's movement as tragic, but the nature of the writing does not bear that out, and that too applies to this quartet. While it has the power to be moving, he did not invest it with dark or profound meaning that should bring the listener to tears, despite what actually happened to Leo Tolstoy, who sat beside the composer at the first public performance of the work. He felt flattered by Tolstoy's reaction, but probably thought the great writer was having some difficulty controlling his emotions—or simply liked to respond with that type of overt emotionalism. In fact, for the tune at the beginning of this movement, he cribbed one he had used before, in his *Fifty Russian Folk Songs*, a folk song with the text "Vanya was sitting on the divan, smoking a pipe with tobacco" (another version gives it this way: "Upon the divan Vanya sat and filled a glass with rum; before he'd poured out half a tot, he ordered Katenka to come"). Whether about tobacco or rum, it should not have the effect of inducing tears. Like Mozart, who could write something that sounds moving without investing anything personal into it, Tchaikovsky appears to have attempted the same here, and he even got somewhat annoyed hearing it played over and over, usually without the rest of the quartet, including in a violin-and-piano arrangement popularized by Leopold Auer. The peculiar rhythm of the first movement in a varied way carries over to this movement.

The third movement, a scherzo, now finally with a fast tempo, suggests something closer to Haydn than Mozart. Mozart typically writes more sophisticated minuets—a courtly dance—for this movement, whereas Haydn preferred the lighter and more rustic scherzo, which literally means "joke" in Italian. Jokes happen not uncommonly in Haydn's quartets, and while Mozart occasionally throws them in, his tend to be more subtle or toned down. Tchaikovsky very much gets into the comical spirit in his scherzo, using rhythms typical of folk dances, and playing tricks on the listener with incongruous figures or surprise key changes. The fourth-movement finale, also fast, continues something of the light spirit of the previous movement, taking that to the extreme near the end of the work. After a very loud rising figure with a folk-dance rhythm, everything stops on an incongruous chord, followed by two bars of silence, with a fermata over the last rest, meaning the silence could be held almost indefinitely. When the players re-enter, they do so *andante* in contrast to the prior *allegro*, and very quietly proceed with harmonizations that seem awkward and out of place. This fades out into another extended rest, also with a fermata, and the Haas Quartet draws this out appropriately (almost absurdly) long. When they again re-enter, they make a mad dash for the end, *allegro vivace* and *fortissimo*, bringing the quartet to a close with a witty musical jest. Before the final unison on D, Tchaikovsky gives five huge D-major chords, with triple and quadruple stops, instead of four voices throwing in a staggering thirteen. Often before, including from the first bar of the work, we have heard more than four voices, sometimes giving the feeling of a quintet or sextet, but at the end he makes it sound like a string orchestra playing divisi (with parts dividing into sub-parts). You can only imagine that Tchaikovsky had fun writing this quartet, and the Haas Quartet delightfully captured the right spirit.

Chamber music never became an obsession for Tchaikovsky, although he did attempt various types until near the end of his life; the more of it he wrote, the less it bore any resemblance to Mozart. As a student he had a go at various types, aside from string quartet movements—one for four horns, another a wind octet, a quartet with harp, and a string trio as well as two string quintets—but the First String Quartet marked his initial serious effort. He followed this with two more string quartets, the Second (Op. 22) in 1874, and the Third (Op. 30) in 1876. Both of these veer more in the direction of Beethoven, especially the Third with its slow movement as a funeral march. That configuration of instruments no longer tempted him after 1876, but in later years he wrote a trio for piano, violin, and cello (Op. 42, in 1882), which he dedicated to Nikolay Rubinstein after his death, and a sextet for strings (Op. 70), which he did not complete until a year before his own death. The latter, named *Souvenir de Florence*, came immediately after *The Queen of Spades*, and in contrast to the dark character of the opera, it returns to the lighter atmosphere of his first quartet, finding that relief he had previously found in the type of musical detachment that chamber music permitted him to explore. As the name suggests, it allowed a musical reflection on the happier times he spent in Florence, one of his favorite spots of the many in which he found fairly frequent refuge outside of Russia.

ORCHESTRAL SUITES

By 1778 Tchaikovsky had reached a high level with two different types of orchestral writing, one on a large scale—the symphony—and the other more compact—the symphonic poem—both with the possibilities for high drama and also personal expression. That year he introduced a third type as well, the orchestral suite, diverging significantly from the other two in leaving aside the tension and angst they embodied. If Mozart did not directly have an influence on these, the eighteenth century certainly did, as they can in many respects be called neoclassical works. In his own way of thinking the eighteenth century represented something pure and unfettered, and while that in part may have been a misreading of the previous century, the possibility of writing such works appealed to his most basic compositional instincts. In some ways the symphonies and symphonic poems took him deeper into his own anxieties and distress, and while the act of writing such works could provide some relief from these, a type of musical escapism also had a powerful appeal; the imagined purity of eighteenth-century forms, dances, gestures, and techniques seemed to offer that possibility of escape. Since sonata form with its own high degree of drama and tension belonged to Mozart's generation, he needed to look earlier to find what he wanted, to the half century before Mozart's birth dominated instrumentally by different dance types, preludes and fugues, and themes and variations. Mozart of course continued to use these procedures, but not as the previous half century had; for him they proved more of a diversion, so in that respect he remained on Mozart's wavelength. While the first three suites look to that earlier time, the fourth moves ahead to his idol, very specifically as an homage to Mozart.

With his first suite started in 1878, Tchaikovsky wrote to his brother Modest that "I want to compose a suite so that I may have a good rest from symphonic music" (B3 19). The next two came in 1883 and 1884, and have a similar spirit, although progressively they became more complex if not more personal. The titles of the movements make clear what they are, although at times—especially with the orchestration—they sound like late-nineteenth-century reinterpretations of eighteenth-century procedures. The fugue had been a mainstay for composers such as Bach, and even Mozart became interested in fugues after being introduced to the music of Bach and Handel by Baron von Swieten in Vienna; Tchaikovsky's Suite No. 1 begins with the Introduzione e fuga, with a sufficiently complex fugue to be worthy of the name. Fugues tended not to occur in eighteenth-century suites, where dances predominated, and the next five movements fall more typically into line: 2) Divertimento; 3) Intermezzo; 4) Marche miniature (not always included); 5) Scherzo; and 6) Gavotte. The gavotte had very little life outside of the eighteenth century, and it's less clear that he had a real sense of the gavotte's character in terms of the dance gestures. Only in the twentieth century would a type of purist fascination compel performers and composers to understand and feel those gestures before attempting to perform them or integrate them into new works.

Already in Suite No. 2 he had moved more toward the nineteenth century, with less dance music from the previous century as it now consists of a series of character pieces—almost in the manner of Schumann. It starts with a piece called *Jeu de sons* (Sound game), which plays with exchanges among strings and winds, as he would do in other symphonic works where those exchanges could be highly dramatic. The next movement, *Valse*, also belongs to the composer's century, since the waltz did not yet exist in Mozart's time. Even the third movement, the *Scherzo burlesque*, steers toward the present by modifying the idea of the scherzo with a specific character. The fourth movement, called *Rêves d'enfant*, takes the character-piece flavor even further, exploring the fantastical dreams of a child. Only the title of the fifth and final movement seems grounded in the earlier century, *Danse baroque*, although even here the sound moves much closer to the present.

Similarly, Suite No. 3 has left Mozart's century behind, with the first two movements veering toward what could be construed as personal expression with an element of angst; it starts with an *Elégie*, and that moves to a *Valse mélancolique*, not merely a waltz, but one with a pensive atmosphere. The work ends with a large-scale theme and variations, but in no way do these invoke those of the eighteenth century, usually for keyboard with different types of figuration for each variation. In this suite each variation generates its own atmosphere, not unlike the manner of Beethoven in his *Diabelli Variations*. With this treatment he had come a long way since Suite No. 1.

SERENADE FOR STRING ORCHESTRA IN C

During the time that Tchaikovsky wrote his suites, he composed one of his most familiar pieces, the Serenade for String Orchestra in C, Op. 48 (1880). Scored for violins I and II, viola, cello, and bass, it could be thought of as a string quintet, although he preferred to have as many strings on each part as possible, and that also makes possible the not infrequent divisi. Like the suites following the first, he thought of the Serenade as arising from an inner compulsion, although he never revealed what that might be. He did, though, have Mozart in mind, going so far as to claim that "in the first movement I paid tribute to my worship of Mozart; this is an intentional imitation of his manner" (WT 236). Perhaps, but in listening to the Serenade, we hear very little that will remind us of Mozart's sound. The connection with Mozart in the first movement may not go beyond him calling it a *Pezzo in forma di sonatina* (piece in the form of a sonatina), a format familiar to short piano pieces in Mozart's time, and formally it lacks a development section. The movement may not be very long, but "small," as the title implies, does not describe what we hear; it starts with four prominent chords, *forte* and emphasized by divisi in most of the parts, and the phrase ends on a huge chord, *fff* with a total of sixteen parts. This opening material happens in a slow (*andante*) introduction, giving the sonatina symphonic scope. In the *allegro* section the chords, part writing, fast flourishes, and melodic breadth also suggest something big. The coda at the end of the movement returns to the introduction, with the slow tempo and same expansive chords of the opening.

For the second movement he gives us a waltz, with the expressive marking *dolce e molto grazioso* (sweetly with much charm). Mozart would not have written a waltz, which in fact did not exist in his time, but for the second or third movement dance he favored the minuet over the scherzo, preferring grace and charm instead of the more raucous scherzo. The slow movement, an elegy, appears to add to the inner-compulsion dimension. The final ten bars of this movement quietly launch a rising pattern, taking all the parts (with the exception of the bass, which drops out) just about as high as they can go, even using harmonics in the last five bars (the ° over the notes instructs the players to press their strings lightly so as to sound a note two octaves higher than written). At the beginning of the finale the two violins give the same note (D) heard at the end of the previous movement (without the harmonics), allowing a continuity between these movements. The finale has the subtitle "Russian Theme," and perhaps the elegy just heard places his overt introduction of something Russian in context, also including the rise to ethereal heights. He quotes actual Russian folk tunes in the finale, which also starts with a slow introduction. The folk character of the *allegro con spirito* will not escape anyone, with distinctive folk rhythms, and at times the use of *pizzicato* along with the nature of the writing imitates the balalaika. For this movement he does provide a development section, and he even weaves in a connection with the first movement, allowing the opening chords of that movement to return near the end of the work, bringing back the slow tempo and asking them to be played as loudly as possible. No doubt a programmatic character could be inferred for the entire work, perhaps involving his sometimes double life between Russia and Italy, or maybe even having to do with the recent upheaval in his life involving the failed marriage. He does not discourage us from superimposing such interpretations, and I leave it to listeners to come up with their own.

SUITE NO. 4: *MOZARTIANA*

With his Suite No. 4 (*Mozartiana*), Tchaikovsky paid his ultimate veneration to Mozart. For a few years he thought of doing something to commemorate the one-hundredth anniversary of his favorite opera, *Don Giovanni*, but only during that year, 1887, did he throw himself into it. He planned to create a suite that would be orchestrations of keyboard works by Mozart, and the choices may seem surprising since mostly he opted for relatively unknown pieces; with these selections he went where no one else likely would. Of course he hoped to profit from this work, anticipating there would be an audience for it, but to his publisher Jurgenson he deferred to his idol: "My position as regards Mozartiana is very delicate, for how can I receive much money for the fact that Mozart was a genius, and yet on the other hand my labor is worth something" (WT 326–327). Liszt would play a role in one of the movements, but unlike Liszt he did not write transcriptions that reinterpret the borrowed pieces, for the most part simply giving them in orchestrated versions. He wanted there to be more Mozart than Tchaikovsky in these, and aside from a few unlikely orchestrations and added material, he came very close to succeeding in this. His own preface to the published score read as follows: "A great many of Mozart's outstanding short pieces are, for some incomprehensible reason, little known not only to the public but to many musicians also. The author who has arranged this suite entitled *Mozartiana* had in mind to provide a new occasion for the more frequent performance of these pearls of musical art, unpretentious in form, but filled with unrivalled beauties" (B4 113).

The first of the four movements shows just how short the target pieces could be, in this case the Gigue in G Major, K574, a mere thirty-eight bars long. Normally in early-eighteenth-century suites the gigue came as the last movement, but as a lively dance, often with leaps, Tchaikovsky placed it first to achieve a cheerful opening. Mozart kept the texture very thin, and despite using a full orchestra, Tchaikovsky preserved the original essence, also retaining the original key and of course the time signature of 6/8. Mozart gave no dynamic markings, so Tchaikovsky's, ranging from *p* to *fff*, are his own. The angular and often leaping melody at times becomes fairly chromatic, and chromaticism runs through the entire suite, possibly being one of the factors that prompted the choice of these pieces. The second movement, the Minuet, from Mozart's Minuet in D Major, K355, almost as short as the Gigue, has the distinctive elegance of Mozart's minuets. In this one Mozart uses some expression markings, and while Tchaikovsky adds more of his own, he follows the spirit of the original, especially the opening marking of *dolce*. The chromatic motion here immediately emerges in the smooth legato lines of the first few bars.

The third movement, entitled Prayer, or Preghiera, has a somewhat more convoluted origin, and this is where Liszt comes in. It's based on the exceptionally short choral motet, the "Ave verum corpus," for soprano, alto, tenor, bass, strings, and organ, and surely possesses one of the most glorious melodies that Mozart ever wrote; like the Minuet it develops a chromatic line in the second bar. As a motet it of course has a text, and even though Tchaikovsky did not take it directly from this source, he may have had the text in mind when calling it a prayer: "Hail, true body born of the Virgin Mary, who truly suffered, sacrificed on the cross for man, whose pierced side overflowed with water and blood, be for us a foretaste in the test of death." This being a relatively late work for Tchaikovsky, who found himself often haunted by thoughts of his own mortality, the premonition in this text could have stirred him particularly. Even without the text the music could not be more moving.

His source, though, turned out to be a piano transcription by Liszt, *A la Chapelle Sixtine*, in which Liszt reinterpreted both Allegri's *Miserere* (the work Mozart wrote down after hearing it only once in the Sistine

Chapel) and "Ave verum corpus"; Tchaikovsky used only the latter, which makes up the second half of Liszt's work. Now he orchestrated Liszt instead of Mozart, and since Liszt wrote a transcription that re-interprets Mozart, this works in a manner unlike the other movements. In fact, he even went beyond Liszt; instead of Liszt's two-bar introduction he added a longer one, of eight bars, and he opted for a flat key as well, changing Liszt's B major to B flat (Mozart wrote it in D). The plaintive nature of it demonstrates how ably Mozart captured this character in the major key as well as the minor, something he did consistently in his operas as well, for example with the Countess's first cavatina in *The Marriage of Figaro*. Of course the use of chromatic lines helped to achieve that. Some have found Tchaikovsky's use of the harp overly sentimental, perhaps undoing what Mozart manages with great simplicity; in his defense, he's prompted to add the harp where Liszt puts in large rolled chords, and the treatment of the harp has similarities to other works, such as his *Romeo and Juliet*. It may not be Mozartian, but that should not necessarily taint our view of his homage. At the end, after four bars of rapid broken chords in the harp, it concludes with the strings in very high registers, fading away to nothing (*pppp*). This also connects it with parts of *Romeo and Juliet* where he wanted an ethereal, heavenly atmosphere, and anticipated what he would do in the last year of his life in the *Pathétique* Symphony as it fades into nothingness at the end. His reworking here may very well have taken on personal significance for him.

Unlike the Serenade in C, where the high notes at the end of the Elegy led directly into the high notes at the beginning of the Finale, here a clear break occurs between the movements, with the fourth-movement finale full of fun and silliness. Now he returns to the piano pieces, a Theme and Variations using Mozart's Variations on "Unser dummer Pöbel meint" (What our stupid Pöpel thinks) by Gluck (K455). Mozart generally took for his themes variations from other composers, often because they were well known, and players at the time would enjoy the playful expansion on something they probably knew and loved. In this case he took it from Gluck's opera *Le recontre impévue* (The unexpected encounter, or The pilgrims to Mecca), specifically an air near the beginning for the comical character Le Calender, a dervish (bass), not unlike Osmin in his own *The Abduction from the Seraglio*. Le Calender sings here about the expectations of a stupid population in contrast to the life of good food and wine that he enjoys. Gluck had heard Mozart's *The Abduction* and complimented him on it, and to return the favor, Mozart, probably in Gluck's presence, took the funny little theme from this air and improvised variations on it, no doubt to Gluck's amusement. Mozart's variations usually came into being this way, as improvisations, and only later would he write them down, to be published and played by amateur pianists.

Unlike variations by Beethoven and later composers, ones from the eighteenth century followed a well-defined format, first presenting the theme as simply as possible. The typical format, which this one follows, goes something like this: variation I, right-hand figuration in sixteenth notes; II, left-hand figuration; III, R.H. triplets; IV, R.H./L.H. exchanges; V, in the parallel minor; VI, added ornamentation; VII, more harmonic writing; VIII, L.H./R.H. crossing over each other with rapid figuration; IX, *adagio*; X, *allegro*. This final *allegro* will be longer than the other variations and may add new treatments; Mozart gets fairly carried away with that, adding a cadenza, of course delightfully in jest considering the humble tune that gave the theme, now making it sound like a fantasy, if not a concerto. Part of the fun he could have with the theme originated from Gluck's, which starts with a series of parallel octaves—a no-no in part writing that can be accounted for by the grammatical ineptitude of the dervish singing the part. Mozart uses only four bars from the original theme, emphasizing the parallel octaves in the first two bars, then adds a four-bar B section, and finally returns to the A theme, adding an extra doubling to the octaves.

For Tchaikovsky the fun in orchestrating this lay in trying to hear what instrumentations the keyboard writing implies. For the theme itself he does this by separating strings and winds, letting the strings play the two bars of parallel octaves, and then giving the winds the answering cadence; for the B section instead of two and two the strings and winds separate one and one, adding a cheerful contrast. Each variation then follows Mozart's figurations, the right hand of the first going to the clarinet, and the left hand of the second to the viola; the triplets of the third variation flow nicely in the flute, and the exchanges of the fourth engage the full orchestra. The orchestration becomes especially interesting later on with cadenzas or cadenza-like passages. Mozart connects variations VIII and IX (the *adagio*) with a rapid single-line flourish, and Tchaikovsky logically hears this as a solo violin line, setting up what will happen in the *adagio*. Here too Mozart implies a solo line, which Tchaikovsky keeps for the solo violin, now pushed well beyond the ornamental flourishes of the piano, in fact allowing the violin to behave as though it's in a violin concerto. Mozart already had his fun with this somewhat fatuous writing considering the inane theme it comes from, and Tchaikovsky takes that even further by mockingly pulling on the heartstrings with the solo violin. The violin has had its romp, so the big cadenza in the finale goes instead to a solo clarinet. The work ends like the whirling dervish it should be, and Tchaikovsky has given a delightful re-enactment of Mozart having fun with Gluck, certainly living up to the adoration he felt for Mozart.

4

BALLET'S NEW WAY

Swan Lake

Camille Saint-Saëns visited Moscow in November 1875 to conduct and perform some of his own music, and when he met Tchaikovsky, the two of them hit it off beautifully. Their friendship did not follow a normal path, and Tchaikovsky's brother Modest remembered this delightful incident about a mania they had in common:

> In their youth both had been enthusiastic admirers of the ballet, and had often tried to imitate the art of the dancers. This suggested the idea of dancing together, and they brought out a little ballet, *Pygmalion and Galatea*, on the stage of the Conservatoire. Saint-Saëns, aged forty, played the part of Galatea most conscientiously, while Tchaikovsky, aged thirty-five, appeared as Pygmalion. N. Rubinstein formed the orchestra. Unfortunately, besides the three performers, no spectators witnessed this singular entertainment. (LL 176)

What a pity that no one else saw it, since it must have been hilarious. If nothing else, it tells us that when Tchaikovsky started to compose his first ballet in August of the year he met Saint-Saëns, he came to it with a passion that went back to his childhood, not only for the music of ballet but also dancing.

Before 1875 no one could deny the popularity of ballet in large European cities, as both court and public entertainments, but not a single major composer contributed to this—in Russia, France, or anywhere else. Ballet belonged to dancers and choreographers, who intended their art to be visually pleasing, which meant the music should be simple so as not to get in the way of the dancers' performances. With music as little more than a necessary evil, ballet-specialist composers provided scores that met the requirements of choreographers, who told them what meters, tempos, dance types, and every other characteristic they needed. They wrote straightforward and repetitive music, providing no problems for the often musically challenged conductors who led from the pit. The ballets themselves had little by way of dramatic plot or continuity, but tended to be pastiches of dances strung together serendipitously, allowing the dancers to reveal their prowess. This started to change in the 1870s, first in France with Léo Delibes's *Sylvia* and *Coppélia*, two works Tchaikovsky admired without reservation, but while writing *Swan Lake* he did not yet know them. In making his foray into ballet he did so in many ways without any clear sense of what he was doing.

Not surprisingly, serious composers and musicians held ballet music in very low regard, and that spread beyond the medium itself to intrusions of ballet music into other types of composition. After the premiere of the Fourth Symphony, Tchaikovsky's former student and later good friend Sergey Taneyev expressed reservations about that work because parts of it—especially the trio in the third movement—sounded to him too much like ballet music: "I don't like the trio which is like a dance out of a ballet." This succeeded in getting Tchaikovsky thoroughly annoyed, evoking this reply: "I simply do not understand how in the term *ballet* there can be anything *censorious*" (B2 162). This exchange will be looked at more closely in chapter 6, but at this point few colleagues could grasp why Tchaikovsky would wish to venture into the musically lowbrow area of ballet. In the short term they turned out to be right, since the experience of getting *Swan Lake* produced did not suggest much of a future for him as a ballet composer. Only after his death would it be produced in a way that pointed to it becoming the most popular ballet of all time; thankfully he loved ballet enough that his experience did not put him off from trying his hand at it again, with *The Sleeping Beauty* and *The Nutcracker*. He could very easily have given up on the medium.

Tchaikovsky said very little to anyone about his work on *Swan Lake*, aside from the fact that the Bolshoy in Moscow commissioned it and that he took it on partly for the money (eight hundred roubles), but also because "I have long had a wish to try my hand at this kind of music" (LL 173). According to Modest it took him only two weeks to write the first two acts once he had started. No one really knows if he took a scenario provided to him, possibly by Vladimir Begichev, the supervisor of the Moscow Imperial Theaters, and the dancer Vasily Geltser, or if he invented the idea himself, perhaps using the German collection of folktales by Johann Musäus, *Volksmärchen der Deutschen*. The possibility of it being his idea seems more plausible since a few years earlier while spending a summer at his sister Alexandra's house in Kamenka he wrote a children's one-act ballet by the same name for family amusement, and even used the now famous swan theme for that. Whether or not he collaborated with the choreographer Julius Reisinger to come up with suitable music we do not know, although it seems unlikely that he did despite his inexperience in the medium. Before starting to write he studied other ballet scores, and probably felt that a mediocre choreographer such as Reisinger would only get in the way of the music he wanted to write. When it came to rehearsals, the dancers complained about the complexity of the music, as did the conductor, Stepan Ryabov, who had never dealt with music of this difficulty before. Tchaikovsky knew perfectly well how dismal ballet music had been prior to this, and how disconnected the music of these works had been from the scenario, assuming one existed at all. A composer of his stature could not get involved with ballet simply to continue a shabby tradition; he resolved to bring something new, with music at a high level that, like opera, carries within itself the most important sense of the drama. He appears to have concluded that choreographers and dancers would simply have to adapt to his new way.

Unfortunately he overestimated the abilities of the others involved with the production to think beyond the bleak landscape that defined ballet at the time. Aside from the complaints of the dancers and the musicians, Reisinger not only came up with a pedestrian choreography but he took a slash-and-burn approach to the score as well, getting rid of Tchaikovsky's music that he considered too awkward to dance to, and substituting music by some of the lesser ballet composers he normally dealt with. In the end about one-third of Tchaikovsky's music had been excised. The pastiche that remained brought very little praise from reviewers, but being as good or better than anything else in the repertory, it lasted a number of years, until the poorly constructed sets finally disintegrated.

In this state the ballet would never have come down to us as the great work we know it to be. Not long after Tchaikovsky's death the brilliant St. Petersburg choreographer Marius Petipa, with whom Tchaikovsky collaborated on *The Sleeping Beauty*, recognized the quality of the work and set about revising it completely with a new choreography, along with his assistant Lev Ivanov. The new director of the Imperial Theaters, Ivan Alexandrovich Vsevolozhsky, persuaded Modest to rewrite the scenario as well, and that resulted in the generally superior scenario as we now know it—although even today parts of it, and especially the ending, continue to be changed.

Aside from his own fascination with dancing, ballet seemed to appeal to Tchaikovsky because it represented a world of fairy tales removed from the burdens of life—that audiences young and old could absorb with childlike innocence. Operas and symphonies could deal with the discordant aspects of life, but ballet allowed something different, along the lines perhaps of the lighter music in his Fourth Symphony, the second theme of the first movement, for example, as he described it to Nadezhda von Meck: "Would it not be better to turn away from reality and give yourself up to daydreams. . . . The daydreams have gradually taken possession of the soul completely. Everything gloomy and joyless is forgotten. Here it is, here is happiness!" (TM 186). In chapter 6 I will discuss how this description of the work missed the mark, and applying that to ballet, especially *Swan Lake*, may also do a disservice. His next two ballets would keep things lighter, with happy endings, but *Swan Lake* clearly has a darker side, evident not only in the scenario but also in the music. Even here he could not keep free of his presentiments about fate and the impossibility of real love ever being achieved.

The story, as Modest revised it, starts out as a lovely fairy tale: a young prince, Siegfried, enjoying the companionship of his friends and tutor, is told by his princess mother that on his twenty-first birthday he must choose a bride and settle into more responsible pursuits. He sees some swans flying overhead, and with his friends he goes to the nearby lake to hunt. He aims at one of the swans, but she, suddenly transformed into a beautiful young woman, demands to know why he torments her. He discards his weapon and soon falls in love with her; when her companions come to her aid, she assures them he will not harm her.

She, Odette, has been captured by an evil genie, Rothbart, who has condemned her to be a swan by day and woman by night, and only love with a sacrifice of death can free her from the spell. The Prince invites her to come to the castle the next day, to the ball at which he will choose her as his bride, but she reminds him of the condition of her release. At the ball the most beautiful young women of the land dance for him, but none of these appeal to him. A mysterious man with a beautiful woman dressed in black appears, and believing her to be Odette, Siegfried selects her, to the delight of his mother. The mysterious man reveals himself to be Rothbart, and the woman, Odile, turns out to be his daughter; her resemblance to Odette has duped Siegfried, who then sees a rising image of Odette. He rushes to the lake to find her and ask forgiveness, but since he has broken his promise to love only her, she can do nothing. In the original version she bids him farewell in grief, but a great storm causes waves to sweep them into the lake, where they both die. In the end swans can be seen on the lake. In Modest's version the two lovers take their lives together, breaking Rothbart's evil spell.

Throughout the scenario, both old and new, various touches of Wagner can be found, perhaps surprising for a composer who claimed to have very little use for Wagner's music. In 1876 Tchaikovsky attended the first performance of the Ring Cycle, which he did not like, and the name Siegfried may have stuck in his mind. Hunting swans would have resonance in *Parsifal*, although Wagner would not complete that until much later. Riding a swan, though, happens in *Lohengrin*, and from that opera we find some possible musical borrowing as well. The idea of being released from a curse by a sacrifice of death comes from *The Flying Dutchman*. Any of these could be coincidental, simply possibilities from the vast array of myths, legends, and fairy tales, but perhaps not. Like many of Wagner's operas, *Swan Lake* does not end happily, and despite his thoughts about ballet, it's hard to say how he would have reacted to an Orpheus type of ending, or, as we will see in the Maryinsky production to be described in the next section, a genuinely happy ending.

Tchaikovsky's spectacular achievement with *Swan Lake*, completely unrecognized at its premiere, was to make ballet dramatic in a way it had never been before, and to accomplish that with the fusion of music and scenario, allowing the music itself to carry much of the drama. We should not imagine, though, that this led to some sort of through-composed music drama à la Wagner or anyone else, or that he somehow turned ballet into opera with movement instead of song. Ballet had certain conventions that could not be abandoned, and Tchaikovsky keeps these intact, such as constructing the work as a series of discrete numbers for dancing, never too long because of the limits to what any one dancer or the corps de ballet can manage without collapsing physically. Tchaikovsky may have actually provided too many of these numbers, and it's unlikely that any production will include them all. He does write discrete pieces to be danced, but he goes far beyond this, integrating the music in ways that the ballet composers before him could not possibly have imagined. Some of these features will be audible to the entire audience, while others will be caught by only the most sophisticated listeners, such as key schemes that unify, or at times make things unstable. Even if most listeners will not be aware of these, they are worth noting since they reveal the lengths to which he went to make his ballet dramatic, with a type of underlying treatment that may affect us even if we do not necessarily hear it. This may be similar to montage in film, which works on our emotional responses in ways that few filmgoers would be able to describe, despite the careful construction of it by directors such as Griffith, Eisenstein, or Hitchcock.

On the fully audible level, though, Tchaikovsky uses thematic continuity—most notably the swan theme that we first hear at the end of Act 1, and then in each subsequent act of the ballet. Not only do we hear this, but it makes a direct emotional impact, in the beautiful wistfulness of its first appearance, and later as he changes or distorts it, allowing us to remember its original impression as it takes on other meanings, even becoming grotesque. Between these extremes he brings to bear on the drama other procedures, involving themes, rhythms, meters, orchestration, and the use of specific types of dances, some of which have distinctive meanings or associations, all of which will be considered in the next section. He surged ahead of his time in envisaging what ballet could be, and thanks to Petipa and his colleagues, the world has been able to enjoy this most popular of all ballets.

INTRODUCTION AND ACT I

It's Sunday, 21 January 2007, and you have come to London on a business trip from the United States, to oversee the development of an American subsidiary office in the United Kingdom. You have no business or social responsibilities on this Sunday afternoon, so after a stroll around the British Museum and some of your other favorite Bloomsbury haunts, you return to your hotel at Russell Square to watch a 3:15 p.m. BBC television broadcast of *Swan Lake*, which you saw announced the day before in *The Guardian*. This broadcast, filmed by the BBC at the Maryinsky Theater in St. Petersburg earlier in 2006, stars Ulyana Lopatkina, one of the great ballerinas of the time, as Odette/Odile, and is conducted by Valery Gergiev, the internationally known musical director of the Maryinsky. For you, a woman fully entrenched in the corporate world, spending the afternoon watching a ballet is not in the least unusual. Like thousands of other young girls in North America—to say nothing of Europe and the rest of the world—you started going to ballet classes at the age of seven, and since you loved it and showed considerable promise, you continued until the age of fifteen, even landing roles in local productions of *The Nutcracker*. Because of your height in your early teens, which kept climbing higher and higher, it became clear that a career in ballet would not be an option, but that did not stop you from continuing until your mid-teens, since you enjoyed the camaraderie of the other dancers along with the fantastic physical condition it kept you in. During the early years of your dancing only one of your fellow dancers was a boy, who no doubt enjoyed the attention of so many girls, but at twelve he left, with disappointment, because the Saturday lesson time conflicted with his little league baseball games.

One of the aspects of ballet you find most fascinating is the way dancers can disguise extraordinarily difficult physical activity to make it somehow seem effortless. In eight years you became sufficiently advanced to begin to realize what goes into that, coached by a teacher who had been a successful dancer herself and knew exactly how to impart this quality. In fact, few other physical activities require as much effort as ballet, as dancers seem at times to defy gravity, but to uninitiated viewers, they do not appear to be expending all that much energy. You also enjoy watching Olympic sports, both summer and winter, some of which similarly defy the laws of gravity, but mostly these athletes make no pretense of the effort, resting after intense exertion from the high jump or long jump. Floor exercises in gymnastics and figure skating have more in common with ballet than other sports, and you remember well when figure skating started to emulate ballet, especially the British skater John Curry, who won the Olympic gold medal in 1976, and also the Canadian Toller Cranston, who won the bronze. After these two, figure skating never returned to a display of athletic spins and other maneuvers, but the artistic element became fundamental to it, and with that also came the disguise of the physical effort. Opera singers in fact do something very similar, using a great amount of energy to sing, especially with the control of muscles in the solar plexus area to regulate the even flow of air, but Placido Domingo and Jon Vickers made their high A flats seem effortless.

Like anyone interested in ballet, you know *Swan Lake* well, having seen more than one live production of it, and you also own a DVD of the famous version danced by Margot Fonteyn and Rudolf Nureyev, a performance you could not imagine being surpassed. Even if the two principals do not top these, you still look forward to what the Maryinsky will do with it, the company that brought this ballet to life in 1895 and has featured it more than any other work in the century since. Also, much more goes on than simply the two principals, with difficult parts for the corps de ballet and numerous secondary soloists; practically no other company in the world has the depth to do justice to all these other parts.

At 3:15 you turn on the telly to Beebs I, as your British friends call it, and after the titles introducing the work, the theater, and the composer, a wide-angle shot of the magnificent Maryinsky Theater shows the stage curtain, the orchestra, a section of loge boxes, and some of the audience. After a close-up of Gergiev walking to the podium and then bowing, which the orchestra also does, you see a brief close-up of the oboe soloist, of course for good reason, since he gets the first of the memorable melodies, starting in bar 1. Gergiev begins, and as that beautiful melody flows, you sees close-ups of his batonless hands, with fingers fluttering in his characteristic way; you have no idea how the musicians can follow his finger paroxysms, but since he's in demand around the world, including at the Met, he's obviously doing something right. Perhaps what he does best involves what happens at rehearsals and the level of understanding he brings to the works he conducts.

The work begins with a very short introduction, a mere sixty-one bars—less than three minutes in duration, but you know from *Eugene Onegin* how salient these short intros can be, telling us important things about what will follow, setting the tone, introducing thematically crucial material, and possibly embodying a small drama in itself. The first impression of tone comes from the plaintive melody in B minor sounded by the oboe and then taken up by the clarinet followed by the cello, with nothing arousing cheerful expectations, but instead nostalgia for something already lost. Starting with the oboe may itself be significant, considering how he treats that instrument in two works to follow shortly after this, in the slow movement of the Fourth Symphony and as the obbligato accompaniment to Tatiana in her letter-writing scene in Act 1 of *Onegin*. The melody itself, the minor key, and the instrumentation all leave a sense of foreboding, and it does not take long for the darkness to set in. After the violins have had a go at the melody, bassoons and violas get stuck on a fragment of it, allowing it to disintegrate, and a crashing *fortissimo* chord after this completely shatters the atmosphere. No sweetness remains as the full orchestra drives home jarring rhythmic figures and tremolo triplets in the strings, not only destroying the previous atmosphere, but getting even louder as it builds to *fff* with nonmelodic hammering. Clearly in an ABA form, the pounding of the B section leads directly into a return of the opening theme, still at *fff*, and at that volume it has lost all its charm as the brutality of the B section has permeated it. In this short intro we have a précis of the entire scenario, as we start with beauty and see it destroyed, with any attempt to return to the earlier beauty disallowed. Many of the dance numbers that follow will not participate in this symphonic overview of the drama, but in the first three minutes Tchaikovsky has told us what we need to know before the ballet unfolds. If the production gives it a happy ending, as this one does, we need to remember not only the music at the end but also in the third part of the introduction.

The gloomy mood of the end of the intro transitions almost imperceptibly into the beginning of Act 1 by way of a low A in the double basses and timpani, with two bars of nothing but this to start scene 1, and this continues for another fourteen bars as the atmosphere tries to change. This should be a scene of rejoicing, for the celebration of Siegfried's coming of age, and while it becomes that, even here the music as it opens foreshadows dark clouds. Things lighten up as the corps de ballet cheerfully floods the stage, a jester brilliantly danced by Andrei Ivanov adds to the mirth, and finally Siegfried (Danila Korsuntsev) makes his entrance. The second scene, a waltz, one of many in the work, continues the festive atmosphere, although as the discussion of that dance in *Onegin* will confirm (see chapter 6), waltzes in the nineteenth century could have negative connotations. Some hint of that comes in scene 3 with the entrance of Siegfried's mother, the Princess, who tells him he must now choose a wife and settle down, leaving behind the good life of the bachelor he has enjoyed to this point. If you think that Alexandra Gronskaya playing the non-dancing role of the Princess looks too young to be Siegfried's mother, you're entirely right: in fact, Gronskaya is one year younger than Korsuntsev. Similar miraculous conceptions happen not infrequently in the theater or movies. In *North by Northwest*, Jessie Royce Landis, playing the mother of Roger Thornhill (Cary Grant), was only one year older than Grant.

Most productions have a companion, Benno, a knight, who tries to console Siegfried in his loss, but this production replaces him with a jester, making less of the regret about the carefree existence now to be left behind. Waltzing, though, thought by some in the nineteenth century to be too lascivious, may symbolize at this point something of the frivolity that Siegfried must abandon. During the waltz, Wolfgang, his tutor, becomes progressively more tipsy, the jester dances exuberantly and flirtatiously, and Siegfried enjoys dancing with peasant women—usually more than one at a time. After the departure of the Princess the festivities continue, first with a *pas de trois*, musically a set of variations, as happens elsewhere (the *pas de deux* and *pas de six*), allowing some spectacular dancing from other soloists in the company. In Tchaikovsky's original design for the ballet the *pas de deux* comes immediately after the *pas de trois*, with Siegfried dancing with a peasant girl, a plausible place for him to be more indulgent in a Don Juan–like way, but here, as in most productions, this has been moved to Act 3 for the Siegfried/Odile love dance. Instead of the *pas de deux* we jump to a *pas d'action*, where Siegfried can continue to flirt with the peasant girls, they can have some fun with the now drunken tutor, and the jester pirouettes in physically unimaginable ways. A brief *sujet*, or pantomime, leads to a polonaise, the Goblet Dance, the last fling for Siegfried of wine, women, and song. The placement of the polonaise here may have some connection to *Onegin* where the final act begins with that dance, which leads to the onset of the heavy hand of fate and the downward spiral to the end.

The merrymakers have left, and the solitary Siegfried, seeing swans overhead, picks up his crossbow with the intention of hunting at the beginning of the finale to Act 1. Tchaikovsky now introduces the famous swan theme, which more than any other music defines this ballet, with the melody given by solo oboe accompanied by harp and tremolo strings. After some tonal wandering he now returns to the key of the intro, B minor, and while the melody has its own distinctive character, it does bear some resemblance to the intro's opening theme: both start on a half-note F sharp, followed by four eighth notes (ascending in the swan theme instead of descending, as in the intro), and both then continue with the same rhythmic motif. That wistful, nostalgic atmosphere of the intro, at a similarly moderate tempo, now returns, with the same key giving a type of structural unity to the movement. At the beginning of the intro you could not help but feel a certain amount of sadness, and the destructiveness of what followed confirms that all was not well. Using the swan theme for the finale may seem misdirected, since Siegfried, in the highest of spirits, now sets out to enjoy an activity he loves—hunting waterfowl. The music tells us something else, not only that he should not be hunting these swans, but that events on a much grander scale will occur shortly. Considering the destructive path of the intro, we now can anticipate that something similar of importance may happen in the future, and his encounter with swans will be at the heart of it. In fact, when the winds take over the melody (horns, flutes, and clarinets in unison) at a *fortissimo* level, you get some inkling that trouble may be brewing.

ACT 2

The second act starts as a continuation of the first, and while you hear the same swan theme just heard, you see close-ups of the oboist as well as Gergiev with his quivering fingers (this Maryinsky production, like the Petipa/Modest revision, treats Act 2 as scene 2 of the first act). While that music may have seemed a little mysterious at the end of the previous act, it now gets linked directly to swans as the first visuals after the shots of the orchestra show a deep-blue lake in the forest with swans gliding on its smooth surface, so smooth that they cast a perfect reflection in the water. The link with the intro becomes much more pronounced in the opening scene of Act 2 as the music follows a similar three-part pattern, moving away from the swan theme to something with a more ominous sound. Tchaikovsky starts that transition with rapid triplets first in the winds and then shifting to the strings before a descending passage in the lower instruments that leads to a crashing chord at *fff*. That chord sets off a loud and frightful repetition of the swan theme, offering an ideal point for the menacing Rothbart in the form of a black owl to make his sinister first appearance. At the end of the scene the swan theme tries to re-establish itself, but fails to launch as it becomes fragmented in the lower strings and bassoon, just as the melody in the intro died. Now the destructive B section can be given a visual essence, in the form of Rothbart, whose presence will prevent the swan theme from regaining its former shape and beauty.

Siegfried enters after this musically self-contained opening scene, in scene 11 oblivious to the intimidating Rothbart, as the jaunty new theme with its dotted rhythm presents him as the blithe hunter. The music slips back into a triplet pattern and then to a sped-up two-note dotted figure that caused the disintegration of the swan theme at the end of the previous scene; this culminates in a loud chord that gives a good opportunity for Rothbart to flit by. Siegfried still seems oblivious to his surroundings as his quick dotted rhythm returns, but Tchaikovsky stops him short with three bars of tremolo chords, at which point Odette, changed from a daytime swan into a nighttime woman, makes her grand appearance, moving toward him on rapid points. Tchaikovsky now sets up a musical dialogue between Odette and Siegfried, as she begins, represented by the oboe, of course, asking a plaintive question. Her descending line has characteristics of both the theme of the intro and the swan theme, without being too obvious about the connections. Her question, as we know from the libretto, is, Why do you persecute me and my companions with your weapon? He replies eight bars later, his melody in the violas starting as an inversion of hers, astounded to find a woman instead of a swan, and begging her forgiveness for his unpardonable error. Aside from the opening inversion they have almost identical lines, allowing them very quickly musically to become almost as one. For a little while the dialogue continues, never with any disagreement until their parts, hers in the winds and his in the strings, become fused as one into a love duet; the music allows them to dance a *pas d'amour*, with motions becoming progressively more intimate. Lopatkina may seem a little icy in her response to him, certainly more so than Fonteyn's to Nureyev at this point, but the distance she maintains may very well reflect the impossibility of their love, since she must remain swan by day and woman by night until released by a sacrifice of death. With more menacing passages in the music, Rothbart intrudes on them with this reminder. The composer calls this scene a waltz, but as a waltz it clearly has a deceptive nature, being in 4/4 time instead of the standard triple meter; again the waltz plays something of a duplicitous role.

In scene 12 the swans as women make their entrance, and seeing this ensemble of first twenty-four and then thirty-two dancers you know you made a good choice to watch this performance: the precision of the ensemble work and the artistry of each dancer seem as though they would be all but impossible to top. When Siegfried enters their midst, they shun him, no doubt fearful of someone who came among them as a hunter. As he retreats the twenty-four dancers form two parallel rows, and eight more enter in two groups of four, joining one of the rows at an angle at the front, forming the shape of a swan's wing. Odette glides between the parallel rows, and by her gestures assures the others not only that he will not harm them but that they love each other. With that resolved the swans can begin their dances without fear, and Tchaikovsky sets this in seven parts, starting with a waltz that will return, along with other solo and duet numbers. Again the ensemble dancing can only be described as stunning.

Changing the original order of numbers, this production now proceeds to the *pas d'action*, a duet for the two principals, commonly referred to as the "White Swan" dance. After a lengthy harp introduction, the duet proper sets off with a violin solo, not simply the appearance of an obbligato part, as would have been fairly normal in Russian ballets prior to this one, but a violin part that sounds much more like a violin concerto. Between the solo passages he returns to some orchestration he used in the first act for the winds, both in the *pas de trois* and in the Goblet Dance, now with slightly more intricate rhythms. In Act 1 these passages accompanied the frivolity of his birthday celebrations, the playful seductions while flirting with peasant girls, and generally the delights of his single life. Now they occur in their new mode when he has found true love, and the violin solo gives substance to their feelings going well beyond anything in Act 1. As this love exchange continues, it miraculously becomes transformed into an actual love duet, with the solo violin joined by a solo cello; independent lines for the two soloists nevertheless blend in perfect harmony and accord, making the music itself a spectacular representation of the action on stage. Tchaikovsky goes even one step further with this number, putting it in the fairly unusual key of G flat. Perhaps the most famous piece in that key is Schubert's Impromptu Op. 90, No. 3, also *andante*, and essentially a song without words; Tchaikovsky's *pas d'action* also gives that impression. Few pieces are more moving than this impromptu by Schubert, and one has the feeling that Tchaikovsky infused this ballet number with the same spirit. G flat, the enharmonic equivalent of F sharp, also relates comfortably to the home key of B minor as the dominant area.

After such intensity a strong change of tone seems called for, so instead of returning to the waltz just danced by the ensemble, this production jumps back to the comic relief of the Allegro moderato, known since Petipa choreographed it in 1895 as the *Danse des petits cygnes*, or the *pas de quatre*. Clearly Tchaikovsky had mischief on his mind in the way it starts, with the bassoons playing a patter pattern (alternating F sharp and C sharp in eighth notes) for the first ten bars. This type of usage of bassoons comes straight out of eighteenth-century comic opera for buffa characters or situations, and composers such as Haydn used it when they wanted to represent something comical in operas or symphonies. Oboes have been used seriously prior to this, but now they enter on the second bar as a cheeky little duet, with other winds soon joining in. Rhythm becomes a factor too, giving the oboe duo its cheekiness, and then with syncopations that suggest a bit of a pre-jazz beat. The choreography to this could not be more delightful, as the four women, arms locked, dance in unison with highly intricate patterns, some of which seem a little more rustic than what normally happens in ballet. It never fails to be a showstopper, and as danced for the Maryinsky, with Yevgenia Obraztsova, Svetlana Ivanova, Irina Golub, and Olesya Novikova, it could not be more enjoyable. A return to the waltz just heard features a different group of four, now with all the sophistication and gracefulness of classical ballet. There must be an opportunity for Odette to dance solo, and instead of that coming near the beginning of the swans' sequence, the Maryinsky places it near the end, shifting the emphasis to her over the ensemble. The corps de ballet returns in the coda, along with Odette, and at the end of the coda Siegfried joins her, as they enjoy their last moments before daybreak in their human form.

The finale to Act 2 brings back the now familiar swan theme with its touch of melancholy as the women with the first light of dawn must return to their swan form. The love-struck Siegfried would like Odette to come to the ball the next evening so he can choose her as his bride, but she knows the impossibility of this, as she cannot be freed from the curse that changes her into a swan by day. As the two of them embrace center stage, the ensemble forms a perfect, rapidly moving circle around them, and the circle breaks as they exit, unfurling around them and then vanishing. With all of them but Odette offstage, the actual swans appear on the lake, as the backdrop to the two lovers in their last embrace. She too must leave, exiting on points as she first entered, leaving him alone onstage; as she leaves the music becomes fragmented as it did in the introduction to this act, now not only melancholy but coming unstuck, lacking any sense of certainty about the future. Tchaikovsky intended this finale to be a full repetition of the introduction to the act, and for good reason, since the destructiveness of its middle section gives meaning to the fragmentation and impossibility of recovering its earlier essence at the end. That sense of foreboding should be even more pronounced at the end as Odette has no grounds to believe this love can be real, but in this Maryinsky production the finale has been truncated, basically excising the middle B section, which removes the feeling of menace. Because of the way this production ends, it appears to have been a strategic choice to delete the ominous music at this point, and not simply a matter of economizing.

ACT 3

Key relationships appear to have been a matter of some importance to Tchaikovsky in this ballet, a notion entirely unique in Russian ballet at this time, and while most in the audience will be blissfully unaware of it, for the composer it had significance. The key connections come most into focus in the third act, although the common practice since Petipa's production in 1895 of moving the *pas de deux* from Act 1 (No. 5) to be the *pas d'amour* for Siegfried and Odile (the black swan) undermines the coherence of keys in Act 3. Should we be concerned about this? It may bother musicologists, but few others, considering the need for a *pas de deux* in Act 3. Tchaikovsky himself had to come to terms with this when the prima ballerina Anna Sobeshchanskaya took on the role of Odette, and her objection to the *pas de six* in this act led to an added *pas de deux* by the specialist ballet composer Leon Minkus. Tchaikovsky got wind of this and, insisting the music should be his own, composed a *pas de deux* conforming to Minkus's so Petipa's choreography would not have to be altered. This added number, 19a, lacks the musical strength of the *pas de deux* from Act 1, although some choreographers continue to use 19a, for example Nureyev for his 1966 Vienna version, which you have on DVD (Deutsche Grammophon, 2005). The *pas de six* has not fared well either, generally replaced by the *pas de deux* from Act 1.

As for the key relationships, the defining key of the work, B minor, happens at the beginning, the ending, and crucial points en route, and this sets up associations with other keys, especially the prominence of F in Act 3. The interval of a perfect fifth defines closely related keys, along with the extension of that in a progression of fifths away from the home key. In this circle-of-fifths scheme, the furthest key from home is a tritone (augmented fourth), in this case F in relation to B. Composers of early music went to great lengths to avoid the remoteness of the tritone, even giving it a nefarious or duplicitous connotation, referred to as the *diabolus in musica* (the devil in music), and some of that thinking carried over into the nineteenth century. Tchaikovsky may in fact have been using the key of F in this act in that way, since here the evil Rothbart comes to the fore as he succeeds in deceiving Siegfried by passing off his daughter Odile as Odette, destroying any vestige of hope for the love that the Prince and Odette found in Act 2. With this we can simply step back and admire the dramatic and structural approach of the composer, which he and sophisticated musicians will hear, but not many other members of the audience. In some ways it's more the possible intent than the realization that counts, which need not prevent us from enjoying productions that do not stick to the original score.

After the disheartening tone of the end of the previous act, Act 3 begins entirely upbeat, with a bright invocation to dance like those found in many works by Tchaikovsky, here (No. 15) announcing the ball about to start in which Siegfried will choose his bride. With most of the assemblage in place, a curious number leads things off (No. 16), the *Danses du corps de ballet et des nains* (dwarfs). A dance for the full assembly along with a group of dwarfs should keep things light, but the appearance of dwarfs may seem a little too strange. Nureyev drops this one altogether, while the Maryinsky, having introduced a jester in Act 1, makes this the jester's dance—in the key of F, keeping the high spirits and allowing some brilliant dancing from Ivanov. Another rhythmic call to dance starting with the trumpets leads to a waltz, a dance now used strategically with the excising of the *pas de six*. Six princesses dance for Siegfried to catch his eye as potential brides, and if the *pas de six* were used, with its Intrada and five variations, each princess would be allowed to dance individually to show her prowess to make her case. The Maryinsky instead makes them completely uniform, all dressed identically and all dancing in unison, leaving nothing for him to select in one over the others.

In the scene that follows (18), his mother wishes to know which one he prefers, but with nothing to distinguish any of them, he can do nothing but shrug his shoulders, not in the least interested in arbitrarily taking one above any of the others. As oboe and flute pass the melody back and forth, at times in counterpoint, syncopations encroach, making for a somewhat sticky situation, in a flat key (D flat) not close to the home key of B minor. Again the trumpets give a fanfare, rescuing the son from a scene of tension with his mother, doing this in E flat to announce new guests. Aside from the strain generated by F in relation to the home key, Tchaikovsky also appears to use flat keys for ominous situations in contrast to the sharp keys for Odette and the genuine sentiment of love. This time we have no invocation to a dance but instead the dramatic entrance of Rothbart in a black cape with a young woman also in black who looks remarkably like Odette. The music greeting their entrance starts with a rapid descending figure leading directly into a loud dissonant chord, with more chords connected by short passages in the low strings and bassoons that lack melodic lines but are defined by syncopation, as though the early offbeats now come to full fruition. Tonally this is unstable until it settles in F, and then instead of another dissonant chord we hear an even louder (*fff*) entry of the swan theme, in F, the key for this work of deception and evil; now fast, loud, in a major key, and accompanied by tremolo strings, it sounds misshapen and grotesque. At this point Odile dances, led by Rothbart, immediately presenting herself in a way that attracts Siegfried to her, unlike any of the six prosaically identical princesses (in all modern performances the same dancer does both Odette and Odile). Siegfried's appetite has been whetted, and he needs some time to comprehend what he has just observed, believing by the resemblance that he now sees Odette.

Instead of the *pas de six* (19) or the added *pas de deux* (19a), a brief interpolated transition plunges immediately into entertainment for the guests—a series of international dances starting in this production with the *Danse espagnole*, followed by the *Danse napolitaine*, then a Czardas (*Danse hongroise*), and finally a Mazurka. A certain amount of patriotic pressure also compelled Tchaikovsky to write a *Danse russe* for this sequence, and this one seldom makes it into modern performances, despite the extensive solo violin part. This exciting sequence of dances lasts long enough (about ten minutes) for Siegfried to be convinced that good fortune has struck, despite what he knows about the nasty Rothbart—that Odette has fallen right into his lap. Finally the "Black Swan" *pas de deux* borrowed from Act 1 comes, and you notice that Lopatkina has now lost her icy demeanor, even smiling a little, which she never did as Odette. Musically the *pas de deux* has four parts, of which the first and third are waltzes, making this especially suitable for the action. Odile has been thrust in as an interloper, intent on carrying out Rothbart's wish that she deceive Siegfried, and in her dance she must therefore seduce him, not in a lurid way but with an allure that will result in her having the highest position of any woman in the land. In the opening waltz they dance together, but he takes a secondary role, with most of the emphasis on her as she ties him around her little finger. He responds ecstatically; when he dances alone he does so reactively, expressing the joy he feels that he has found the right woman. They alternate solos and dancing together, always with virtuosity as their union appears imminent, and the solo violin seems to make it convincing.

The *pas de deux* ends with a strong cadence, in the key of G, making it seem to be in the right place since the finale that follows (scene 24) proceeds in the key of C, the closest possible key relationship (in the original score this finale is preceded by the Mazurka, also in G). Key proves to be a factor, since Siegfried has been duped into thinking he now has Odette; he tells his mother, to her delight, that he wishes her as his bride, all of this happening in the key of C—the dominant of F, the key of deception. The solo oboe, Odette's instrument, reinforces his illusion of her, and the melody the oboe plays has a similar rhythm and contour to the melody of the waltz in scene 17. Here too, as when Odile danced earlier, the oboe melody goes into counterpoint with syncopations first in the flute and then pervading the melody itself, the offbeats giving cause for doubt. This scene of her acceptance does not last long, as the original score moves to the waltz just described, giving the lovers one more chance to embrace, but the Maryinsky production skips the waltz altogether, jumping ahead to a loud chord that stops the current pleasantries as it jolts Siegfried into the realization that he has been deceived. He now sees an image of the real Odette, and the dissemblers flee. Tchaikovsky drives this home with a return of the swan theme, as loud as possible in the winds (*fff*), in the key of C minor, emphasizing the grotesqueness and counterfeit nature of the music, as when Odile first appeared earlier in the act. Tonally the theme becomes unstable, metrically it loses the beat, and a chromatic progression results in C becoming the dominant of F, with F arriving on the loudest possible chord. The act ends chaotically, in F, with triplet figures that remind us of the odious hand of fate, striking its ultimate blow against Siegfried and the possibility of love with Odette. He unwittingly has not remained faithful to her, and that appears to seal her doom.

ACT 4

As Tchaikovsky originally conceived the work it cannot possibly have a happy ending, despite being a fairy tale, which could be manipulated in any way its authors chose. The music as it has progressed to the end of the third act does not bode well, and Tchaikovsky's ending for the original scenario confirms this. In the final act Siegfried returns to the lake to find Odette and beg forgiveness, but she lacks the power to accept; a fierce storm breaks out and the lake overflows. In attempting to keep her with him, he takes the crown from her head and throws it into the churning water, but this presages certain death for her as the owl snatches up the crown. He holds her in his arms as they succumb to the fury of the lake, drowning as we hear the swan theme one more time; at the end a band of white swans swims on a calm lake. For the composer fairy tale has given way to reality as the impossibility of love has been borne out—certainly the story of his own life, and no doubt the source of much of the melancholy in his music.

The revised scenario of 1895, with the assistance of Modest, also ends badly for the lovers, but with twists that improve it. The crown no longer stands as an issue, and when Siegfried rushes to Odette by the lake, he responds to her regret about his betrayal by claiming that he believed he chose her at the ball, not Odile. She forgives him, but the evil genie interrupts their joyful embrace to change her back to a swan as dawn breaks. She resolves to die instead of letting this happen, and because of his love for her he will die with her. From the top of a cliff they together throw themselves to their death in the stormy lake, and because of the sacrifice of death, the owl not only loses his control but also falls to his own death. This did not fundamentally change Tchaikovsky's ending, and may have actually made it better. The same cannot be said of other later versions, for example one that projects beyond their death to (figuratively) the fields of Elysium, where they can be seen wandering blissfully together. If they can be happy in heaven, why not on earth, and thus we have the Hollywood ending from the Maryinsky.

In order to end the ballet as the Maryinsky has chosen, some of Tchaikovsky's music from the fourth act simply will not do. The opening entr'acte remains intact, but they axe the two scenes following (Nos. 26 and 27), especially the somber *Danses des petits cygnes* (27) in B-flat minor. In this production the young swans (both white and black) do not mope about waiting for Odette to join them, but dance much more cheerfully to a substituted number. Odette's entrance begins with the music we expect (scene 28), allowing the owl menacingly to swoop in after some disjointed offbeats, and his music emphasizes that fate will take its course. Siegfried rushes in at the beginning of the finale to ask forgiveness, but before the return of the swan theme where that should happen, another cheerful dance has been inserted. When the swan theme finally arrives, in the distant key to A minor to underlie the hopelessness of his pleading, this production treats it as the beginning of the conflict between the Prince and Rothbart. Dawn can be seen creeping across the dark sky, and while Odette lies on the ground waiting to be transformed back into a swan, the Prince attacks Rothbart the owl, tearing off his right wing. With the last statement of the swan theme, back in B minor, we expect to see Odette dying in the Prince's arms, but here the Hollywood ending kicks in. A final section with harp and repeated notes in the strings should reveal swans on the lake, but here the Prince takes Odette in his arms, and since Rothbart's feathers have been plucked (he writhes in pain and dies), Odette revives as a woman, no longer under the curse. Instead of dying, the joyful couple embraces, to live happily ever after. Much has been done to distort Tchaikovsky's ballet, but if he had lived to see this production, you can only imagine he would have been appalled. He wrote the music that he did for good reason, especially the continuity that the mournful (and at time belligerent) swan theme provides, and to turn that into peaches and cream at the end defies the slightest understanding of the music.

5

PUSHKIN'S GENTLE MOCKERY, TCHAIKOVSKY'S IMMODERATE ARDOR

Eugene Onegin

PUSHKIN AND TCHAIKOVSKY

Some countries have one writer who stands head and shoulders above all others. Even England, despite no shortage of greatness, can vault Shakespeare onto that pinnacle, and Germany can do the same with Goethe. Similarly Russia has such a writer, Alexander Pushkin (1799–1837), revered throughout the nineteenth century, and no less during the Soviet era as the great icon of Russian literary achievement. Many Russians, even now, can claim to know large amounts of his verse from memory, and that includes substantial passages of his most loved work, *Eugene Onegin*. Like any educated Russian, Tchaikovsky shared that reverence for and knowledge of Pushkin, and it probably should not surprise us that he would choose this tale, told as a novel in verse, for the subject of one of his operas. Prior to this one Tchaikovsky had already written four operas, three of which had been fully staged in either Moscow or St. Petersburg, but none of those suggested that he had what it took to be one of the great composers of opera. Something changed with *Onegin*, composed in 1777–1778 from his own libretto with the assistance of his poet friend Konstantin Shilovsky, and at least in part we can thank Pushkin for that.

Great writers such as Shakespeare, Goethe, and Pushkin leave their mark in various ways, not the least of which is in giving us characters in their plays or novels that defy predictability—characters we will discuss endlessly in trying to plumb their depth. Just when we think we know Hamlet, Desdemona, or Werther, we discover something that turns everything upside down, and we may not even be able to agree on which characters are the most important ones. When Tchaikovsky read *Onegin*, he clearly did not see in it what most readers do, as he completely ignored some of Pushkin's most basic cues, including the title itself. Pushkin takes us through a chapter and a half of his eight chapters—a full 20 percent of his verse novel—before we encounter the name Tatiana, placing the focus squarely on Eugene. That does not make her a lesser character, but with forty pages of introduction to him, we can assume that Pushkin intended the spotlight to fall on Eugene, with large amounts of information to let us know what sort of a person he is. Not only does that information give a somewhat dim view of a dissipated being with not much of a backbone, who happens to be bored most of the time, but Pushkin pokes fun at him in the way he presents him to us, giving us remarkably little to admire. The tale itself could not be simpler: The adolescent Tatiana, at home in the country on her mother's estate, falls madly in love with the urbane Eugene, whose inherited estate has made them neighbors; she writes a letter declaring her love, and he gently rebuffs her. His friend Lensky intends to marry Tatiana's sister Olga, but at a name day celebration for Tatiana, Onegin, simply looking for sport (and wishing to get even with Lensky for dragging him there), prevents Olga from dancing with Lensky by keeping her to himself, which enrages Lensky to the point of insisting on a duel that results in his death. A few years later Onegin returns to society and discovers the now sophisticated, wealthy, ennobled, and married Tatiana; he falls madly in love with her, but she now rejects him.

In turning the work into an opera, Tchaikovsky deviates so substantially from Pushkin that we may have difficulty recognizing the work; in fact, it seems doubtful that he got the title right. Unlike the long introduction to Onegin in the novel, Tchaikovsky makes Tatiana the first character to be heard in the opera, in a duet with her sister that soon becomes a quartet when her mother and nurse join in. They do not sing of anything terribly important, or at least so it seems, but Tchaikovsky has made a seismic shift away from Pushkin, first introducing us to the four most important women, not the two leading men. Lensky brings Onegin for a visit to his new neighbors at the Larin estate, and only then, after we have become thoroughly acquainted with the women, and an entertainment by peasants returning from a hard day's work, do we encounter the men. Lensky, we soon discover, loves Olga so passionately he can barely contain himself, but on this visit we learn very little about Onegin, aside from his boredom with country life, and his assumption that Tatiana, with whom he takes a short walk, must feel similarly bored. As for the dreamy and somewhat reclusive Tatiana, in contrast to her effusively vivacious sister, it has never occurred to her to be bored on this land she treasures so dearly, surrounded by the people she loves most in the world (her father died some years earlier). Besides, she has her books to read, novels especially, by both English and French authors, and from these she has created a fantasy world for herself that seems more poignant than the real one.

Both Pushkin and Tchaikovsky make her an avid reader, since this is crucial to her misjudgment of Onegin, although Tchaikovsky refers only to English writers such as Samuel Richardson, omitting French novels, for example Rousseau's *Emile*, that Pushkin has her reading. For Pushkin, the national distinctions in literature play a large part in his narrative, since the national traits also help to define certain aspects of character. Eugene, as a case in point, was well tutored in French as a child, by Monsieur l'Abbé, "the mediocre," who "treated his lessons as a ploy. No moralizing from this joker." This French education left its mark on him as a youth: "In French Onegin had perfected / proficiency to speak and write, / in the mazurka he was light, / his bow was wholly unaffected. / The World found this enough to treat / Eugene as clever, and quite sweet." The youthful Eugene found English styles appealing; after Monsieur l'Abbé he became "free, and as a dresser / made London's *dandy* his professor." Only his boredom seemed peculiarly Russian. In complete contrast, the passionate and poetic Lensky's "creator / was Göttingen, his *alma mater*. . . . / He'd brought back all the fruits of learning / from German realms of mist and steam, / freedom's enthusiastic dream, / a spirit strange, a spirit burning, / an eloquence of fevered strength,/ and raven curls of shoulder-length." The two young men had nothing in common, and for his Russian readers Pushkin could make this most apparent by having one blasé, attracted by French and

English styles, while the other's intensity comes from German inclinations. In so doing he can poke fun at both of them, assuming the affectations of the national stereotypes.

Aside from Tatiana's reading English epistolary novels by Richardson, Tchaikovsky gives no indication of different national predilections, since this did not fit into his plan. For him to mock anything French clearly would not have flown since in part his own passionate nature had something of a French origin, considering his mother's French ancestry and the fact that she proved to be the strongest influence on him as a child and youth. His family's French governess Fanny Dürbach also played an important role in his upbringing and early education. In fact, he avoids the way that Pushkin holds even Tatiana up to a certain amount of ridicule, in that Pushkin makes much of the fact that Tatiana writes the fateful letter pouring out her love to Eugene not in Russian but in French: "her Russian was as thin as vapour, / she never read a Russian paper, / our native speech had never sprung / unhesitating from her tongue, / she wrote in French . . . what a confession! / . . . till now our language—proud, God knows— / has hardly mastered postal prose." Of course he could have fun with readers at this point, chiding that "they should be forced to read in Russian, / I hear you say," but definitely at her expense. Before giving the letter to the reader, in "a weak" Russian version (in a facetious translation from French), he speculates, "Who taught her all this mad, slapdash, / heartfelt, imploring, touching trash / fraught with enticement and disaster?" The preoccupation of the adolescent Tatiana with novels has played a nasty trick on her, since the appearance of the urbane and handsome Eugene causes her to create the person in her own mind based on the characters she knows from Richardson and others, completely missing the few signals that he throws her way. Tchaikovsky may dispense with the background about him that Pushkin gives, but even in the opera he comes off as detached and bored in the little he utters, in no possible way the man she imagines him to be. The letter she writes, following the epistolary mode of the novels it comes from, indulges in an attempt to write her own novel, one that has no chance of ending any way but badly.

A story can be told in different ways, and Pushkin's way did not work for Tchaikovsky. At least three points in the story appear to call for high drama and pathos, and with each of these Pushkin defuses that with commentary that jests, gibes, and derides. The first of these, Tatiana's "heartfelt" letter, he calls "touching trash," reducing it to the language of a sentimental novel, not likely to evoke the response she desires; luckily for her, Eugene brings her down to earth with a gentle landing, claiming to have been moved by it. The second intense moment occurs after the friends have dueled, and Lensky, the poet of great promise, lies dead—his voice silenced and his passion extinguished. Pushkin grants the possibility of thinking of him in this way: "Perhaps to improve the world's condition, / perhaps for fame, he was endowed; / his lyre, now stilled, in its high mission / might have resounded long and loud / for aeons." Pushkin, though, cannot resist the other option, and completely deflates the possibility just put forward in the canto that follows: "Perhaps however, to be truthful, / he would have found a normal fate. / The years would pass; no longer youthful, / he'd see his soul cool in its grate; / his nature would be changed and steadied, / he'd sack the Muses and get wedded; / and in the country, blissful, horned, in quilted dressing-gown adorned, / life's real meaning would have found him; / at forty he'd have got the gout, / drunk, eaten, yawned, grown weak and stout, / at length, midst children swarming round him, / mist crones with endless tears to shed, / and doctors, he'd have died in bed."

The third comes at the end of the work, with Eugene now abandoned by Tatiana, after he has mustered passion similar to hers earlier on, professing his love to her and for the first time in his life apparently finding meaning. But has he? He now pursues a married woman, whose life in nineteenth-century Russia, like Anna Karenina in Tolstoy's novel later in the century, can only be ruined by conceding in any way to his advances. She may still love him, but has no appetite for ruin, living with him in disgrace; surely he sees that as well, or is simply trying to chalk up a prestigious conquest. Pushkin must now end his story, but if we feel inclined toward pathos, he quickly changes the tone: "She went—and Eugene, all emotion, / stood thunder-struck. In what wild round / of tempests, in what raging ocean / his heart was plunged. . . . But from the hero of my tale, / just at this crisis of his gale, / reader, we must be separating, / for long . . . for evermore. We've chased / him far enough through wild and waste, / Hurrah! Let's start congratulating / ourselves on our landfall. It's true, / our vessel's long been overdue." He still has three cantos to go, and continues the light banter with the reader, whom he still addresses directly: "Reader, I wish that, as we parted— / whoever you may be, a friend, / a foe—our mood should be warm-hearted. / Goodbye, for now we make an end. / Whatever in this rough confection / you sought—tumultuous recollection, / a rest from toil and all its aches, / or just grammatical mistakes. / . . . God grant you took at least a grain. / On this we'll part; goodbye again."

Tchaikovsky would have nothing of this flippancy. The voice of the narrator he replaces with the music of the opera, and while the music occasionally has light touches, none of these happen at the three points of high tension just noted. Instead of the sentimental outpouring of a teenager writing in French, Tchaikovsky turns her letter-writing scene into the epicenter of the opera, not only lavishing it with melody at its very best, but backing that up with orchestral ebullience that gives this its place as the Russian cynosure of the opera. When Lensky dies, we have no choice but to feel the pathos of the great loss, as the composer gives him an aria before the duel that almost rivals Tatiana's letter-writing scene, a number that stands up as one of the great arias of the entire operatic repertory, in which he laments his own impending death and ponders the great potential that will never be realized. We have no sacked muses here. For the turned tables at the end of the work, Tatiana may speculate on the dignity of Eugene's motives in pursuing her, but Tchaikovsky banishes this speculation with his music, with a final climax that allows us only to pity him. After not entirely knowing what to do with Eugene for much of the opera, Tchaikovsky at the end brings him up close to the emotional level of Tatiana, but not close enough for the title of the opera to ring true: unlike Pushkin's work it should be *Tatiana*.

ACT I

It's Saturday, 5 October 2013, in the historic town of Waterville, Maine, and you have been looking forward to the opening of the fall season of the Metropolitan Opera's Live in HD broadcasts, which this year starts with *Eugene Onegin*. As a resident of this town you don't have a long walk to the elegant, newly renovated red-brick Waterville Opera House on Common Street at Front Street, with a pleasant view of the Kennebec River. You can think of nothing more delightful than seeing the opera transmission from New York in an actual opera house, built in 1902, when live performances of operas actually took place here. Many towns the size of Waterville had opera houses built back then, but the operators soon discovered that mounting productions proved excessively difficult, forcing these houses to become venues for more populist entertainments and also for silent movies. With the advent of feature-length films around 1912—for example, the Italian *Cabiria*, which circulated throughout the United States—audiences could enjoy something fairly close to opera, and when shown in a small-town opera house, the music could be played by a modest orchestra instead of just a piano or organ, since the theater actually had a pit. When American directors such as Cecil B. DeMille introduced silent feature films a couple of years later, such as *Carmen*, starring America's favorite opera diva Geraldine Farrar, the projection in an opera house seemed entirely appropriate.

Now, thanks to the Met, opera can once again take its rightful place in the Waterville Opera House, not in a modern Cineplex with bare concrete walls, but in a beautiful theater with a decorated proscenium, plush red seats, boxes lining the side walls, and a spacious balcony. Even though the house has over eight hundred seats, large enough to hold 5 percent of the entire town's population, you know from experience that if you want a good seat, you need to arrive at least forty-five minutes early, since people will come from Oakland, Belgrade, Fairfield, and other surrounding towns. Well before the 1:00 p.m. starting time, the house will be full, and you arrive early enough to get one of the best seats in the house, right in the middle of the front row of the balcony.

You have seen this opera before, and have concerns about this production for a number of reasons. Most recently you saw it in New York at the Met, on Tuesday, 20 February 2007, and being thoroughly disappointed with what you saw, you watched it back in Waterville on the following Saturday on the Live in HD transmission. You can think of few operas with a more intimate tone than this one, and because of that, you could make no sense of the set—or lack of it—on the Met's stage in 2007. With the minimalist set, the dark-blue walls of the stage seemed like a chasm, making the singers appear as insignificant dots in a massive abyss. Even Tatiana had her letter-writing scene framed more by light than anything else, and that did not really help to shrink the vast emptiness surrounding her. In fact the HD broadcast worked better, since the close-up camera shots did eliminate the emptiness of the stage. Now, only six years later, you know this will be a new production, but that does not entirely rule out the possibility of seeing the same set.

Years earlier you had the good fortune to see two outstanding productions of this opera, and both addressed its performance problems in different ways. One of the issues concerns Tatiana herself, clearly the focus of the opera, and the fact that the character is exceptionally young—no more than about sixteen or seventeen at the beginning and perhaps twenty or twenty-one at the end. Because of the vocal demands of the role, no one that age could actually sing it, and in most cases the singer playing the part is two or three decades (or even more) older than the character she portrays. You saw it on 7 May 1976 at the Royal Opera House, Covent Garden, in London with Kiri Te Kanawa as Tatiana, still near the beginning of her career, and well before she reached the status of one of the greatest of all sopranos. At the age of thirty-two she had little difficulty looking the age of the character she portrayed, and with the technical demands of the role, especially for a singer that young, a vulnerability could be heard in her voice, perhaps inadvertently capturing something of her character's susceptibility, especially in the first act.

Roughly two decades later, in June 1994, you saw it again, in Vienna at the Kammeroper (Chamber Opera) with an (almost) all-Russian cast, not one of the large opera houses in Vienna but an exceptionally small one, as the name implies, so small that members of the audience almost feel they are on the stage. You cannot imagine the intimacy of the work being better captured than in this production, and another important factor played a large role in that. Many years earlier the great Russian dramaturge Konstantin Stanislavsky had directed this opera, and with his special interest in it had also written at length about how he believed it should be done, in his book *Stanislavsky on Opera*. We in the West may not be all that familiar with him, but we know his legacy in the United States well, through the Actors Studio modeled on his method acting, founded in 1947 in New York by Elia Kazan, Cheryl Crawford, and Robert Lewis, with distinguished alumni including the likes of Marlon Brando, Ellen Burstyn, Harvey Keitel, and Al Pacino. The Vienna performance of *Eugene Onegin* you saw in fact was a reconstruction of Stanislavsky's 1922 chamber production, using his sets and direction, based on archival material surviving from then as well as his own well-preserved writing about it. Stanislavsky stressed the intimate nature of the relationships among the characters, as well as portrayals that bring us as close as possible to the inner life of each character, something that of course can also be gleaned from Tchaikovsky's music. After seeing it in Vienna you doubted you could ever again experience it in such a satisfying way. The 2007 Met version, which seemed to go out of its way to be anti-intimate, confirmed your worst fears about how badly it could be done.

Being an avid reader of *The New York Times*, you have another concern about this new production. On Sunday, 22 September, Zachary Woolfe's article "Backstage Drama, Worthy of Opera," appeared in the Arts & Leisure section, describing some of the trials of getting this production mounted. Deborah Warner had been engaged to direct the staging of the opera, but health issues had forced her to cancel. At the last moment Fiona Shaw stepped in, but with other engagements in the U.K., she could spend very little time in New York, not making it through the entire work, and not even able to attend the premiere of the first opera of the season. A potential fiasco could be looming, although from the musical side all appeared to be well, with Valery Gergiev, artistic director of the Maryinsky in St. Petersburg, conducting, along with Anna Netrebko, a Russian and one of the finest sopranos now active, as Tatiana. Two outstanding Polish singers, Mariusz Kwiecien as Onegin and Piotr Beczala as Lensky, round out the leading roles, both of whom speak fluent Russian. Another matter has come up, which the Met's management considers an unfortunate distraction, but many others do not. Russia's president, Vladimir Putin, recently pushed through anti-gay legislation in the Russian parliament, banning "propaganda on nontraditional sexual relationships," and an online petition has garnered thousands of signatures not only criticizing this, but calling on the Met to dedicate the opening-night performance to this issue in light of Tchaikovsky's own homosexuality (which Woolfe takes as mere conjecture). Aside from the management's lack of interest in any type of activism, even some of the performers have become involved, with Gergiev, closely associated with Putin, remaining silent, while Netrebko, feeling ambivalence toward her former mentor, stated, "I have never and will never discriminate against anyone." The situation seems charged for anything to happen.

After host Deborah Voigt's opening introductions, the camera follows Gergiev to the podium, and Tchaikovsky's music begins with the camera following the conductor and orchestra. Traditionally operas start with an overture, but Tchaikovsky calls this relatively short one an Introduction (only thirty-eight bars, lasting no more than a few minutes). It may be short, but it could not be more potent. Those more familiar with movies than opera, especially classic films from the 1930s and 1940s, may be able to connect this type of short intro with the titles music at the beginning of films, at least prior to the onset of the use of popular songs as titles music. The music provided at this point by some of the finest film composers, such as Max Steiner, Bernard Herrmann, Erich Wolfgang Korngold, or David Raksin, may give us our first inkling of the type of film we are about to watch, and that can be very important for setting the appropriate tone or atmosphere. A title such as *Mildred Pierce* tells us very little, but Steiner's titles music sets a serious and even melodramatic tone, perhaps with its lugubriousness even beginning to undermine Mildred's attempts to gain independence. Raksin goes further with *Laura*, not only setting a sensuous tone, but giving a leitmotif—a recurring theme—to be heard over and over throughout the film. With that musical idea fixed in our minds, he can alter and distort it, shifting the effect it should have on us.

Despite writing a Duke Ellington–like theme, Raksin may very well have gotten his inspiration from *Eugene Onegin* for his recurring Laura theme. Right from the first bar Tchaikovsky gives us his Tatiana theme, which of course we do not know at this point, but the music immediately draws us into its web. It has a gentle and dreamy tone, with agitation as well, but never losing the dreaminess of the opening. He gives us a very short theme, less than two bars long, which can be manipulated in many ways, but it never loses its recognizable essence. Part of that essence relates to the direction of the melodic line, always downward, and the harmony moves in the same direction by way of descending sequences. The theme may on subsequent hearings start on higher notes, but the downward motion remains constant, and in fact when it starts higher, it simply has further to go in its descent. Tchaikovsky gives us a theme simple in the extreme and memorable, and when we hear it later in the opera, we will not mistake it, even if he alters it in various ways. Already in the intro we sense its pliability, that the composer will be able to develop it, stretch it, or make it more compact. Without us knowing it, he has made us fall in love with Tatiana before the end of the intro, and when we first hear this music associated with her, it works on us like déjà vu, allowing us to feel we already know her at a surprisingly intimate level. With the first few bars we hear Tchaikovsky at his melodic and harmonic best, not just writing melody for the sake of melody, but achieving a deep-rooted dramatic function that will carry throughout the entire opera.

The intro comes to a full close, quietly, and that takes us directly to a terrace of the Larin house, nicely catching a mixture of indoors and outdoors in Tom Pye's Met set. Madame Larina (Elena Zaremba) and Tatiana's nurse Filipyevna (Larissa Diadkova)—alas, neither of them singing close to the standard of the principals—take the foreground, preparing food, but the first voices heard come from Tatiana in a duet with her sister Olga (Oksana Volkova), as they offstage sing a familiar old song of the forest nightingale and a shepherd's flute. We have no hint of Pushkin's Eugene here. This evokes nostalgia from Larina, recalling how she in her youth sang this song as well, and also, like Tatiana, devoured the novels of Grandison and Richardson, with Filipyevna's running commentary rounding out the quartet. The thought of these writers reminds her of her own youthful dreams, and how they even prompted her to dress, but also how marriage brought her down to earth, with custom replacing dreams. Her not entirely happy recollections take on the aura of a lament, and at least one writer, Roland John Wiley, hears the music at this point as an embedding of Mozart's Introit to his Requiem. It comes to an end with the sounds of a chorus of peasants approaching.

If we imagine that this fairly lengthy peasant chorus and dance has been interjected by Tchaikovsky as mere diversion, we have missed his signals. No such appearance of peasants can be found in Pushkin, and for Tchaikovsky, introducing them before we have actually become acquainted with any of the leading characters, this plays a special role. Here we have the Russia that he identifies with—and Tatiana does as well, as the spirit that makes her love her home in the country and prevents her from feeling any boredom or disgruntlement. The peasants, like the composer and Tatiana, can have rapid mood swings, from weariness and sorrow to elation, and their folk songs fill the air with love. Even politically they define the Russia that Tchaikovsky holds dear, with the comfortable master/servant relationship. They approach Larina completely exhausted, but without hesitation will provide the liveliest possible entertainment, for which she rewards them with good food. This amiable relationship has no hint of resentment or oppression, running completely contrary to the revolutionary thinking by now well entrenched among some intellectuals. This is much more idyllic than what even Mozart shows us in *The Marriage of Figaro*, where undercurrents of revolution cannot be mistaken; Tchaikovsky himself had no such inclinations, and his Russia, whether realistic or not, embodied an idealized social harmony of the classes.

That sense of harmony reveals itself in the music he gives the peasants, not simply plunging into the chorus, but allowing a tenor soloist (and later bass) in a very slow and dignified way to express his weariness and heavyheartedness before the chorus joins in. This tenor may use musical language as elevated as anyone else's, but at the same time it includes a rhythmic figure distinctive to folk music. When they greet Larina, at an *andante* tempo, presenting her with a traditional harvest garland, the folk character becomes more apparent, and her response, to be happy, sing, and enjoy themselves, maintains something of their rhythm. They then sing and dance, using a distinctive Russian folk rhythm, with a ballet scene provided by the Met troupe that tells the story of a girl courted by a young lad (although she's handled somewhat roughly). This dance fits very nicely with a comment Tchaikovsky made to Mrs. von Meck, which will relate to the finale of the Fourth Symphony as well: "As for the Russian element in my music overall that is revealed in melodic and harmonic contours that are related to folksong, this comes about because of my growing up in the wilds, being steeped since early childhood in the indescribable beauty of Russian folk music and its characteristic features, because of my passionate adoration of Russianness in all its manifestations, and because, in brief, I am *Russian* in the fullest sense of the word" (TM 201). He may not always tell her exactly what he thinks, but this time he did.

Tatiana and Olga witness this display of the peasants, and not surprisingly at the end Tatiana gives her opinion, clearly Tchaikovsky's own, of how she loves to listen to their song, how it fills her with dreams, and says that she will follow where they lead. To confirm the importance of her response, Tchaikovsky accompanies her words with the main theme from the intro, and since this is the first time we have heard it since the beginning, he now defines it as a type of leitmotif. As the singer, the melody belongs to her, and not only that but it exemplifies her dreams as well, related to the books she reads—one of which she now holds in her hand. Showing the pliable character of the motif, Tchaikovsky lets it rise more than fall, temporarily buoying her dreams upward. After she sings the orchestra lets it descend, now bringing her back to earth as Olga chides her for dreaming her life away, and she picks up the folk dance just heard with the comment that it makes her laugh. We have now heard the intro's theme return, and while the character of the music is such that we could intuit its meaning at the beginning, Tchaikovsky does not leave this open to mistake, letting us know with Tatiana's words where it will lead—eventually to the most important part of the opera a little later in this act. Olga then gets to sing at length about her happy nature, which contrasts with Tatiana's, but despite what more or less amounts to an aria, musically we will not lose sight of Tatiana's motif. After the peasants leave, Larina asks Tatiana about her dark mood, and Tatiana explains, once again to her familiar motif, that the book she's reading has upset her—it is about the suffering of star-crossed lovers. Now the meaning of the motif becomes even stronger, as the novel she has been reading will become her own life's story, including her own literary effort to propel it along.

By now we know the women fairly well, and only at this point in the opera can Eugene and Lensky appear, on their visit that proves fateful for Tatiana. Lensky has come to see his beloved Olga, and with the two of them together, that leaves Tatiana and Eugene to get acquainted. Before they pair off, they sing a quartet, in which Lensky explains who's who; more importantly, Tatiana, mostly obscured by the presence of the three other voices, believes she sees (in nothing more than his physical appearance) that all her dreams have come true, before so much as a word has been exchanged with Eugene. She almost swoons as she trembles with anticipation, but as only one voice in the four-part counterpoint, we may have difficulty catching her thoughts. When they do split into pairs, and the lovers leave, we get our first impression of Eugene, and it tells us little other than his assumption that Tatiana must be bored with her life in this desolate countryside. She replies naively that she likes to read, accompanied by her motif, so we take much more from her response than he does. He admits she could do worse than reading, but surely there must be more than that. In contrast to his musically bland question, she returns to her motif as she tells him that she likes to wander and dream. That draws him into the motif musically as he wonders what she dreams about, and it continues as she explains dreaming is simply part of her nature. He warns her about dreams becoming obsessions, and that he has had a similar weakness; in this entire discussion about dreams the motif has held sway, drawing him musically to her level in contrast to the fairly vapid writing given to him prior to this. The conversation ends with the reappearance of the two lovebirds, dominated by Lensky's professions of love for Olga. He too speaks of dreaming, of his love for her, but never to Tatiana's motif.

In a final brief chat between Eugene and Tatiana, where he does all the talking, he tells the story of his dying uncle, and how tedious it was to stay at his side during his illness, presenting this in a way similar to Pushkin's. After saying how he resented being stuck in this boring situation until the uncle died, his story ends, and with this he leaves his final impression on her before that night when she writes her impassioned letter. Her most important understanding of him, her first impression almost lost musically in the quartet on his arrival, reveals the complete disconnect between what she should see and what she actually sees. At best he has shown some curiosity about her dreams, but mostly he has told her about his boredom with the countryside that she loves so much, and also his complete lack of human compassion toward a close relative as he died, an uncle whose legacy will allow him to live the good life. Tatiana should have seen a person sketchy at best, but she seems incapable of picking up any of the signals, left only with her first impression of physical appearance, creating in her mind a person who does not exist but whose essence she bases on characters she knows from English novels. We easily forget that she's only sixteen or seventeen years old, and her first encounter with adult reality may be somewhat distorted.

THE LETTER

After Eugene's last deprecating words, all go in to dinner except for Filipyevna, who comments on how timid and dazed Tatiana appears. When she speculates that something may come of this, she does so accompanied by Tatiana's motif, and that lingers in the orchestra after she exits. The new scene takes us to Tatiana's bedroom, and an extended orchestral introduction prepares us for what will happen next; this music is Tchaikovsky's way of setting the atmosphere for the most important scene of the opera. Not only does this scene become the musical epicenter of the opera, with some of Tchaikovsky's most extraordinary writing for both voice and orchestra, but despite being primarily for one singer, it takes up nearly one-sixth of the entire opera. Unlike Pushkin, who chides and even mocks her for writing in French instead of Russian, Tchaikovsky's scene-preparing music has no hint of admonition or irony, in fact taking us almost directly to the motif we already know so well.

Soon action will be taken to transform her illusory dream into something real for her, and her motif now becomes the musical vehicle to drive that forward. As the motif progresses we hear it as we have not before, with triplets encroaching on the duple time, and then, just before Filipyevna encourages Tatiana to go to bed, a descending passage gives way to syncopations, gently presented, but adding more uneasiness to the dream motif. Tatiana pays no attention to her nurse, and, much more than what she says in recitative, that her head spins and she can't breathe, the orchestral interludes—some fairly long—tell us about her agitated state of being, continuing the motif both with triplets and syncopation. Tatiana would like to hear about the old days from Filipyevna, but when the aging nurse claims not to remember, the girl, now hopelessly in love, asks her if she has ever been in love. She gets a fairly long story about the lack of love in the old days—how a matchmaker helped to arrange her marriage, and how at thirteen complete strangers uprooted her from her own family to live with them. Tatiana pays no attention to this monotone drone, and overflowing with emotion asks her nurse to leave her alone after bringing pen and paper.

Now that Tatiana is alone, a new orchestral interlude reveals her state of mind as more agitated than before, with a much faster tempo, and her accompanied recitative signals the hand of fate, which prods her now to act, even if all may be lost as a result. When she sits down to write, the tempo returns to *andante* and the orchestra comes back to her motif, first in a rising pattern and then falling. She gets it wrong and has to start again, now to an unrelenting passage of syncopations in the orchestra, realizing the folly of her action but unable to stop. Shades of the motif are never far removed, but now as she writes the music skirts around the motif, prompting her dream to come out distorted and misshapen. We hear very little of the letter itself, or the frequently discarded bits of it, but mainly what the orchestra tells us about the condition of her mind as she writes. To this point most of her thoughts emerge in accompanied recitative, but with the new *moderato assai quasi andante* section it becomes much more of an aria, reaching a high point of focused emotion. The orchestration too plays a more active role in heightening the intensity, as all violins and violas now give the harmony in syncopation, while the winds become much more pronounced—especially the solo oboe, which takes the predominant melodic lead, enlivened by fragments for flutes, clarinets, horns, and bassoons. When she sings, speculating on what might have been if he had not turned up, fragments of her motif flit in and out, as twisted as the persistent syncopation in the strings. The oboe obbligato continues, as though to create a duet between her and the illusory voice of Eugene.

She builds to a fevered pitch, questioning if he has brought the end of her desperate longing. If the oboe has been his phantom voice, he caricatures her with her own motif at the beginning of the new *andante* section, which she then takes up as she questions if he is an angel or a devil—if this is but an illusion of an inexperienced soul, whose destiny has been confused. Again she builds to new climaxes as she places her fate in his hands, and to heighten this, Anna Netrebko lies on the stage, her prone body almost paralyzed with conflict. Netrebko rises with the upward surging lines for all the strings, takes up pen and paper and writes furiously while she swirls around, and then declares the letter finished. She has one more climactic high note, evoking the fear of the trust she puts in him, before the section ends.

She has not slept when dawn arrives and the shepherd plays a folk tune on his pipes. Filipyevna comes to wake her, surprised to find her already up, and Tchaikovsky interjects some comedy as the nurse can't figure out to which neighbor her grandson should deliver the letter. The letter-writing scene ends when the nurse exits, leaving Tatiana to ponder her fate after this rash act of writing to Eugene. The orchestra has played a large role throughout this lengthy scene, allowing us inside Tatiana's head; we can grasp every nuance of her emotion through the spectacular orchestral writing, and the conclusion works the same way. Tatiana need not do anything but look pensive, but beneath her frozen expression, the orchestra can rise to a final climax for the scene, building to a *fortissimo* peak, and then trailing off to something quiet in the extreme (*ppp*). In this scene more than anywhere else in the opera we see the great symphonist and dramatist at work, showing how effective the orchestra can be in capturing and conveying an inner drama, something he also achieves admirably in his symphonies. This infusion of drama in fact has profound implications for his symphonies, especially the Fourth, more or less written at the same time as this opera.

Tatiana does not doubt that Eugene will come in person to deliver his response to her letter, and as she waits, the reality of what she has exposed herself to begins to sink in. Peasant girls sing as they gather berries in a nearby garden, and their four-part folk song strikes a contrast with Tatiana's own dark thoughts. The girls sing a cheerful song about their tightly knit group, which will tease any young man they entice to come near, teaching him the risks of prying by pelting cherries and currants at his head. Unlike a girl who reads novels all day and makes the mistake of trying to write her own epistolary script, girls who spend all day in the fields prefer a game of taunting and merriment. This song comes straight from Pushkin, where the girls are up to mischief with their masters as well, who presume they cannot eat their berries while singing: "Such rustic cunning can't be wrong." Whether Tatiana hears them or not, her own morbid thoughts expressed after the folk song ends separate her in the extreme from these girls she would otherwise like to identify with. Her own action has removed her from her beloved country life and placed her in a different world, one she will inhabit later in the opera.

As she anticipated, Eugene arrives, and she braces herself for the verdict, which could very well amount to laughter at her foolishness. In the barest recitative, more like speaking than singing, he calmly but coldly asks her not to deny that she wrote to him. A clarinet joins the thin string accompaniment when he admits she aroused emotions long since stilled, but returns to its bareness when he says he will repay her with equal candor. His answer, seeming somewhat less cold, comes as a type of aria, in which he explains he's not the marrying type, and union would simply result in tedium for both of them; if he loves her, it will be as a brother loves a sister. Despite the fuller accompaniment, especially the presence of the clarinet, his aria still has the character of recitative, fairly devoid of emotion, as is true of the text he sings. He sees his role as one who must teach a lesson to a naive soul, who might find herself in a serious jam if the addressee were not as understanding as himself, and musically Tchaikovsky never removes the cold edge. The act ends with the same chorus of peasant girls, now heard by Tatiana, who makes not a peep to Eugene but is clearly in a state of complete devastation.

ACT 2

Act 1, about the same length as the next two acts combined, with its focus on Tatiana, gives us the most substantial part of the opera. Act 2 will deviate sharply away from her, but its first orchestral notes do not allow that to happen, as it starts with the most prominent melody from her letter-writing scene. This orchestral introduction continues about as long as the intro to Act 1, builds to a climax of volume, with some syncopation, and then returns to its original quiet *dolce* character. The scene gives us a ball in the Larin house, with numerous people both young and old, but the music places the focus squarely on Tatiana, even though her role throughout this act will be marginal. Of course she will be present—after all, these people have come to celebrate her name day, but her role shrinks to the point that she has no solo singing in the act—only a relatively small place as an ensemble member. Eugene and Lensky now carry the action, but Tchaikovsky assures us musically at the beginning of the act that we should be thinking more about her than the others, remembering that everything that unfolds relates to Eugene's rejection of her earlier. In fact, the three-part form of the intro in a sense encapsulates the act just heard, taking Tatiana from her dream to the destruction of it, and then to a point where she must calmly live with the result.

Dance and opera work closely together for Tchaikovsky, and this should not surprise us considering his achievements in ballet, with *Swan Lake* already under his belt at this point. In his most recent opera, *Vakula the Smith* (1874), later revised as *Cherevichki* (*The Tsarina's Slippers*)—to be discussed in chapter 7—he included full-scale ballet scenes. The celebration at the Larin house is a ball, and at a ball obviously there will be dancing, both group and individual. After the introduction a waltz strikes up, and amid the dancing, the chorus revels in the gaiety, telling us that a military band provides the divine music (Tchaikovsky's own facetious self-congratulation); the wine flows, and how like the good old times it seems. Tatiana, who discovers that Eugene has come (this is probably the first time she has seen him since he coolly let her down), will certainly not share any of the sentiments of the group. Eugene, completely unaware of her reaction, swoops her up to join him in dancing the waltz, and a group of older women begin to gossip about him—that he's a tyrant, a gambler, boorish, a heavy drinker, and, worst of all, a Freemason. Eugene overhears them, and devises a way to get his revenge on Lensky, whom he blames for bringing him to this house filled with tedious chin wagging. He will accomplish this by preventing Lensky from dancing with Olga; as they dance he steps in to separate them, and he whirls off with her as Lensky protests that she promised the dance to him. She takes it as sport, even flirting a little with Eugene, and thus the evening continues with no more dances for Lensky, abandoned by Olga, as Tatiana has been by Eugene. When the dancing stops Lensky asks Olga what he has done to offend her, and she chides him for making such a fuss over nothing.

Lensky must cool his heels with the arrival of Monsieur Triquet, a French pedant straight out of Pushkin who improvises a couplet for the birthday girl; she grimaces but must take her place of honor for his display. Pushkin could mock the mediocrity of his French verse, and now Tchaikovsky indulges in something similar, allowing some comic relief as he not only spews out his long-winded trivial couplet—twice—but does so on music designed to reinforce the mediocrity. Here Tchaikovsky has no problem laughing at French affectation.

The next dance, a cotillion, in the tempo of a mazurka, gives another opportunity for ballet, and as with the waltz, this dance adds to the drama itself. When the waltz emerged in the middle of the nineteenth century in Vienna, some at first considered it to be subversive, and even though Europeans got over that, when it migrated to the United States, it took Americans much longer to banish the stigma. Tchaikovsky may very well be playing with its subversion in the way that Eugene wrests Olga away from Lensky, causing Lensky to accuse her of behaving like a coquet. Similarly, in the cotillion, a dance of French origin with frequent changes of partner, Olga should be dancing with more than one man, especially with Lensky included, but she dances with no one but Eugene. As these two dance together, Eugene even taunts Lensky with a question about why he's not dancing. All this becomes too much for Lensky, and he loses his cool, accusing Eugene of dishonor and Olga of being unfaithful. When Eugene calls him a lunatic, the insulted Lensky lays down the challenge for a duel, something in Russian tradition that can be prompted by very little. Larina cannot believe the two of them would quarrel like this in her house, but Eugene, now feeling insulted by his friend, considers he has no option but to accept the challenge.

The next morning Lensky appears in a wooded area out of town with his second ready for the duel, but they see no sign of Eugene. Curiously, as his second prepares the weapons, we see that in this production they will use rifles instead of pistols. Lensky now has some time on his hands, and this gives him a chance to reflect on his life, which he does in an aria, after Tatiana's letter-writing aria the next most potent number of the opera. Unlike Pushkin, who gives us two ways of thinking about Lensky—as a writer possibly with great potential, or as a hack who would have died unrecognized—Tchaikovsky prefers a different option. Now taking his imminent death as a foregone conclusion, he reflects on the love with Olga that might have been, and wonders if she—not posterity—will remember him. In taking this option, the composer rejects any possible hint of irony, and allows Lensky to pour out his heart ardently, his last poetic gasp trained on love, life, and death. In a perhaps unexpected nod to Pushkin, Tchaikovsky seems to pick up on his use of musical tone in his verse, especially the flute ("speaking in a melodious, flute-like tone"). In this aria he uses the woodwinds in a special way to enhance the emotions felt by Lensky, certainly the flute, but also the full range of winds as soloists or together. After a duet between the two combatants, which temporarily pulls Eugene up to Lensky's emotional level, the poet falls, and Eugene can say nothing more profound than "He's dead? He's dead!"

ACT 3

A few years have passed, but no more than about three or four. The act opens in a side salon with a view into a grand ballroom, not in a country estate such as the Larin house, but a splendid palace in St. Petersburg. The music begins with a loud trumpet call with a distinctive rhythm, heard twice, heralding an arrival that seems auspicious, although of what we do not yet know. Since Tchaikovsky uses virtually the identical call to begin the Fourth Symphony, only recently completed, we get the sense that this is no ordinary lead-in but in fact an exordium of much greater importance, signifying the beginning of a progression toward something fairly momentous. For the moment it leads to chords ascending chromatically, building in intensity toward more rising passages now with a persistent dotted rhythm. That rhythm suggests a dance, and finally the dance emerges, a polonaise, and dancing couples quickly appear in the background, dressed as members of the nobility. The dance continues at length, and when Eugene emerges in the foreground, others seem to shun him; instead of having a glass of champagne, he takes the whole bottle. As at the beginning of the opera, he's bored, just back from travel abroad, and has found travel just as tedious as balls in the city or life in the country. At the age of twenty-six his life has no aim, and he expresses all of this in recitative reminiscent of the dryness of his earlier interjections. His existence seems as devoid of passion as the music that Tchaikovsky gives him.

A new dance begins, a Schottische (Scotch dance), and now a beautiful, young but sophisticated princess emerges from the background, certainly catching Eugene's eye. As he looks he believes he recognizes her, as none other than the Tatiana he knew and rebuffed in the backwoods of the steppes, now looking grand but simple, even like a queen. She sees him, too, and learning from a friend that it's Eugene, she pretends to scarcely remember him, but at the same time tries to compose herself since she trembles with emotion. Eugene asks Prince Gremin, in whose palace this ball is taking place, to identify the woman, and he confirms this to be Tatiana, the Larin girl from the country—now Gremin's wife. There appears to be some age discrepancy between the married couple since the prince, a decorated military hero, has retired, and Tatiana cannot be more than about twenty years old. The prince (Alexei Tanovitski) wishes to tell his old friend and relative how this woman has changed his life, and he does this with a fairly formally dignified aria, but certainly not lacking in warmth. He has finally at this point in his life discovered love, and lets Eugene know all about it in the somewhat unusual key of G flat, a key Schubert, as I noted earlier, had brought to the fore with one of his most emotionally stirring impromptus for piano. The key of this aria stirs more emotion than the rest of the music, which never departs very far from the deportment of the socially elevated person delivering it. To take the formal tone even further, Tchaikovsky actually puts it in ABA form, not unlike the da capo arias of the eighteenth century, with a B section that gets somewhat more animated before returning to the sedateness of the A section. This aria goes on surprisingly long, and delivers a crucial grounding for the rest of the act.

After Gremin introduces Tatiana to Eugene, she feigns tiredness and leaves, perhaps as a ruse to hide her agitation. It's now Eugene's turn to be stirred, and for the first time in the opera Tchaikovsky gives him music to show him in a daze, first in accompanied recitative, and then as an arioso, or short aria. He now gets music that is melodically distinctive, with rising passages building to climaxes, at times on high notes that push the upper edges of the baritone register. He's hopelessly in love, and as he rushes off, a second Schottische begins.

The final scene of the opera takes place out of doors (instead of in the usual reception room in Gremin's palace), on a cold and snowy evening. The orchestra plays a rising passage similar to the one at the beginning of Gremin's aria, clearly establishing Tatiana's new identity. In most productions she enters carrying the letter Onegin has written to her with his profession of love, balancing hers from Act 1, but not so here. Pushkin makes much of this letter, "penned with passion," almost as long as Tatiana's much earlier, using the epistolary mode as the strongest means of expressing love, in which Eugene ends avowing, "I surrender to my fate." In the opera we have no second passionate writing scene, and in this production not even the paper in Tatiana's hand; needless to say, the music will carry the ardor, more even than the words they say. Before he arrives she ponders her vulnerability, with musical hints of her motif from Act 1, and Eugene then enters, throwing himself at her feet. She speaks first, in recitative, reminding him of his sermon to her a few years earlier, for which he asks forgiveness. Before the duet proper begins, each one of them has a lengthy solo, with Tatiana going first. She recalls the folly of her letter, and how his frigid response still makes her blood run cold, but much more than her words, the music seems to make her position clear, since she begins on the exact melody that Gremin's aria started with, and follows remarkably close to his aria as she continues. If we should doubt the words she speaks, we cannot avoid the fact that she speaks them in her husband's voice. Why, she asks, has Eugene come—because she's now a princess, or simply to ruin her good name in society?

Eugene grants that the optics may seem skewed, but pours out his love, as he did after first seeing her at the beginning of the act. The duet then starts, with Tatiana ruing that once happiness had been so near; we hear little of her motif from Act 1 in this act, but on these words the music comes close, as if to allow at least a fragment of the old dream, with Eugene taking it up as they sing together. She begs him to leave, assuming he still has a modicum of decency left, but he refuses, backed up with music from his earlier outpouring. It's too much for her, and she admits she still loves him, which sets him off on what he imagines to be triumph, and the final stages of the duet have her calling for inner strength to resist, while he thinks love has overcome. He's mistaken: she bids him farewell forever. He cries out, "Despair, regret! Oh, bitter destiny!" as the final curtain falls.

Some would like to imagine that the extraordinary achievement of this opera, vaulting it to a position as one of the greatest of the entire repertory, has something to do with the desperation of Tchaikovsky's own personal situation at the time. Shortly before this he had gotten married, out of the most misguided of motives, as he confided to his brother Modest that an aversion to his homosexuality drove him to it, hoping to find atonement in a life of normality. Like Tatiana, Antonina Milyukova had written him letters professing her love, based every bit as much on delusion since she did not know him, and being determined to marry, he, without knowing her, took this as his opportunity. The marriage ended badly in short order, with him fleeing from her, perhaps as Eugene predicted theirs might end if they did marry. Fate played a major role in both Pushkin's story and the composer's life. Taking these kinds of parallels too far probably leads down the wrong path, and Tchaikovsky did not need such direct similarity between his life and a novel to achieve greatness with his opera.

At the same time, something clearly stirred him in this story on a personal level, especially his own reworking of it, and in a less literal way strong parallels do exist. A theme recurring persistently for Tchaikovsky concerns his own inability to experience the fruits of love—that destiny prevented him from achieving in life what he most desired. In many of his dramatic works, including operas, ballets, and symphonic poems, we see him embracing stories in which love cannot be, in which either one or both of the protagonists want it desperately but some impediment intervenes to make that impossible. Of all such stories, Pushkin's *Onegin* proved to be one of the most powerful, in fact depriving both people in love at different times of their goal, Tatiana at the beginning, and Eugene at the end. The more we try to explain what happens in rational terms, the more fleeting the answers become. We can laugh at Tatiana for her bookish foolishness if we like, as Pushkin at times seems to, but that in no way diminishes her pain. She knows as well as anyone else how misguided her letter is, but no force can stop her from writing it or stop her even as an adult from loving the man who could not possibly have been worthy of her infatuation. It simply could not be, and for this she must suffer; so must he at the end. Tchaikovsky identified with this kind of suffering in the deepest possible way, and not surprisingly, he could transfigure his vision of it, with Tatiana instead of Eugene at the center, into an exceptional opera.

6

SYMPHONY AS OPERA

During the two years following his Third Symphony Tchaikovsky underwent some life-changing experiences, and his music reflected these changes in the strongest possible ways. A large part of the difference between the Fourth Symphony and the previous one has to do with the dramatic effect a symphony should have on an audience in touching the human spirit at the deepest possible level, and he gave much thought to this when he started the Fourth near the beginning of 1877. The drama clearly should arise from within himself, and the more he endowed the works with this, the more an audience could respond. Aside from three earlier symphonies, he had by now thoroughly established himself as a composer of symphonic poems, with notable successes including the Shakespeare-inspired *Romeo and Juliet* (1869) and *The Tempest* (1873); most recently he had written *Francesca da Rimini* (1876), a fantasia based on Dante's *Inferno*. Especially after *Francesca* he may have seen the symphony moving more in the direction of symphonic poems, and by now a long tradition existed of treating symphonies that way, starting with Beethoven's Sixth, and progressing through Berlioz and Liszt. His greatest German contemporary as a symphonist, Johannes Brahms, proceeded along the lines of the German classical tradition, and he not only held no fascination for Tchaikovsky, but even evoked contempt, with what Tchaikovsky considered "pretentions to profundity." That did not stop him from enjoying Brahms's company when the two of them met in Hamburg, even getting drunk with him (he called him "a potbellied boozer"). Tchaikovsky sometimes regretted not being able to fashion his symphonies more on the classical mold, but when it came right down to it, that type of formal rigor did not suit his expressive purposes, since something very different prompted his symphonic language.

FOURTH SYMPHONY: PROGRAMME

In letters just after completing the Fourth he had much to say about this work, and depending on the correspondent, we get some fairly divergent if not contradictory views. Not being in Moscow for the first performance of the symphony, he hoped to receive congratulations from friends by mail, but this came in very small doses. The person whose musical judgment he most trusted, his former student and now colleague Sergey Taneyev, whose brilliant performance of the Piano Concerto had proved Nikolay Rubinstein wrong about it being playable, did not give the kind of praise he hoped to receive. Taneyev complained about the Fourth having the appearance of a symphonic poem—that this somehow made it defective, and that parts of it seemed too much like ballet, again a defect in light of the low regard for ballet music in Russia at this time. Unlike Rubinstein, whose censures could easily throw him into a state of distress and anger, Tchaikovsky appreciated Taneyev's forthright opinion, although he certainly did not agree, wondering what he had against the use of dance-like music since all great composers used it, including Beethoven. Most interesting though is his response to the criticism about it sounding programmatic, and in writing to Taneyev, a friend whose own musical thinking he had helped to shape, we can assume his reply came as close as possible to the truth:

> As for your observation that my symphony is programmatic, I completely agree. The only thing I don't understand is why you consider this a defect. I fear the very opposite situation—i.e. I should not wish symphonic works to come from my pen which express nothing, and which consist of empty playing with chords, rhythms, and modulations. Of course my symphony is programmatic, but this programme is such that it cannot be formulated in words. . . . Ought not a symphony—that is, the most lyrical of all musical forms—to be such a work? Should it not express everything for which there are no words, but which the soul wishes to express, and which requires to

be expressed? . . . Please don't think that I aspire to paint before you a depth of feeling and a grandeur of thought that cannot be easily understood in words. I was not trying to express any new thought. In essence my symphony imitates Beethoven's Fifth; that is, I was not imitating its musical thoughts, but the fundamental idea. Do you think there is a programme in the Fifth Symphony? Not only is there a programme, but in this instance there cannot be any question about its efforts to express itself. My symphony rests upon a foundation that is nearly the same . . . I'll add, moreover, that there is not a note in this symphony (that is, in mine) which I did not feel deeply, and which did not serve as an echo of sincere impulses within my soul. (B2 162–63)

He leaves no question that he has based the work on a programme, but this gets tricky when commentators, or for that matter Tchaikovsky himself, try to define what that programme may actually be. Some have tried to link it directly to his personal life, for example to his disastrous marriage, despite the fact that he had not even heard of Antonina before starting to work on it, or the complications of balancing his homosexuality with social expectations. The linkage of the work with events in his own life at this time will unlikely be very fruitful, although the composer himself gave in to this in a lengthy letter to Nadezhda von Meck in which he actually spelled out a programme. Their stunning correspondence had started about the same time he wrote his first sketches of this work, and by the time he completed it, their epistolary relationship had grown to the point that he wished only to dedicate it to her. She had initiated the correspondence late in 1876 because of her desire to know the person behind the works that moved her so deeply, and Tchaikovsky, ever the sensitive letter writer, indulged this fascination of hers, writing in a way to her that he would not to anyone else. In many respects he tailored his responses to what she made clear she wished to know about him or his approaches to works, and the thought of these in any way becoming public would have been anathema to him. It led him at times to exaggerate, or worse, to say things that bear only a moderate resemblance to reality. As for his descriptions of the Fourth, he could tell Taneyev exactly, within the limitations of spoken or written language, what he intended this work to be; to Mrs. von Meck he gave a very different impression, stressing that it was their work, embodying something of their relationship as friends or perhaps even more, and that in this work she could read him as a person. In fact, it's a great pity that this letter has been published, since it has caused many to fall into the trap of thinking this description accurately reflects the symphony, although that does not preclude it from containing grains of truth.

In a way she goaded him into writing out this programme for her, not only asking for it explicitly but also with comments such as "in your music I hear myself, my condition, I receive echoes of my thoughts, my anguish" (TM 180). It delighted him that "you experienced the same feelings I was full of when I was writing it," but as for describing the programme, that gave him more difficulty, something he would normally refuse to do: "How can one recount the undefined feelings one goes through when an instrumental composition without a definite subject is being written? It's a purely lyric process." Despite the caveat, he agreed to do it, that "there *is* a programme, i.e. it is possible to explain in words what it attempts to express, and to you, only to you, I can and will indicate the meaning." He did not intend this for the rest of us, and we should keep that in mind, as well as his artfulness as a letter writer. He then launched into the programme, with musical examples, starting with the opening motto: "This is *Fate*, this is that fateful force which prevents the impulse towards happiness from achieving its aim, which guards jealously lest well-being and peace should be complete and unclouded, which hangs overhead like the sword of Damocles and unwaveringly and constantly poisons the soul. This force is invincible, and you will never overpower it. All that remains is to resign yourself and languish fruitlessly." With what follows the motto, the Moderato con anima (*in movimento di valse*), "the desolate and hopeless feeling becomes stronger and more corrosive," while the next lighter themes bring "sweet and tender daydreams." And more: "How good! How far away the obsessive first theme of the allegro sounds now? The daydreams have gradually taken possession of the soul completely. Everything gloomy and joyless is forgotten. Here it is, here is happiness!" But with the return of the motto, "No! these were daydreams, and *Fate* wakes you from them. . . . So all life consists of an uninterrupted alternation of harsh reality with fleeting dreams and visions of happiness. . . . There is no refuge. . . . You have to float on this sea until it engulfs you and plunges you to its depths. That, roughly, is the programme of the first movement" (TM 184–86).

In this manner he continues with his description of the other movements, alternating between happiness and sadness, as though pressing buttons on an emotions-measuring meter. Before sealing the letter in the envelope, he saw the fallacy of his attempt: "I have just reread it, and am horrified at the obscurity and inadequacy of the programme I'm sending you. For the first time in my life I have had to put into words and phrases musical thoughts and musical images. I've not managed to say it properly. I was down in the dumps last winter when the symphony was in the writing, and it is a faithful echo of what I was going through at that time." Even in hedging his words he makes a bigger blunder, tying it with how he felt at the time, as though he woke up one morning feeling depressed, and wrote depressing music. Of course this is nonsense. Like any great composer he was not writing only about himself, although he did bring his own experience into an outlook that he could transform into something all humanity could respond to, not just Mrs. von Meck.

As embarrassing as the happy/sad/happy/sad alternating may be, kernels of truth undoubtedly exist, and some of these will be explored. The characterization of the opening motto, for example, seems fair, and also his description of the gloriously melodic second movement (not that it expresses depression, or that "it's the melancholy feeling you get of an evening when, tired after work, you're sitting alone, you've picked up a book but it has slipped from your hand"). He does get it right, though, with this: "There's nostalgia for the past, but no desire to start life over again" (TM 186–88). That nostalgia, and the shattering of it that prevents a return to things as they once were, comes very close to musical procedures that reveal the same thing in some music of his beloved Mozart, and even more remarkably in various slow movements by Schubert.

THE FOURTH AND *ONEGIN*

I would like to put forward a different possibility for getting at the programme of the Fourth, a time-sensitive one, although having nothing to do with being "a faithful echo of what I was going through at that time." While he worked on this symphony he composed another work more or less simultaneously, in fact temporarily suspending progress on one while he switched to the other, and there seems a very real possibility that his thinking on the two became intertwined. He started on the Fourth early in 1877 and had sketches of the first three movements by the middle of May. He then put it aside until near the end of September, for about four months; with the sketches he had a rough idea of how the work would progress, but perhaps not a clear sense of what would set it apart from his previous symphonies to make it one of the great works of the genre. That inspiration may very well have come near the end of May, while visiting his singer friend Elizaveta Lavrovskaya, and she suggested to him the subject for an opera: *Eugene Onegin*. At first the idea seemed doubtful, but within days he had thrown himself into it completely; two days later he met with Konstantin Shilovsky at Glebovo to discuss the libretto, and on 30 May he wrote his brother Modest outlining the full scenario. In June he confessed to Modest that he had fallen in love with the image of Tatiana, as described in the previous chapter, and observed that by the end of the month he had finished composing the first act. He continued at a red-hot pace, completing two-thirds of the opera by mid-July.

On 30 August he wrote to Mrs. von Meck about his own struggle with fate, and quoted Pushkin about the possibility of habit that is "given to us from above as a substitute for happiness." He then launched into a discussion of *Onegin*, doubting its theatricality, but feeling fairly certain that "those who are ready to search within an opera for a musical reproduction of ordinary, simple, universal sensations that are far removed from high tragedy and theatricality may (I hope) find satisfaction in my opera. In a word, it is written sincerely, and I am pinning all my hopes on this sincerity" (TM 41). Work continued over the next few months, first at the estate of his sister and her husband in Ukraine (Kamenka), and then while abroad in Italy and Switzerland, with orchestration continuing until early December. On 28 October, while in Clarens, Switzerland, he wrote to Modest asking him to send the manuscript of the Fourth, and plunged back into that full-time in mid-December, completing the first movement on 20 December, the second movement by the 25th, the Scherzo on the 27th, and the entire symphony by 7 January 1878. Immediately after that he returned to *Onegin*, completing it by the end of January.

It seems entirely plausible that as he surged ahead with the opera, and discovered the ingredients of a great opera—not in high theatricality but instead in something simple, universal, and sincere—it struck him that the same could be done with a symphony, allowing its drama to unfold in a manner consistent with this opera. He dropped a number of clues that seem to bear this out, creating what may amount to musical cameos—passages that appear in both opera and symphony either in identical form or close enough that they cannot be mistaken. The first and most overt, the motto at the beginning of the symphony played by horns and bassoons, is identical to—at least for the first bar—the beginning of Act 3 of the opera, sounded there by trumpets. Both ultimately lead to a dance, or something dance-like in the case of the symphony, and both can be taken to represent fate. We do not hear it again in the opera, but other forces, along with the texts for the singers, carry forward the pervasive effect of fate. Knowing the fateful result of Act 3 can give the sense of fate in the symphony a possible clarity, with the motto returning in the finale. The main theme of the finale, a folk dance, has striking similarities to the motif of the folk dance in Act 1 of the opera, and once again, making that connection, in the context of Tatiana's response to it, suggests possibilities for the way we can think of it in the symphony. A third correlation, although perhaps more in tone than actual melodic shape, concerns Tatiana's motif in the opera, which permeates her letter-writing scene; this also defines the melodic character of the second movement. Even the solo instrument, the oboe, ties in with the oboe obbligato that at times accompanies Tatiana in her famous scene.

The possibility of opera and symphony sharing common dramatic impulses had been around for at least a century by this time, especially going back to Tchaikovsky's beloved Mozart's time, when composers wrote all types of compositions. During the nineteenth century composers tended to become more specialized, and even Beethoven wrote nine symphonies but only one opera. Schumann and Mendelssohn also wrote only one opera each, and Brahms attempted no operas at all. On the other hand, Verdi and Wagner avoided the symphony almost completely. One of the few composers active in both, Berlioz, interested Tchaikovsky very much. In Russia he did not have especially good models, since until the late nineteenth century Russians did not consider composition a worthy profession the way Germans, Italians, and the French did. The only Russian to buck the trend before this time, Mi-

khail Glinka (1804–1857), wrote all types of works, including both operas and symphonies.

For composers of the late eighteenth century, especially Mozart and
Haydn, who wrote both operas and symphonies prolifically, these two
types of composition belonged in a single category that automatically
drew them together. Music for their time, very roughly, divided into
two broad categories (but of course not exclusively): public music, intended for a listening audience, and private music, to be played by
amateurs for their own enjoyment. The latter included just about all
chamber music and solo works, while the former covered opera, symphonies, and concertos. Private music could draw in the players in a
variety of ways, often with an emphasis on the sound itself, but public
works had to engage the interest of an inactive audience, whose attention span would not operate the same as it would for someone actually
playing an instrument or singing. The importance of sound itself should
not be underestimated, but something else needed to captivate the
listener, and most often that could be found in the dramatic nature of
the work. With opera, especially Mozart's, the drama could not be
missed, especially Tchaikovsky's favorite of all operas, *Don Giovanni*,
but certainly all of Mozart's other late operas as well, although it's
questionable if he knew any of these aside from *The Marriage of Figaro*
since they did not re-enter the repertory until a few decades later.
Concertos can achieve their drama in various ways, but one of the most
overt involves the possible dramatic interaction of the solo voice—the
individual—with the tutti section or the orchestra—the many.

Drama in a symphony may not be as obvious to hear, but it can be
every bit as strong, regardless of whether or not the work has a programme. If the symphony has a programme, this may represent a dramatic work of literature, such as Tchaikovsky's *Manfred* Symphony or
his symphonic poems already written, but if it lacks one, pure or absolute music can generate drama just as effectively. The symphonies of
Mozart and Haydn more often than not fell into the latter category, and
Haydn in part created his drama through his treatment of sonata form,
something he did not invent but certainly brought to a new level that
could give the drama broader social implications. In so doing he took
the symphony beyond the type of celebratory piece it had previously
been and turned it into something that prompted listeners to think
about social or religious matters. He could do this by exploiting the

inherent tensions within the form, including contrasting themes, tonal tensions, rhythmic or metric conflicts, and other possibilities, not unlike a dramatic work for the stage, which presents the forces in conflict, develops the tension, and comes to a point of resolution that may resolve the conflict or can simply allow the opposite forces to coexist. Mozart was less inclined than Haydn to treat his this way, but still used sonata form in his symphonic first movements and occasionally some other movements as well.

While sonata form became the backbone of first movements in symphonies in the late eighteenth century, it could be used in opera as well, and here we find a kind of crossover between the two types of composition. Mozart, for example, uses it brilliantly in *The Marriage of Figaro*, in the sextet in Act 3, where the dramatic action of the plot beautifully parallels the form itself, showing how the drama of sonata form can be understood, with words and actions backing up the music. Composers before Mozart had done similar things, and Haydn did too, even using sonata form at times as the formal basis for arias. We also can see that in the development sections of his symphonies, where musical themes can progress in fairly complex counterpoint, the nature of that counterpoint has less to do with formal counterpoint than it does with the ways that the characters interact with each other in operatic ensembles. In different ways at the time opera could take its cues from the symphony, and symphony could do the same from opera; in many ways the two had strong linkages. Tchaikovsky went in a fairly different direction, especially in steering his symphonies toward programme music, but he certainly found himself in good company and part of a long-standing practice by connecting the Fourth with an opera.

THE FOURTH: FIRST MOVEMENT

The motto that begins the symphony (hereafter simply referred to as the motto—in a single bar a quarter note tied to an eighth followed by three sixteenths as a triplet followed by two eighth notes), played *fortissimo* by two horns and two bassoons, as just noted, leads off the third act of *Onegin*. In his description of the symphony to Mrs. von Meck, Tchaikovsky rightly called this motto fate—specifically an invincible sense of fate with destructive power. In the opera he did not have to tell us that, since the action of Act 3 makes it perfectly clear. Eugene has returned from travels abroad, sees Tatiana at a ball, and falls hopelessly in love with the woman he completely rejected a few years earlier. He then spends the rest of the opera trying to win her away from her husband, pressure she now rejects, since her sense of propriety stands as the hand of fate blocking his aspirations. Just before her final farewell to him, she leaves no question about the role of fate in the impossibility of their union: "Onegin, still my vows must bind me! By fate, I am another's wife; unfaithful, he shall never find me!" He persists, characterizing her vows to Gremin as false and therefore non-binding, saying that she should give in to his love, and should "follow where your fate has willed you go." Before leaving him forever, she replies, "That was by fate forbidden!" Tchaikovsky makes fate the most powerful force at the end of the opera, and the trumpet motto at the beginning of the last act represents the inexorable force setting the course toward the final result of fate. Using the same motto to start the symphony confirms its description given to Mrs. von Meck.

In contrast to its treatment in the opera, where the motto quickly leads on to other material, in the symphony it becomes the basis for a slow introduction, not unlike the way Mozart begins his Symphony No. 39 in E flat, or the way Haydn leads off almost all of his late symphonies. As such, the motto takes on a larger life than just the rhythmic figure of the single bar described above, with its extension being as important as the material, which we hear repeated in the second bar. In the third bar it launches into a dotted rhythm (eighth note, dotted eighth, sixteenth—grouped together as a triplet), which becomes the overriding force of the fast part of the movement, because of the triplet anticipating the 9/8 meter of the new section, in contrast to the opening 3/4 meter. Other activities of the introduction also anticipate later events, including the downward motion starting at bar 5, the return of the motto at bar 7, and the syncopations at bar 11 in the upper winds, dislodging the beat in a way that the lower winds and strings cannot overcome. Even without knowing what he said to Mrs. von Meck, we can infer from the music itself that destructive forces are at play, forces that undermine stability and create a sense of unease, which, of course, we will discover permeating much of the symphony.

In both the opera and the symphony the motto leads to a dance, a polonaise in the opera and something dance-like in the symphony (*in movimento di valse*). Now we can also make a connection with Act 2 of the opera, which started with a type of slow introduction, based on Tatiana's theme, and then led into an actual waltz. The choice of something waltz-like for the opening movement of the symphony appears to be significant in the way that it follows the dance sections of the opera (like the waltz, the polonaise also uses a triple meter). In both the second and third acts of the opera, the waltz (or polonaise) appears to be a harbinger of things going badly wrong. All appears to be rosy at the beginning of Act 2, but Eugene soon becomes a negative force, getting his little revenge on Lensky by refusing to let Olga dance with him, with this provoking the challenge to a duel by Lensky; Lensky's death at the end of the act has in a sense been connected to the waltz. The final act works in a similar way, with Eugene seeing the forbidden fruit during the polonaise at the beginning, discovering love for the first time in his life (or was it seduction?), and then fighting a losing battle against fate to win her over.

The waltz may seem an unlikely backdrop for this kind of havoc, especially if we think of it only as a nice social dance for amusement at balls. This dance originated in Vienna in the middle of the nineteenth century, and while it quickly caught on as a craze not only with young people, not everyone at the time thought of it as entirely wholesome, some going so far as to condemn it as lewd and lascivious. On the one hand, the waltz seemed like a paragon of order, constructed with balanced and symmetrical phrases, allowing the dancers to move away from a starting point followed by a balanced return. In actual practice, though, despite the elaborate rules and attempts by dance masters to define decorum, the face-to-face physical contact with men in the lead put women in a somewhat compromising situation. Moral writers reacted strongly, objecting to erotic displays not permitted in polite society; that women might actually enjoy it seemed beyond the pale. Numerous writers had addressed this subversive aspect of the dance, and later some would even couch it as a symbol of the collapse of civilization leading up to World War I, as Ravel does brilliantly in his *La Valse*. Whether Tchaikovsky knew any of these negative views about the waltz we do not know, but considering how he used it in *Onegin*, along with his extensive sojourns to central Europe, it seems entirely possible.

The waltz-like main body of the first movement begins with the dotted-rhythm figure, in 9/8 since the triplet aspect of it has taken over, and while we know this figure because it was introduced earlier, it now behaves in a very different way. In describing it to Mrs. von Meck, Tchaikovsky said, "The desolate and hopeless feeling becomes stronger and more corrosive," and that destabilizing sense of it comes out in the music itself. We no longer have clearly separated figures to give the overall triple meter, but he always puts in a tie connecting the first two beats, in fact preventing the listener from having any clear sense of the beat, and he underlines the instability even more with accompanying syncopations. Of course we cannot describe this as a waltz, since unlike the one in the opera, this could not possibly be danced; it not only lacks the necessary phrase structure but by obscuring the first beat from the second it loses all sense of stability. In the opera we needed the ensuing action to show the waltz as somehow complicit in the movement toward destruction, but in the symphony he builds it into the music immediately, giving it no chance of being taken as something gentle or stabilizing; a minor key (F minor in this case), would also not be used for a light dance. As it proceeds, building to dynamic peaks, that feeling of being dislodged becomes even more intense.

If we expect to find the formal marking points of classical sonata form in this movement, we will be disappointed. Tchaikovsky occasionally regretted not being able to manage that kind of formal clarity, but he had absolutely no need to apologize. In his letter to Taneyev he had compared this symphony to Beethoven's Fifth, and the reason for that will be explored later, but with Beethoven as a possible model, he hardly had to be concerned about any kind of slavish adherence to sonata form. This "form" can best be thought of as a state of mind, or process, where the rules were meant to be broken. Haydn, who more than any other composer defined it, also started the trend of breaking it down, as he did in the first movement of his famous "Farewell" Symphony. Beethoven went much further; by the end of his career we often have nothing more than a vague inkling of the form, lacking both thematic and tonal definition, as happens in the first movement of the Piano Sonata Op. 101. If Beethoven had done this half a century earlier, it should not surprise us that Tchaikovsky would allow other forces to be more important; the only surprise is that he should care about it. Despite that, he does not abandon sonata form entirely, since the movement still partitions into sections that resemble an exposition, development, and recapitulation, but they lack clear points of demarcation, both thematically and tonally.

The material of the dance-like theme behaves much more motivically than as a melody, allowing it to expand and develop, moving from its opening *piano* to a more ominous *fortissimo* well into the movement. At one point in the expositional area, it attempts to become melodic, starting with a solo clarinet and later a bassoon line designated *dolce grazioso* (sweetly, gracefully), but no real melody emerges as the line adheres to the original unstable rhythm. Even though that goes nowhere, these two instruments launch into something more clearly melodic (theme B), sharing a dotted rhythm similar to the one after the motto at the beginning of the opera's third act. There it had been transitional, en route to the polonaise, but in the symphony he makes much more of it as a melody, ending it with a downward flourish of chromatic thirty-second notes, moving that figure from one wind instrument to another. A countermelody tries to emerge in the lower strings, but without much success against this descending figure, and not unlike the first movement of Schubert's "Unfinished" Symphony, we have a struggle emerging between the lyrical instinct and something that seems intent on preventing it.

This struggle will continue throughout the symphony, and as with Schubert, the lyrical writing may be emblematic of the individual with whom the audience can most closely identify. In the opera that had most clearly been Tatiana, although it's not until the letter-writing scene that we encounter her vividly as an individual. Something similar happens in the symphony, in the second movement, but before that happens, attempts to emerge appear to be summarily suppressed. It soon tries again, during a *fff* blast from a modification of the opening theme, at which point the horn tries to rise above it with a melody, but hopelessly overwhelmed, it quickly drops out. The waltz-like theme dominates, often with fierce intensity bolstered by syncopation or *fff*, leaving no opportunity for melodic encroachment. The atmosphere of menace becomes even more intense when the opening motto reappears, also at *fff*, perhaps starting the development. After this reminder of fate the orchestra pulls back to a *piano* level, and against this gentler development, the bassoon and cellos make another attempt at a melody, at *mf* to rise above the rest of the orchestra, but it works only momentarily. The orchestra not only starts to overpower the melody, but even forces the bassoon and cellos to join ranks on their non-melodic figuration. Further attempts at a melody simply lead to disinte-gration, and back at the level of *fff*, the motto again returns with its ominous dismissal of anything melodic. Now the motto comes back more persistently, continuing at *fff* with the dance motif; the two of them have teamed up to muscle out all possibility of anything lyrical.

The lyrical spirit does not give up, as theme B returns in what may be the recap, but once again other forces—including increased volume, syncopation, and eventually again the motto—suppress it; these now take over the entire orchestra. Something melodic makes one more attempt, even designated *cantabile* (in a singing manner), and it holds its own for more than a few bars. That lyrical spirit vanishes with the next *fortissimo* appearance of the motto, in a short section that Tchai-kovsky repeats, progressing into a completely non-lyrical coda. If the movement has in a way been a battle between attempts at lyricism and forces preventing it, with the motto often intervening on behalf of the anti-lyrical forces, lyricism has not stood a chance, since everything has been stacked against it. The interaction of these forces has proceeded not unlike the voices in an operatic ensemble, with intensive drama among players all clearly recognizable. The loud ending to the move-ment signifies nothing triumphant, but instead the beating down of something precious—something individual and personal, which will have to try again to resurface in another movement.

ANDANTINO

Lyricism tried to get a toehold in the first movement, without success, but the lyrical impulse now becomes the raison d'être of the second movement, and in fact receives the title Andantino in modo di canzone (somewhat slowly, in the manner of a song). The soloist of this song, the oboe, has an all-string *pizzicato* accompaniment for the first twenty bars, giving an impression of a singer with a guitar accompaniment. In *Onegin* the most deeply felt vocal music had been for Tatiana's letter-writing scene, and the music that accompanies her writing of the letter features the oboe as an obbligato, with lines very similar to passages from the symphony's second-movement melody, both before she sings and during her singing. Once again Tchaikovsky draws opera and symphony together with his most glorious melodic writing, suggesting that the second movement can be heard in a way similar to Tatiana's outpouring of emotion in Act 1. Tatiana has embarked on an attempt to transform her dream into reality, and while realizing the utter folly of this, she persists, anticipating the negative result. Later in life she can look back on this as the one moment she had a chance to gain happiness, and even though it did not work out, the memory remains precious—not the rejection, but the fantasy itself about love, only an illusion but one that at least in her own mind allowed her to grasp that love may actually exist. She can reflect back on that wistfully, but never replicate it. Any thoughts about it later, as in her duet with Eugene in the last act, can never re-create what she felt earlier. The euphoria briefly existed in her own mind, specifically while she wrote the letter, and with the onset of reality—Eugene's response, and later a marriage more about convention than love—she lost the ecstasy forever.

In the opera we need both the first and last acts to put that together, but in the instrumental writing of a symphonic movement, the focus can become more concentrated, allowing something larger to be perceived more quickly. His remarks to Mrs. von Meck about this movement in part bear out the connection with Tatiana, although his programme provides a fairly poor explanation of the music, especially when he uses words such as "depression" or compares the experience with feeling tired in the evening after work. When he speaks though of "teeming memories," "that so much has been and gone" in reference to youth, and especially "nostalgia for the past" and the impossibility of recapturing this, he gets to the heart of the matter. In the second movement, he shows in music exactly how this can be revealed, both that it's "sweet to immerse yourself in the past," as he explained to Mrs. von Meck, and the "melancholy" of not being able to return. His musical treatment of this comes very close to what Mozart had done in the slow movement of the Piano Concerto in D Minor, K466, where he presents an exceptionally beautiful melody, and then introduces an almost violently destructive force that shatters the nostalgia implicit in the earlier beauty. Following this undermining, the melody cannot return as it was, but must come back as something irrevocably changed, now encumbered with vestiges of the destructive music that first disturbed it. Tchaikovsky undoubtedly knew that work well, since it was the one Mozart piano concerto to remain an active part of the repertory during the nineteenth century. No composer took this format further than Schubert had in numerous slow movements, and even though Tchaikovsky may not have known them, his treatment here comes closer to Schubert's in the String Quintet in C, D956 or the Piano Trio in E flat, D929, allowing the disruptive forces to return more than once.

The first section of this movement features the wonderful melody (A) introduced by the oboe, which then hands it off to the cello, now with added wind accompaniment excluding the oboe, all of this lasting a full forty bars. An episode with new material (B) begins immediately after this, much less melodic in character, also more rhythmically defined, and unlike the *piano* melody, this increases in volume from *mf* through *f* to *ff*, intruding aggressively on the opening melody as a hostile force. The A melody returns, now with a very different accompaniment, but once again B cuts in, not as aggressively as before, but still disruptively, until the melody simply fades out. This leads to a new episode (C), less melodic than B, with a vague resemblance to the dance-like theme of the first movement, a resemblance that becomes closer when the dotted rhythmic cells get tied over the bar lines, generating syncopation as it obscures the beat. Other forces participate in the destabilization taking place, especially the persistent triplets set against the theme, as well as the building to *fortissimo* at the most disruptive points. This goes on much longer than the B episode had, and it finally disappears by fading away. When the A melody returns, now in the first violins with the *pizzicato* accompaniment in the rest of the strings, a new accompaniment in the winds encroaches, in fact borrowed directly from the first movement—the descending thirty-second-note figure, now occasionally ascending as well, adding an uneasiness as it did in the first movement.

Once again an abbreviated B prevents the melody from continuing, and when A does attempt to return, it appears to have lost its way; it has become a series of two-bar altered fragments that lack the eight-bar phrase structure of A, and it changes much more radically as it continues. Near the end the A melody makes one more attempt to re-establish itself, now in the bassoon and continuing for sixteen bars, but the attempt falters as the short fragments take over, finally fading into oblivion. The entire movement has presented a dramatic (even operatic) struggle between the beautiful melody—the embodiment of nostalgia—and non-lyrical forces attempting to undermine it, which in the end succeed. Not only can the melody not be what it had been before, but it ends up as broken shards on the floor, graphically destroyed by the antagonists. Like Tatiana dismantled by Eugene's coldness, unable for obvious reasons to return to her dream later, the melody of this movement collapses under the weight of the antagonistic strain. If we hoped for relief from the first movement, the Andantino gives none, with the lyrical impulse now entirely suppressed.

SCHERZO

The Andantino did not provide a diversion, but the Scherzo most certainly does, with about three-quarters of it written in a highly unusual and most delightful way—for *pizzicato* strings. A few years ago I had the great pleasure of meeting the young Canadian violinist Adrian Anantawan when he came to Halifax to play Mendelssohn's Violin Concerto with Symphony Nova Scotia. My wife, Linda, arranged for us to have coffee together the night before the performance since she felt a special connection with him. Both of them had been students at the Curtis Institute of Music in Philadelphia, and while there Adrian studied with Yumi Ninomiya Scott, who had been Linda's roommate during her time as a student. At the concert we were most surprised to see him after playing the concerto join the orchestra in the violin section for Tchaikovsky's Fourth, and when I saw him take his seat, unusual in the extreme for someone who has just dazzled us as a concerto soloist, my mind immediately jumped to the Scherzo as I wondered how on earth he would play it. Unlike just about every other violinist in the world, Adrian has only one arm (his left), so he plays with a prosthesis attached to his right arm between his shoulder and elbow, and a device on the end of this to grip the bow. Despite this, he handles the bow with great finesse, but *pizzicato* presents a different problem. Most violinists do it holding the bow and using the index finger for short passages, while for longer ones such as this Scherzo they set the bow down. Adrian has no right index finger, and no arm joints below his shoulder. Surely, I thought, he would sit out the Scherzo.

He did not join the symphony to sit and watch. To my amazement he played the entire *allegro* movement using his left hand only. At that fast pace it's difficult enough to coordinate the left-hand fingering with the right-hand plucking, but he did both with his left hand, fingering the notes with three fingers and plucking with his index finger, a feat I had not believed possible. I never felt more satisfied listening to the delightful wizardry of this movement.

Even in a work dominated by fate and the impossibility of returning to happier times, a diversion can be possible, allowing some merriment before the darker clouds return, an occurrence Tchaikovsky himself compared to having "a drop of wine to drink and you're experiencing the first phase of inebriation." He had done this in *Onegin*, with some of the dances early in the last two acts, and even more so in the Act 2 episode with Monsieur Triquet, mocking his French affectations. In this movement the sense of dance emerges most notably, especially in the middle—the trio section, which sounds as though it had been written specifically for a ballet. Taneyev had objected to this, complaining that he did not "like the trio which is like a dance out of a ballet." Taneyev was not alone in voicing this objection, and it provoked a strong defense from Tchaikovsky, in the same letter to Taneyev justifying the programmatic nature of the work:

> Do you understand as ballet music every cheerful tune that has a dance rhythm? If that's the case, you must also be unable to reconcile yourself to the majority of Beethoven's symphonies in which you encounter such things at every step. . . . I simply do not understand how in the term *ballet music* there can be anything *censorious*. . . . I do not comprehend why a dance tune may not appear occasionally in a symphony, even if only when it has a deliberate shade of vulgar coarse humour. (B2 162)

Perhaps even more than in *Onegin* his treatment of ballet music here has something in common with his opera *Vakula the Smith*, written only four years before this, in which Act 3 starts and ends with ballets. Ballet had been essential in French operas from the eighteenth century, and Tchaikovsky saw more potential for himself in these than he did in German or Italian opera.

In his description of the Scherzo to Mrs. von Meck, he characterized it as being made up of "capricious arabesques," with vivid images that flash through the music, including carousing peasants and a street song, as well as a military procession passing by in the distance. After 132 bars of *pizzicato* strings at the beginning, the oboe introduces the ballet scene with lively rustic rhythms, and as the melody passes from one instrument to another, including the piccolo, it's easy to envisage the ballet before the *pizzicato* strings return. Later in the movement the rustic dance comes back, now with strings and winds no longer separated but brought together, with the dance in the winds and the *pizzicato* accompaniment in the strings. The movement ends as cheerfully as it started.

FINALE

In the finale Tchaikovsky returns much more directly to *Onegin*, near the beginning of the movement using the Russian folk song "In the Field a Little Birch Tree Stood," which he had included in a recent collection of songs. This familiar tune had also been used by Balakirev in his *Overture on Three Russian Themes*. The tune also has much in common with the folk song sung and danced by the peasants who have just returned from the fields in Act 1 of *Onegin*, and the direction of the symphony's movement can in some ways be seen to parallel the unfolding of the opera. Taneyev objected to this movement as well, disagreeing with Rubinstein about its quality: "Knowing how you treated 'The Crane' ['Zhuravel' in the finale of the Second Symphony], knowing what you are able to make out of a Russian theme, I think your variations on 'Vo polye beryozinka stoyala' too slight and insufficiently interesting" (B2 162). Others have shared Taneyev's view, ignoring the programmatic aspect of the work while placing the emphasis on the music somehow detached from this. Objecting on these grounds seems similar to panning the finale of Beethoven's Ninth because Beethoven turned to Schiller instead of writing an elaborate and complex instrumental conclusion. In drawing the parallel with *Onegin*, a possible programmatic direction for Tchaikovsky can be envisaged.

In the opera he needed to invoke a specifically Russian spirit near the beginning, since that emerged as a distinctive contrast between Tatiana and Eugene. Tchaikovsky sided completely with Tatiana, as he wrote to his colleague Nikolay Kashkin while starting to work on the opera: "Being completely immersed in composition, I so thoroughly identified myself with the image of Tatyana that she became for me like a living person, together with everything that surrounded her. I loved

Tatyana, and was furiously indignant with *Onegin* who seemed to me a cold, heartless fop" (B2 143). She embraced what surrounded her: the Russia she loved, the country life, the peasants on their estate, and the music that emanated from them; Eugene had no use for any of these things, disdainfully finding them nothing but boring. To establish that spirit of Russia in the opera, the singing and dancing of the peasants proved to be the ideal vehicle, and specifically with a folk tune that could resonate throughout their pantomime and beyond that as well. In the symphony too he wanted that spirit of Russia to be present, not something as trivial as what he suggested to Mrs. von Meck—"a picture of folk celebrating a festival," but a force that stirs the soul at a deeper level, as the Russian landscape had touched Tatiana as a person, to say nothing of many of the greatest nineteenth-century Russian writers. Of course Tchaikovsky shared this sense of Russia, something he had in his blood that always drew him home during his frequent trips abroad, but with an element of tension as well, prompting him to make his trips abroad to get away from its pull. Many sensitive Russians shared exactly the same dilemma, and could identify with the composer's ambivalence.

Tatiana's love of Russia, though, parallels her love of novels, the illusions these generate for her, and the inevitable disillusionment that results from following up on her fantasies. The placement of the folk pantomime near the beginning works in tandem with her literary-fed illusions, and provides a backdrop for the disintegration that will soon follow. Immediately after the peasants leave the stage, Eugene arrives, and Tatiana launches into her flawed assessment of him as the man she has always dreamed of. From that point on all goes badly between the two of them, as he rejects her love the next time they meet, she must witness with embarrassment his behavior at her name day celebration, and in the end she must deal with his persistent and now unwanted advances. In being transformed into the elegant princess, she now finds herself divorced from the countryside she once loved so dearly, in an urban and urbane existence in which formality and custom have trumped passion for another person and love of the simple things in life. We could find her ardor in the first act believable because of the music embodying her dreams and the genuine simplicity of the folk music surrounding her. When the tables turn in Act 3, she has of necessity become more officious, and Eugene appears to be the one who has found passion; that seems much less believable since he does not have the quality of music to surround him that she did in Act 1. Disintegration unfolds over the entire course of the opera, and that includes the folk spirit of Russia, completely absent from the last act.

As has been true of other movements, the finale can encapsulate this disintegration much more quickly, and that includes the Russian spirit prominently displayed at the beginning of the movement. The choice of the song "In the Field a Little Birch Tree Stood" may have another connection with the opera, related to the text of the song. As Roland John Wiley points out, peasants portrayed in the text gather twigs from a tree and straw to make wreaths, and in the opera the peasants present a sheaf to Larina as a traditional token of their respect, which she happily accepts. When they sing the tune similar to the one in the symphony, they dance around the sheaf and start their love pantomime with a story that begins under a tree. The finale begins with an eight-bar fanfare, loud and frenetic, before the folk song begins, and a similar fanfare occurs in the opera before the parallel music, in which Larina heartily thanks them for coming. She asks them to sing a joyful song, and they gladly lift their voices to offer it.

As with the first two movements of the symphony, disintegration sets in fairly quickly, initially with a type of foreground and background, with the foreground as the folk song in the winds and the background a rapid up-and-down scale passage in the strings between the phrases. The background soon becomes more persistent and reduces the song to a characterless two-note figure; the scale passages then take over completely, reaching a *fortissimo* level. The fanfare returns, attempting to kick-start the folk song, but without success, building to something even more frenetic at *fff* with triplets that dominate completely. The folk song does return, only to be quickly overwhelmed by more scale passages, triplets, and a return to *fortissimo*. Amid this fiendishly intrusive background, the folk song's attempts to return give the impression of the idée fixe in Berlioz's *Symphonie fantastique*, an encroachment Wiley has also noted, as it too becomes loud and grotesque. The fanfare can do little to rescue it, and the next time we hear the folk song, it has lapsed into a minor key—D minor, a key often traditionally associated with storms or death.

It does not take long for the frenzied witches' Sabbath to subvert it again, and this time it's cut off by the fate motto from the beginning of the symphony, at the loudest possible level (*fff*). The comparison with

Beethoven's Fifth now makes sense, since Beethoven too brought back the rhythm of his opening fate motif from the first movement in the third and fourth movements. The idea of bringing back material from the first movement did not start with Beethoven, since Haydn had done it in his Symphony No. 101 and also less overtly in No. 104, but Beethoven took the possibility to a new level, allowing a dramatic continuity throughout all the movements of a work. In later ones he would take this even further, for example in the Piano Sonata Op. 101, where he solves a problem posed in the first few bars of the first movement much later in the finale. A case can be made in the late string quartets that he does it not only in individual works but in the whole group of quartets. Tchaikovsky clearly brings the fate motto back near the end for dramatic purposes, as the menacing stick wielded by fate hammers the final destructive blow to the beautiful illusions from the past. Now even the rosy picture of the Russian landscape has been removed, and like the end of *Onegin*, there's nothing left but regret. The entire symphony has been packed with drama, with clashing forces in almost constant opposition, forces that can work either from within or from the outside. With the Fourth and *Onegin* Tchaikovsky defined his own "new way," as Beethoven had with his *Eroica* Symphony, and in writing them simultaneously, he infused the spirit of one into the other.

SIXTH SYMPHONY, *PATHÉTIQUE*

It's 16 October 1893, in St. Petersburg, Russia, and you have passed through the grand entrance of the Assembly Hall of the Nobility, in anticipation of an extraordinary event—the premiere of a new symphony to be conducted by the composer himself. He is one of the two most famous living Russians at this time, and you know both of their works well: Leo Tolstoy and Pyotr Ilich Tchaikovsky. As you make your way to your seat in this spectacularly beautiful hall to hear Tchaikovsky's Sixth Symphony, sponsored by the Russian Musical Society, you overhear numerous conversations about this occasion, and some about the work itself. From this composer, now an international sensation having recently made successful tours to New York, Warsaw, Hamburg, London, and Cambridge (where he received an honorary doctorate), and considering the reception at home of his *Hamlet* Overture, *The Sleeping*

Beauty, The Queen of Spades, Iolanta, and *The Nutcracker,* only the best can be expected. It has been five years since his last symphony, the Fifth, a work universally praised, and after the Fourth and the Fifth, both of which you know well, the sense of anticipation for this one could not be higher. Some of the buzz in the hall concerns the possibility of the Sixth being programmatic, considering that the previous two clearly were. Unlike the practice of some earlier composers and those currently active of making a program available in advance, or at least giving the symphony a descriptive name, as Berlioz, Beethoven, Mendelssohn, and Liszt had done, nothing in this case has come forward, although rumors abound about a programme. Even the name *Pathétique* has not yet been given, and the source of that name remains murky.

Arriving at your seat you wait for the concert to begin after the orchestra has tuned, and an eruption in the hall ensues as a lone figure slowly heads for the podium. Everyone leaps to their feet, and the applause seems to go on forever; he bows awkwardly and turns to the orchestra hoping the ovation will cease, but it does not. He turns again to the audience, and it strikes you that despite his age, now fifty-three, his gaunt face and hair more white than gray make him look like a man of eighty. When the applause finally stops, he faces the orchestra and lifts his baton, holding that pose for a few seconds until no sounds can be heard in the hall, something he does for good reason. He turns to the lower strings and gives them the cue to start, and you hear nothing but sustained open fifths in the cellos and basses, so quiet you can barely hear them. The beginning of Beethoven's Ninth immediately comes to mind since it also starts with open fifths in the lower strings, although tremolo instead of sustained, leaving a feeling of ambiguity about both the key and meter. When a solo bassoon enters with a melody (A), low in its register and quietly, it becomes apparent he has started with a slow introduction. Against that slow melodic bass line, reminiscent of the opening of Beethoven's own *Pathétique* Sonata for Piano, the low strings move downward chromatically. The intro lasts only eighteen bars, but at the slow tempo it seems to last much longer as it creates a funereal atmosphere.

After an extended pause the *allegro* section begins, at first with low strings only, and the violas as melodic instruments play the same four-note motif heard in the intro, carrying the dark atmosphere from the beginning into the new section. Now he invokes a procedure similar to Haydn's, who routinely in his late symphonies started with slow intro-ductions of a funereal character (in No. 103 he even cites the *Dies Irae*), and then carries the motif into the fast section. Despite a lighter feeling the *allegro* here seems shaded by the intro, remaining edgy, with the fate motif even making a brief appearance as the music builds in waves, mostly avoiding anything melodic. That changes with the arri-val of a real melody in the strings (B), introducing for the first time a genuine lyrical spirit, marked *teneramente* (tenderly), *molto cantabile, con espansione* in case the musicians don't get it, and slowed down to *andante*. The orchestral musicians proved to be a real problem for Tchaikovsky in this premiere since not only did they seem not to get it, but they even exhibited hostility. As this melody proceeds you hear traces in it of one of Tchaikovsky's favorite operas, *Carmen*, specifically the "Flower Song" that Don José sings to convince Carmen that he loves her. Aside from his other favorite, *Don Giovanni*, he had written to Mrs. von Meck in detail why he loved *Carmen* so much, with its passages that

> please the ear, but at the same time they touch and trouble. . . . Bizet is an artist who pays tribute to modernity, but he is warmed by true inspiration. And what a wonderful subject for an opera! I can't play the last scene without tears. Here is the mob at the bullfight with its coarse merriment and excitement—and to offset this, a terrible trag-edy and the death of the two principals, who through fate—*fatum*—reach at length a climax and their own miserable end. I am con-vinced that in about ten years *Carmen* will have become the most popular opera in the world. (BF 374–375)

He could not have been more right about its popularity, not only for the end of the nineteenth century, but ever since.

By invoking the "Flower Song," he adds another dimension to a possible programme, making this theme distinctly a love theme, and a very peculiar one at that. Carmen succeeded in seducing José with her Seguidilla in Act 1, and alone with him at Pastia's tavern after his re-lease from prison in Act 2, she dances seductively for him, coming as close as music can get to being erotic (Mozart had also done it in *Don Giovanni*, with the duet "Là ci darem la mano"). She should have José wrapped around her little finger, but the trumpet signaling time to return to the barracks distracts him, and she is furious that he rejects what she has to offer. He tries to convince her he loves her with the "Flower Song," telling how he kept the flower she threw at him when they first met in his breast pocket, and that it got him through his month in prison. He sings of this with passion, but she wants real physical love, not a glorified gesture of gallantry, and she rejects it as ardently as he professes to love her. This scene seals their fate as doomed lovers. With her impetuous southern mindset she opts to move on to someone who will give her what she wants—an Escamilio; José, with his northern ethos, believes she should be his forever, and in the end prefers her dead instead of with another man.

It does not take long in the symphony for antagonistic forces to intrude, with triplets, dotted rhythms, an extended rising chromatic line in the horns, and building crescendos. After much agitation, the love melody returns, *adagio* in the clarinet (*dolce possibile*), becoming quieter to the point that the composer indicates *pppppp*, so quiet it should be virtually inaudible. With the bassoon finishing the melody, a sound that hushed simply isn't possible. Tchaikovsky appears to be representing love in an impossible way, with lovers whose desires can never come together, where the inevitable conclusion will be desolation, if not tragedy. Whether he intends this to have personal meaning or thinks of it more broadly, you have no idea, but the possibility of it having an autobiographical element, based on what you know about his other works, seems entirely plausible.

The development begins with a crashing chord, as rudely as possible demolishing the lyrical atmosphere. At *allegro vivo* things become frenetic while staying loud, with lots of syncopation and other rhythmic invasions that leave you feeling as uneasy as possible. Amid the fairly complex counterpoint, the A motif makes an appearance, building to a furious *fortissimo*. This finally dies away, and as a Russian familiar with the Russian Orthodox liturgy, you can hardly believe what you hear next: he quotes the traditional chant from the Russian requiem, which has the text "With thy saints, O Christ, give peace to the soul of thy servant." Death has been lurking over this movement, but now he makes it explicit with a quotation that Russians at the time would recognize, but probably no one else; in fact, that quotation will return later in the development, after more furious driving forward. The movement ends with as much ambiguity as it began, after returning to both themes

A and B, fading away with open fifths in trombones and tuba, as it started. Tchaikovsky may have remembered the use of the trombone in Mozart's Requiem, in the "Tuba mirum," where that instrument, as part of an eighteenth-century tradition, represented death. Until it ends the first movement paints a very somber—even eschatological—picture.

The second movement, *allegro con grazia* (fast with gracefulness), may seem much lighter than the first, but in its own way it carries the drama of that movement forward. It does not take long with its gestures and phrasing pattern to establish itself as a type of waltz, but certainly a very unusual one as you quickly pick up that instead of a 3/4 meter it proceeds in 5/4. Some have called it a limping waltz, with its gracefulness maimed, although that does not seem entirely appropriate. It moves fluidly, not limping in the least, and while as a waltz it may be warped or misshapen, nothing about it appears to suffer from an injury. Once again allusions to *Carmen* creep in, both with thematic fragments and orchestration, this time not the "Flower Song," but Carmen's dance that elicits José's profession of love. Some productions of *Carmen* show her dance as nothing short of a striptease, and for Tchaikovsky to represent the dance as a deviant waltz seems to hit the mark, considering that the waltz itself can have subversive and licentious connotations. At times the warped character of this one becomes even more pronounced as the melody must compete with syncopations. Fate itself may very well make an appearance in this movement.

After the distorted waltz we get a twisted march, not a stable military march but instead one that has the earmarks of Berlioz's march to the scaffold from *Symphonie fantastique*. A tremendous amount of rapid figuration goes on in the third movement, and at *allegro molto vivace*, played at one time or another by every instrument, this would not have endeared the composer to the orchestra; these lines are devilishly difficult to get together. Amid all this frenetic figuration the march melody must try to be heard, which it does not always do successfully, and sometimes even sounds somewhat grotesque. The timpani also plays a prominent role, at times sounding alone, again invoking the scaffold. Berlioz had treated his as a bad dream, and after the destructive impulse of the first movement and the perverse waltz of the second, the impossibility of love put forward earlier may have lapsed into a nightmare. Fate makes inroads at a couple of points in this movement, as the recognizable triplet figure from *Eugene Onegin* and the Fourth, and with the last four very loud notes of the movement, Beethoven's fate motif from his Fifth also comes through.

For the finale, Tchaikovsky tells the musicians what they need to know with the heading "Adagio lamentoso," and since the audience does not see that, unless it happens to be printed in a program, the musicians have the responsibility of getting across the feeling of lament, which can include all of grieving, mourning, sorrow, and regret. He starts with a six-note descending figure, and does something highly unusual with it, which raises a question about orchestral seating. Each note of this figure alternates between first and second violins. If the two sections sit side by side, we will hardly notice the alternation, but if they sit on opposite sides of the platform, the effect comes across as somewhat tortured, with a curious tension permeating the theme itself. Only much later, halfway through the movement, does the returning theme become unbroken. A pulling in different directions runs through the entire movement, sometimes downward into apparent oblivion, but also with upward surges that suggest hope. At times the presence of fate becomes so overbearing that nothing can withstand it, and in the final stages the triplet figures in the lower strings are always tied together, as they obscure the beat more persistently than the main theme of the first movement had. That lasts to the end of the work, with only the low strings left, which die away to nothing (*pppp*).

If the work has been a battle with fate, fate has won. If the work has been about death, death has arrived. If the work has been about the impossibility of love, love has vanished. If the work has been about life, life is gone. If the work has been autobiographical, the composer would oblige by dying nine days after conducting this performance. If the work had a programme, which Tchaikovsky insisted it did, without revealing it, its secret programme would die with him, and we are at liberty to supply our own. Next morning in the St. Petersburg newspaper you find a review of the concert by Tchaikovsky's longtime friend Hermann Laroche, who, among other things, describes the first movement's second group as "more operatic in style than symphonic." He sees a similar operatic disposition in the finale, where the listener can perceive "an accompaniment to something occurring on stage, such as, for instance, the slow death of the hero; here too . . . one senses not so much a symphonic as an operatic character" (LD 57). A dear friend and colleague saw how operatic a symphony could be, and Tchaikovsky did not need something as specific as the parallel between *Eugene Onegin* and the Fourth to make this operative in his sixth and final symphony.

7

SORCERY, CAPRICE, BLINDNESS, SAINTS, AND STACKED DECKS

More Operas

Aside from *Eugene Onegin*, few of Tchaikovsky's operas gained a firm toehold in the repertory outside of Russia, although he remained preoccupied with opera throughout his entire career, writing ten and contemplating others. Only a year after graduating from the St. Petersburg Conservatory, in 1867, he started on his first opera, *Voevoda*, with little else under his belt at this point aside from the overture *The Storm*, the Characteristic Dances, and his First Symphony. This opera actually got performed, but not so his second one, *Undine* (1869), although that did not discourage him from trying his hand again not much later, with *The Oprichnik*, started in 1870, completed in 1872, and staged with some success in 1874. Years later he looked back at these earliest efforts with considerable embarrassment, and even tried to destroy the scores of the first two. When a competition was announced in 1874 to write an opera with the title *Vakula the Smith*, with a libretto based on Nikolay Gogol's delightfully witty story "Christmas Eve," he leapt at the opportunity, mistakenly completing it over half a year before the due date. Despite the speed of composition, this time he started to find his operatic voice, and easily won the competition, which led to staging and a not insignificant monetary prize. Clearly on to something good this time, he came back to it in 1885 with a substantial revision and new title: *Cherevichki*.

His next opera after *Vakula* has already been discussed, based on Pushkin's *Eugene Onegin*, and with this, although not really suspecting it at the time, he created one of the greatest works of the entire operatic repertory. Other composers who achieved brilliant success in opera early in their careers and pursued the genre, such as Mozart or Verdi, managed one spectacular achievement after another, and Tchaikovsky no doubt assumed he could do the same, writing five more until a year before he died, in 1893: *The Maid of Orleans* (1879), *Mazepa* (1883), *The Enchantress* (1886), *The Queen of Spades* (1890), and *Iolanta* (1891). Except for *The Queen of Spades* these remain almost completely unknown outside of Russia, so what happened? Have we in the West simply missed something, or did Tchaikovsky himself not come through with the goods? If it's the latter, then it surely boggles the mind how the composer of such an extraordinary work as *Onegin* could not do it again, after discovering with that opera the ingredients of what it takes to create a masterpiece. We do not see anything like this with the other major types of composition, such as ballets, symphonies, or symphonic poems, where once on track he generally continued at a high standard (although perhaps piano concertos showed a similar faltering).

The answer to the questions just posed may very well fall somewhere between our perception in the West and Tchaikovsky's own shortcomings. Of the last five, or six if we include the revised *Cherevichki*, we have overlooked some gems, and aside from *The Queen of Spades*, which has a place in the repertory, others are gradually getting the recognition they deserve. *Cherevichki*, for one, received a first-rate performance at the Royal Opera House, Covent Garden, in London in 2009, and in the 2014–2015 season, *Iolanta* will be performed at the Metropolitan Opera in New York with Anna Netrebko in the starring role, a long overdue acknowledgment of a wonderful work at North America's leading house (it will be transmitted on Live in HD). As noted in the discussion on *Onegin*, Tchaikovsky needed to be stirred by the story itself in a personal way to put his best musical and dramatic efforts forward, and we can see that happening, although perhaps not quite as much as in *Onegin*, in the two just mentioned. It should have worked in *The Maid of Orleans*, because of Tchaikovsky's strong interest in Joan of Arc, but for the most part it did not. *Mazepa*, also based on a Pushkin work (*Poltava*), a story filled with cruelty, blood, and gore based on actual history, simply did not work, and it's hard to imagine what prompted Tchaikovsky to take it on. Similarly *The Enchantress*, a story that begins as a comedy and ends with murder upon murder, could not likely inspire him to give his best music, and it did not.

The Queen of Spades, next to *Onegin* the most often performed of the operas, presents a puzzling case. Tchaikovsky worked on it feverishly and quickly, claiming to identify with the characters and situations, but despite that he did not come up with his most inspired music. Like *Onegin* it comes from a story by Pushkin, and similarly he and his brother Modest created a libretto that deviates from the original. Pushkin's Hermann hopes to gain a fortune by learning a winning combination of cards from an elderly countess, and he courts the old woman's niece Lizaveta for the sole purpose of getting access to the source of the information he desires. Again Pushkin gently mocks his characters: Hermann's fixation with money (and absence of interest in love) arises from his German heritage, Lizaveta lacks marriage prospects and even partners at dances, and the Countess's irascibility makes her a disagreeable old hag (who dies of shock when Hermann pulls out a gun to persuade her to give up the secret). Throughout the story Pushkin laughs at himself and others, asking if such a thing as a Russian novel exists, making Hermann's professions of love to Lizaveta translations from German novels (which she will not recognize because she doesn't read German), and poking fun at the obsession of the upper classes with gambling. At the end Hermann gets the last card wrong and loses everything, ending up in an insane asylum, while Lizaveta disappears from the story; Pushkin tells us in an epilogue that she marries a young civil servant. In his own distinctive way Pushkin writes a tale more comical than serious.

Tchaikovsky makes it completely serious, as he did with *Onegin*. That worked in *Onegin*, where he could take one character—Tatiana—and give her depth, first of all in the libretto, and then overwhelmingly with the music. No such possibility existed for Hermann. Tchaikovsky and his brother did not really succeed in trying to create a love story between Hermann and Lise (Pushkin's Lizaveta, who's already engaged to someone else), since only money motivates him, and we can see no possible reason why she should love him. When he claims not to recognize her before going to the casino to place his wagers, she throws herself into the canal; when he loses at cards, holding the queen of spades instead of an ace, he too commits suicide. The Countess remains fairly similar to Pushkin's, including her ghost, who reveals the secret of the cards, and she ends up being the most interesting character in the opera.

Despite his claims about engagement with the story, much of the music sounds routine, seldom with the musical depth, emotions, and appeal that carries throughout *Onegin*. The music did, though, along with that of *The Enchantress* and most convincingly *Iolanta*, reveal the beginnings of a new direction that took it to a higher level of sophistication. Much of the drama and underlying emotions fell to the orchestra to sustain, yielding a greater musical continuity as the orchestra took on a more prominent character partially divorced from the immediate role of accompaniment (this will be explored further in the descriptions of *Iolanta* below). Despite the movement in this new direction, the strong place of *The Queen of Spades* in the repertory seems curious, and it's gratifying to see others such as *Cherevichki* and *Iolanta* coming to the fore; those two will be the focus of this chapter.

CHEREVICHKI (REVISION OF VAKULA THE SMITH, AKA OXANA'S CAPRICES OR THE TSARINA'S SLIPPERS)

With *Cherevichki* Tchaikovsky found himself in unfamiliar territory for a nineteenth-century composer of opera, facing the challenge of writing a comic opera. That century saw the medium of opera rise to its greatest heights, with hundreds written, giving us the core of the modern repertory with many at an extraordinarily high level, but of that deluge, one could more or less count the total number of comic operas on the fingers of two hands. In fact, if we remove Rossini and Donizetti from the mix, both active in the earlier part of the century, the number fits nicely on the fingers of one hand. Comedy simply did not correspond with the mindset of the century, where grandness dominated and tragedy reigned, unlike the eighteenth century, in which virtually every composer wrote comedy, and developed a musical language for doing it, a language Mozart perfected above all others. Even Rossini, writing his comedies in the first two decades of the nineteenth century, worked in large measure with that language from the previous century, with his *Il barbiere di Siviglia* (1816) a worthy successor to Paisiello's adaptation of that play by Beaumarchais, or Mozart's *The Marriage of Figaro*, part of the same trilogy of plays. That language, as exemplified by Mozart, could be simple or complex, dominated by ensembles, and could tell us much of what we needed to know through the music itself. Characters could be intelligibly delineated, in large ensembles with half a dozen characters singing at once, or in duets such as the first two of *Figaro*, where contrasting dance styles differentiate the characters. Aside from dance, other types of borrowed music could be integrated into the language, borrowings the audience would recognize and could think, "I got it," when listening; these could also work subliminally, for example making a dance undanceable by jimmying the phrase structure.

Three-quarters of the way through the nineteenth century that language no longer existed, and despite the enormous admiration that Tchaikovsky had for Mozart, he could not revert to the brilliant intelligibility of that language. Looking at perhaps the greatest of all nineteenth-century opera composers, Giuseppe Verdi, illustrates amply the scope of the problem. No composer was as prolific or successful as Verdi, with masterpieces such as *Nabucco*, *Macbeth*, *La forza del destino*, *La traviata*, *Rigoletto*, and *Otello*, to mention only a few, but only after over half a century of composing did Verdi attempt a comic work, *Falstaff* (1893), in fact his last opera. Even though he could not use Mozart's language, he perhaps understood better than anyone what Mozart had done to make his comic music work, obviously keeping the music light, but more importantly focusing on ensembles—exceptionally complex music that undoubtedly proved much more difficult to write than beautiful arias, of which *Falstaff* has virtually none. Verdi had written brilliant ensembles before, such as the quartet in *Rigoletto*, but nothing close to an entire opera of ensembles, and with his achievement, we can see why few others went there. He may very well have felt that he needed a half century of experience before attempting something of this scope, and it worked because of the craftsmanship of the composer doing it.

Unlike the eighty-year-old Verdi, Tchaikovsky wrote his comic opera at thirty-five, a mere decade after his Conservatory graduation. He loved Mozart with a passion, and around this time even made his own translation of *Figaro*, which students at the Moscow Conservatory performed, but he knew perfectly well he could not write *Vakula* in that style, despite what the librettist Polonsky hoped. Mozart's relationship with his librettists, as early as *Idomeneo* and *The Abduction from the*

Seraglio, was always collaborative, usually with the composer holding the upper hand in shaping the work, and the same held for Verdi and his librettists throughout his career. Both composers had a clear sense of what they wanted, and insisted that their librettists provide the texts they needed, cajoling them to make the necessary revisions or supply new numbers. In both cases they often took the texts from literary masterpieces, as with Mozart's *Figaro* and Verdi's *Otello*, and the composers always had their own sense of what the work should become as an opera, sometimes making it very different from the original work. Verdi, for example, made his *Otello* much more about Desdemona than Othello, focusing on her pathos more than his tragedy. Tchaikovsky would do the same with his *Onegin*, shifting the emphasis to Tatiana, but at this stage he had no such options. He wrote this opera for a competition that came into existence because the composer who intended to write it, Alexander Serov, died shortly after beginning, and the competitors had to use Yakov Polonsky's pre-existing libretto, depriving them of any type of collaboration.

As with the works by Mozart and Verdi just noted, Polonsky based his libretto on a story by one of the literary giants, Nikolay Gogol's "Christmas Eve," perhaps not one of Gogol's better-known works, but certainly one full of his characteristic wit, humor, and satiric barbs. Vakula, the blacksmith in a remote Ukrainian village, and the son of a woman (Solokha) thought to be a witch, loves the vain and self-possessed Oxana, the daughter of the usually inebriated Chub. An upright young man, Vakula has a hobby of painting religious murals, which annoys the Devil, a major player in the work, to no end. Solokha has many lovers, all of whom she encourages to greater or lesser degrees, and on Christmas Eve they all one by one come to her house looking for more than dumplings and vodka. The Devil arrives first, followed by the mayor, the schoolmaster, and then Chub, and each time the rascal arriving knocks at the door, the one in the house crawls into a sack, until all four hide in sacks. Gogol has great fun with the hypocrisy of some of these men (a deacon, for example), cheating on their wives on this religious holiday.

Oxana takes great pleasure in teasing and tormenting Vakula, to the extent that she's not sure if she actually loves him, and when carolers come to her house and she admires the elegant boots of one of the women, complaining that she has no one to provide her with such luxuries, Vakula boasts that he will get her slippers (*cherevichki*) as ornate as the ones worn by the Tsarina. She mocks his promise, saying she will marry him if he succeeds in this, and this pushes him over the edge, as he vows he will get rid of his obsession with her by killing himself. He tries to move the sacks from his own home to clean up for Christmas, surmising they must be filled with coal, and inadvertently ends up dragging one with him as he heads for the river to take his life. In this sack he discovers the Devil, and with the Devil in his power, he extracts a promise from him to take him to the court in St. Petersburg to get a pair of the Tsarina's slippers. On arriving in the capital he meets some Cossacks, who have business with Catherine, and when he makes his request to the court, he almost immediately receives the slippers. He and the Devil return to his village, where all believe him to be dead. He goes to Chub with gifts and asks for his daughter's hand, while Oxana regrets how badly she has treated him, realizing she loves him. They meet, and he presents the slippers, but she says she doesn't want them—that she will marry him regardless. In the happy reunion, she cheerfully accepts the slippers anyway.

In this lighthearted story, Gogol pokes fun at just about everyone, including the Devil, taking expressions such as "what the devil" or "that's a devil of a . . . ," etc., and personifies the Devil, who turns out not to be such a bad guy. He induces people to sin, but their lives would be boring without sin, which they all enjoy. Setting the story on Christmas Eve takes religion for a special ride, and in fact it brings out the pagan customs associated with Christmas much more than anything holy. Village life in Ukraine abounds with colorful characters, hearty drinking, superstition, sensuality, and the fantastical, in some ways ideal backdrops for opera, where we need to suspend disbelief in accepting flying witches and devils; the Devil steals the moon or creates blizzards, resulting in what can be called a devilishly dark night or a devil of a storm. That part works well for Tchaikovsky, but much more difficult if not impossible to capture is Gogol's tone, which gently mocks the village customs, such as the attempts by Cossacks to use language at court that isn't crude, the portrayal of a beautiful girl full of herself, the amusement of the high and mighty with the peasants, the religious hypocrisy, the loose morals, and even the notion of aspiring to wear decorative *cherevichki* like the Tsarina's. Tchaikovsky tried to keep the musical language light, but instinctively he slipped into serious writing, whether Vakula really intended to commit suicide or not, whether So-lokha actually cared if her son lived or died, or whether Oxana believed he would do such a thing. In duets, unlike Mozart's, he was hard-pressed to separate his characters musically, all too often making them musical reflections of each other.

Tchaikovsky himself never gave up on this work, unlike his earlier efforts, and for good reason he picked it up again in 1885, revising, cropping, and adding to it to address some of the earlier defects. The work clearly has charm and potential, and with his own double life between the two major cities of Russia and his love of Kamenka in Ukraine, with its rural landscape, peasants, and the feeling of refuge these gave him, he could easily identify with the rural/urban split in "Christmas Eve," in fact reflective of Gogol's own life. Just as Gogol could use high and rustic language to exemplify the division, Tchaikov-sky did this with musical language, with extensive borrowing from Ukrainian folk music for village life and a sophisticated Western style for the capital. In this work more than any other he revealed his inclina-tion toward the manifesto of the Mighty Five, infusing much of the work with a folk atmosphere, especially the gopak (a Ukrainian folk dance), and letting the two styles clash delightfully with Vakula and the Cossacks at court. In fact, others have identified at least four known folk songs in the opera, as well as other tunes derived from Ukrainian folk styles.

Much of the folk music is specifically dance music, like the gopak, actually danced by Solokha and the Devil in Act 2, and the notion of dance in many ways gives this opera its special character, with inserted ballet scenes. Of course a long tradition of combining opera and ballet existed, present in virtually all French operas from the seventeenth and eighteenth centuries, and necessarily added by non-French composers working in Paris, such as Gluck. Mozart also included it in *Figaro* and *Don Giovanni*, with specific interpretive meaning in the Act 1 finale of the latter, and Tchaikovsky's contemporaries used it effectively as well, for example Ponchielli in *La gioconda* (1876). Without dances such as the habañera and seguidilla, which Carmen herself sings and dances, Bizet's *Carmen* (1875), Tchaikovsky's favorite opera along with *Don Giovanni*, would not have been nearly as effective. Tchaikovsky had many treatments to draw from, and here he went about his use of dance in a distinctively Russian way, even placing classical and more rustic ballet side by side, for example the Russian dance and Cossack dance in Act 3.

ACTS 1 AND 2

It's 23 November 2009, and on this chilly evening in London you have come to the Royal Opera House, Covent Garden, for a rare treat—a performance of Tchaikovsky's *Cherevichki (The Tsarina's Slippers)*. How rare? Not even in Russia is this work in the current repertory of any theater, and this production would not be happening were it not for the director of the Royal Opera House, Elaine Padmore, who, in 1993 as director of the Wexford Festival, to celebrate the centennial of Tchaikovsky's death, mounted a production of it there. Now with the resources available to her in London, including the Royal Ballet, it can be staged as she believed it should be. Despite Tchaikovsky's own admission of this being his favorite of his ten operas, the work inexplicably has not taken root in the Bolshoy, the Maryinsky, or any other company in Russia. Thanks to Padmore, the work will be getting the airing it deserves at a major international house, and on this night the BBC is filming it for television (a DVD will be released in 2010). As usually happens with Russian works at houses such as this or the Met in New York, the principal positions and conducting need to be provided by Russians, and that has happened in this case. Alexander Polianichko is conducting, and of the ten main roles, only two lesser ones have gone to non-Russians. Leading the cast are Olga Guryakova as Oxana, Vsevolod Grivnov as Vakula, and Larissa Diadkova as Solokha; the set designer, Mikhail Mokrov, and costume designer, Tatiana Noginova, have brought respectively the fantasy world of Gogol and an authentic look from Ukraine and Russia.

With Polianichko at the podium, the overture begins, and familiar with the comic bite of Gogol's story, you expect the overture will set the appropriate atmosphere, as did the overture to *Onegin*—which you know well. To your surprise, the opening of the overture does not sound in the least bit comical, and you therefore assume Tchaikovsky will be doing something else with this opera, perhaps emphasizing the seriousness of the relationship between the lovers, or in some other way changing the tone of the source work. He does that with *Onegin*, which he wrote a few years later, turning Pushkin's satire into something serious, and that may also be his strategy here. Some lighter touches do come later in the overture, with distinctive melodies that you suspect will recur later in the opera, allowing the overture to give a little musical précis of things to come. Also, some of these melodies have a distinctively Russian or Ukrainian folk flavor, and in that respect Tchaikovsky follows Gogol, as well as his colleagues making up the Mighty Five, from the beginning lacing the work with a Russian folk atmosphere.

In the opening scene Vakula as muralist finishes up one of his satirical representations of the Devil, making him look like a skinny pig with horns, painted on the church wall of the delightfully portrayed village. The scene shifts immediately to Solokha, hoping for a storm so she can lure a man into her cottage, and despite the comical action, the music seems slightly at odds with this (based on one of the borrowed folk songs), even when the Devil appears and talks a little dirty about her, which is exactly what she wants. Unlike the rapid-fire exchanges in Verdi's *Falstaff*, Tchaikovsky lets these characters develop something longer and more melodic, with the orchestra playing a significant role in the background. It appears he found the characters charming and engaging—even the Devil—and gave them music that would endear them to the audience, music that seemed more symphonic than dramatic, as the characters singing together often get painted with the same musical brush. He realized this, and in writing to Nadezhda von Meck in 1878, he pointed out the problem: "Lord, what unforgivable mistakes there are in this opera, made by me and me alone. I've done everything to cripple the good effect of all the passages which might have been pleasing in themselves had I restrained my purely musical inspiration and been less forgetful of the *theatrical and visual* requirements of operatic style" (TM 363). Writing to her a year later, he hit the nail on the head: "The operatic style must be marked by breadth, simplicity, and some scenic effectiveness. *Vakula*'s style is not operatic but symphonic, even chamber-like" (B1 313). That may be true, but not because of any lack of understanding resulting in a defect; he knew what he wanted, and wrote accordingly. What he wanted, it appears, was not comedy in any conventional manner, but comedy with flesh-and-blood characters, with personalities revealed through the music. Here he could draw from his much loved *Figaro*, where Mozart gives depth of character, especially to the women Susanne and the Countess.

By no means does he abandon comedy. After Solokha and the Devil enjoy their somewhat racy duet, the style becomes whimsical as she brings out her mode of transportation—a broomstick—and they joke about the chase as well as the fact that she wears her age well. Costumes and makeup have been done with care, especially her traditional peasant Ukrainian apparel and hairstyle (her flaming red hair has horns knitted into it); the Devil, with a snout for a nose and protruding potbelly, could almost look avuncular were it not for his horns and long tail. Very quickly the libretto picks up on the fun that Gogol has with expressions, such as the fact that she flies on her broomstick so well that "the devil won't catch me," or "this devil's in luck." When they sing of soaring to the heavens, the music enjoys the irony with appropriately high passages and orchestration.

Even in recitative Tchaikovsky gives the orchestra a prominent role, allowing its accompaniment to interpret the characters' words. This happens immediately after Solokha leaves, and the Devil remembers why he came out of hell on that day. It's because of the nasty images of him painted by Vakula, making him the laughingstock of other devils, and he hopes to get his revenge. He intends to do this deviously by stealing the moon and whipping up a blizzard; under these conditions Oxana's father, Chub, will not go out to the tavern to drink, and if he's stuck at home, Vakula, who does not get along with him, will not dare to come to spend his evening with Oxana. With the Devil so delightfully personified, God necessarily takes a backseat. Instead of God intervening in the day-to-day activities of people, here it's the Devil, who arranges things down to the smallest details. He tells of his plan in recitative, but backing this up Tchaikovsky provides appropriately comical music. Instead of the Devil being the fiend of Dante or Milton, he's more like a cheerful peasant who's had a trick played on him, and tries to get his own back by hoodwinking that person. He looks silly, and thanks to the music, he sounds silly. The punishment, far from eternal damnation, is one night less of carousing for some, and an interruption in wooing for another. When he steals the moon and summons the blizzard with the aid of his impish helpers, Tchaikovsky has his own bit of fun. Needing blustering, storm-evoking music for this, Tchaikovsky all but directly quotes "The Ride of the Walkuries," including the orchestration, even letting Solokha respond to it in a Brünnhilde-like manner. Tchaikovsky seldom had anything complimentary to say about

Wagner, especially at this point in his life, finding his music pompous and overblown, and with this little jest he could say musically what he thought.

Peasant dances abound throughout the opera, and one precedes the entrance of the aging Cossack Chub and his drinking buddy Panas, now lost en route to the tavern because of the moonless sky and ferocious blizzard. The opera acquaints us with these delightful characters prior to the appearance of the beautiful Oxana at home, and before she sings about the nasty weather, Tchaikovsky introduces her recitative with a brief fugato, a clever touch for the scene, considering the interactions about to happen. Before Vakula comes courting, she gets an aria as striking as any that Tchaikovsky ever wrote, and despite her preening and satisfaction with her own beauty, she puts these in terms of her dead mother's expectations for her, musically changing her from Gogol's silly self-adulating goose to someone who under the right circumstances may actually have some depth. A few years later he would do something similar with Tatiana, changing her from a foolish girl who reads too many novels to a dream of a woman who should be irresistible. Oxana deserves to be mocked, but the music simply does not allow it. The circumstances for her to show her depth will come much later, but not yet, as she sets about systematically tormenting Vakula when he arrives at her door. Only at the end of the act, when he leaves in a huff, does she wonder if she has been too hard on him.

Much of Act 2 is pure comedy, and Tchaikovsky has his share of fun with it. It starts at Solokha's cottage, where the Devil has followed her (down the chimney), and as he moves in ready for lovemaking, she gets up to dance a gopak, a Cossack peasant dance considered the national dance of Ukraine. Originally intended only for men, it later became acceptable for women also, and with its rustic leaps and energetic motion it here becomes the ideal vehicle for their sexual sport. As they dance close to each other, in this production he wraps his phallic tail around her, with no objections from her. With both of them ready for more, they move to take things from vertical to horizontal, but just then a knock at the door prevents them from going any further. This sets off the sequence of men, some married and clearly cheating on their wives, coming to her house expecting more than a drink, and as each one arrives, the previous one climbs into a coal sack. None of them (the mayor, the schoolmaster, and Chub), including the Devil, risk being found out by the others. When Vakula returns home, after his spat with Oxana, he finds four large sacks that need to be moved before Christmas day, and he wonders why he can't lift them as easily as usual. At one point all four men sing, in counterpoint, from the sacks. The act ends outdoors with all the village folk who have been caroling, Oxana still teasing, and Vakula, after promising to bring her slippers like the Tsarina's, slinking off believing death would be better than the abuse he takes from her.

ACTS 3 AND 4

Act 3 begins with an entr'acte (interlude), a three-and-a-half-minute orchestral piece on which Tchaikovsky lavishes some of his best writing, giving it a somewhat pensive character. In the original performance this may have simply been done with the curtain still closed, setting the atmosphere for the scene about to come, but this production takes full advantage of this music, turning it into a ballet. When the curtain rises you see what appears to be an underwater scene, with aquamarine reeds and a murky riverbed; the dancers as water nymphs, including a very young one, move gracefully in the water. After the entr'acte the ballet continues, and a chorus now gives the rusalkas voices, as they sing of being imprisoned in the murky depths, trapped beneath the ice. Lest we should take their plaintive pleas too seriously, a fat wood goblin with a solo role pops ups, and he complains about all the fuss they're making, not giving him a moment's rest. The ballet works beautifully with this chorus, making the rusalkas come alive, not simply having to be disembodied voices. Since ballet will in fact be necessary later in the act, it makes perfect sense for it to be seen at the beginning.

Before Vakula appears, we understand why we have an underwater scene, as the fat goblin tells of a man walking by the river's edge, close to a spot where the ice has melted. Vakula's threats about suicide have been serious, and he now sings an aria—in fact more of a Ukrainian ballad or lament (also one of the borrowed folk melodies)—as he bids Oxana farewell with the icy water in sight. His aria continues in the spirit of the entr'acte and chorus, giving it depth, which Tchaikovsky bolsters with his rich orchestration. Even throughout this number the ballet continues, beautifully blending opera and ballet as the rusalkas lure him toward the water, one taking his hand to draw him in. All the while Vakula has been dragging a sack, from which the Devil now crawls out, and seeing Vakula ready for his own death, the Devil proposes a bargain, whereby Vakula will win Oxana if he signs himself in blood over to him. Here ballet works especially effectively, as a rusalka pulls Vakula toward the water while the Devil yanks him the other way. Given the options, Vakula opts to go with the Devil, but on the pretext of searching for a pen, he grabs the Devil by the tail, now with all the demonic power in his control. The Devil can do nothing but offer anything he wants, and Vakula demands he be taken to the Tsarina's Hermitage in St. Petersburg. The Devil tells him to get on board for the flight, and the witch's flying broomstick music returns, a Ukrainian folk dance that gets the Devil's impish entourage in motion.

Dance has been the focus of Act 3 in this production, and that is now taken to the point of cutting the next scene, steering things in the opposite direction from Gogol's satire. In the cut scene, as in Gogol's story, Vakula meets some Cossacks at court, men he has recently met in his own village, who have a petition to bring to the Tsarina; some delightful exchanges occur as they stumble over each other to try to master a semblance of the courtly language. The give-and-take between peasants and the people of court yields here to the nobles dancing a polonaise and then singing the praises of the Tsarina, whose forces have just been successful in battle. Having mocked the Cossacks at this point, Tchaikovsky does not let the court off the hook, with a gentle lampoon in the form of an ode by a still half-baked poet, performed by a member of the royal family. He backs the pedestrian poetry up with fairly banal music, not unlike M. Triquet's offering in *Onegin*, spiced up a little with the occasional pompous military trumpet call, subtle enough that the court in 1874 may not have caught the jest; a second stanza, echoed by the chorus, makes it seem interminable.

High and low culture then intersect as Vakula comes forward to make his request for slippers like the Tsarina's, set against the backdrop of the courtiers dancing a minuet—a dance only engaged in by the nobility. Vakula sounds a little more monotone than usual, hinting at his peasant roots, although he manages something more expressive as he lifts the skirts of women to look at their slippers, wondering, to the amusement of the onlookers, if they are made of gold, silver, or sugar. The nobles find his simplicity charming, and promise he will receive a pair of slippers. Then opera and ballet come together, this time clearly intended by Tchaikovsky, as the master of ceremonies announces two ballets to be performed, first a Russian dance belonging to high culture, followed by a Cossack dance for the peasants. For the Russian dance the corps de ballet of the Royal Ballet in noble attire can perform at their most sophisticated level, giving classical ballet to be associated with the court. The four Cossacks, suitably clad and with handlebar moustaches, dance as a group, in pairs, or as soloists, with gravity-defying leaps or double-leg kicks while balancing on their hands; for this dance Vakula shows enthusiasm. Instead of the language given to the two cultures by Gogol, Tchaikovsky lets them reveal their differences with dance, and both are equally exciting. After this display Vakula gets the slippers, which he briefly loses, and then the Devil transports him back to his home village.

Act 4 begins with a brief orchestral introduction that sets the tone for Solokha's lament about her son she presumes to be dead, and Oxana regrets how badly she has treated Vakula, with the music once again favoring the emotions of individuals. The audience knows he's safe, but the music does not become maudlin as their emotions come across as genuine. The villagers cannot console Oxana, and Tchaikovsky milks her moping to make Vakula's return more festive. The villagers don't let the celebration of the evening distract them, and their joy now includes the lively motion of the Cossack dancers. With the lovers happily reunited, and Chub ready for a drink, the triumphant ending becomes a wild dance scene, with participation not only from the villagers but in this production from the ballet dancers as well.

IOLANTA

With much operatic water already under the bridge, Tchaikovsky wrote his one-act opera *Iolanta* in 1891, two years before he died, although instead of an ending it may have been the beginning of a new direction had he lived longer. As with *The Queen of Spades* a year earlier, which gained considerable success, he once again turned to his brother Modest as the librettist. Since no one knew his inclinations as well as Modest, their collaboration could be as close as he could get to being both librettist and composer. Wagner, of course, wrote all of his own librettos, and more than most of Tchaikovsky's earlier operas (although we see it beginning in *The Enchantress* and *The Queen of Spades*), *Iolanta* has a Wagnerian leaning in the way the orchestral writing has been treated. Another factor sets this one apart from most of his earlier operas: since *Onegin*, most of his subjects had been highly dramatic, with treachery, deception, murder, political intrigue, and, as ever, the hand of fate. *Iolanta*, taken from the 1850 play *King René's Daughter* by the Danish playwright Henrik Hertz, has no such bombast. In fact, it has something strikingly in common with *Onegin*; despite moments of high drama (which Pushkin tended to mock), *Onegin* had the potential to focus on a vulnerable young woman, embraced much more by Tchaikovsky than the character whose name the verse novel bears. In the case of Hertz's story, the title of the opera gives the name of the young woman in question, and her vulnerability—resulting from her blindness and her father's obsession with protecting her, so extreme that it does much more damage than good—presents a character that Tchaikovsky could embrace as he did Tatiana. With spectacle Tchaikovsky had mixed results, but with lyric or chamber opera, and a central female character with whom he could identify, the odds of success went up considerably. Surprisingly he did not seem to see this for almost a decade and a half with the four operas following *Onegin*, but this time, aided by Modest, he found himself on the right track.

Iolanta, the blind daughter of a king in fifteenth-century Spain, neither suspects her own blindness nor knows that her father is a king. He, René, has gone to elaborate lengths to keep this information from her, surrounding her with attendants who avoid the subjects and completely pamper her, and she has been led to believe that eyes have no purpose other than for crying. Unlike the play, where she does not appear onstage until almost halfway through, the opera begins with her in the glorious garden her father has created for her, surrounded by her loving attendants, clearly placing the focus on her from the outset. The distinguished Moorish physician Ibn-Hakia has determined (based on her horoscope) that her blindness, which seems more psychosomatic than physical, can only be cured at the age of sixteen, and that she must know about her blindness and want it to end for the cure to work. René will hear nothing of the latter, and dismisses the doctor, who stays at the castle just in case René changes his mind.

Meanwhile, two strangers venture into the garden, where Iolanta has fallen asleep by herself (entry to the garden has been forbidden to all outsiders), and one of them, Robert, was betrothed to her while still a child. He now loves someone else, and has come from Burgundy to Provence to get out of the marriage contract. His companion, Vaudémont, falls madly in love with Iolanta when he sees her, wakens her when Robert (who thinks they may be in danger) leaves to get help, and soon discovers her blindness. He knows nothing of René's edict, and tries to explain light as well as sight to her, which fascinates her in an uncomprehending way. When René discovers what has happened, he reacts with horror, but the doctor could not be happier, since he believes she has now met the critical condition to regain her sight. René doubts this will work, and unlike in the play, he informs Iolanta that Vaudémont must pay with his life if the doctor's procedure does not succeed, thinking this will provide the incentive she needs to make it happen; he later explains the deception to Vaudémont. Not surprisingly, the procedure succeeds, and the opera ends happily, with the two lovers free to marry.

It's a charming story, but one requiring more than the usual amount of suspension of disbelief. How, we wonder, could she live for sixteen years and not suspect that sight exists? She seems completely devoted to her father (who in the play keeps her hidden in the garden so her betrothed will not discover her blindness until it's too late), but his obsession with keeping her ignorant of her condition seems more like cruelty than anything else, especially since that ignorance will prevent the cure. His threat in her presence to execute Vaudémont, who has awakened love in her, also seems cruel, and with this callous streak he certainly provided challenges for a musical setting. Iolanta starts out as even more innocent than Tatiana, living in a virtual cocoon (perhaps another act of cruelty on Rene's part), since aside from ignorance of sight she also knows nothing even about the possibility of love (which Tatiana at least has read about in novels). Now she suddenly finds herself facing a monumental challenge, with eyesight dependent on extraordinary willpower, and the daunting prospect that the one she loves (a phenomenon she has only known about for a couple of hours) may die if she is not able to see. All this may invoke suspension of disbelief, but the emotions surrounding what she must overcome—an inward drama instead of something external—fired Tchaikovsky's musical imagination as the subjects of few of the previous four operas had. He did not succeed as he had with *Onegin*, but the result, perhaps pointing to the direction he would have taken with opera in the future, if that possibility had existed, proved compelling.

A strong indicator of Tchaikovsky being on a new track comes with the first sounds we hear—the brief orchestral introduction. This starts with a single English horn, not giving anything melodic as it goes into a chromatic descending pattern. Following the first bar, two bassoons enter, one of them playing a clashing dissonance with the English horn, only resolving at the end of the bar when the English horn moves down by a half step. After three bars a clarinet comes in, very low in its register, creating the most unlikely instrumentation, sounding so strange we may think Tchaikovsky belongs to the twentieth century instead of the nineteenth. Avid filmgoers may recall something similar from the beginning of *Citizen Kane*, which composer Bernard Herrmann starts with nothing but three bassoons and three muted trombones, creating an eerie effect apropos of the strange images on-screen. In the opera we have seen nothing yet to justify this music, which gets even more bewildering as it continues. After the slow-paced and quiet opening, a rapid and loud flourish from most of the winds jolts in, with simultaneous upward and downward scales on thirty-second notes, again sounding modern with a lack of anything melodic or harmonic. This flourish leads into a low chugging repetition in clarinets, bassoons, and horns, all near the bottom of their registers, providing a mystifying accompaniment to the same descending chromatic pattern with the English horn, now joined by the oboe a perfect fourth above. And so continues the introduction, using winds only and therefore lacking the warmth of the string sound, as well as shunning intelligible melody and harmony throughout; this is not the Tchaikovsky we know, and we may very well wonder if he has lost his wits.

In previous operas, his overtures had always been linked thematically to other parts of the work, and the tone of the overture told us much about the nature of the opera, as, for example, the prelude to *Onegin*, giving us more than a glimpse into Tatiana's mindset. Once again we may assume that this distorted music has something to do with the girl the opera focuses on, and we soon discover after the introduction what that may be. Unlike the Iolanta of the play, Tchaikovsky's heroine seems conscious from the outset of something lacking in her life, and it weighs heavily on her. She wonders, for example, how her nurse Martha can know when she sheds tears if Martha does not touch her eyes. Perhaps the music devoid of orchestral strings, harmony, and melody represents that lack, emphasized by chromatic movement and dissonance, but one suspects it goes beyond that to include the misguided and unrelenting protectiveness of her father.

As the curtain rises to reveal Iolanta in her beautiful garden surrounded by her adoring attendants, the music changes to the extreme opposite of the introduction, now with strings only and harp (some winds join later), and lusciously melodic and harmonic. Against this music Iolanta explains her longings to Martha, and we immediately discover that this music emanates from troubadours playing it onstage, music therefore extraneous to the opera. In fact, this music, so alien to her being, has upset Iolanta, and she tactfully asks the troubadours to stop. With these two musical extremes placed side by side at the beginning, one difficult to listen to and the other sanguine to a fault, we suspect that the solution may ultimately bring some kind of fusion of the two, going beyond both opposites into a sound universe with full orchestra, melody, and harmony, without biting tension or overbearing sentimentality.

In this opening scene, both before and after the troubadours, another aspect of Tchaikovsky's new music language becomes apparent, one that takes him closer to Wagner without actually becoming Wagnerian. Earlier works such as *The Enchantress* and *The Queen of Spades* already moved in this direction. The orchestral music appears to have a life of its own, providing an underlying continuity not in any way shaped by the vocal lines with their arioso/recitative-like sound loosely adapted to the orchestra, and not the other way round. The orchestra will play a role in providing the psychological underpinning for the scenes, gaining independence that may draw our attention even more than the singers, giving a type of music drama more in step with the highly influential approaches of Wagner than what Tchaikovsky had previously admired most, coming from Mozart, Verdi, or Bizet. The sound of the troubadours' music may anachronistically sound eighteenth century, or at least neoclassical, but in fact it creates something decidedly modern, allowing the next generations of Russian composers including Prokofiev, Shostakovich, and even Stravinsky to recognize Tchaikovsky as their musical forbear if not mentor.

Despite the laying of a new musical framework, Tchaikovsky by no means gives up on the tradition of distinctive solo numbers, as he provides at least one for each of the principal characters as well as a remarkable duet for the lovers. Even these, though, flow almost seamlessly from the orchestral fabric, which places the "arias" within a larger continuity, and the first of these goes to Iolanta, yearning for what she believes to be missing from her life. That yearning belongs to what precedes and follows, and the orchestral writing can therefore put her aria within that continuum, allowing no break in the psychological underpinning of the scene. After this outpouring her attendants bring her flowers with a song of praise and then sing her a lullaby to put her to sleep, and here Tchaikovsky comes as close as he can to the type of Russian folk music that added so much to *Onegin* or *Cherevichki*. In an opera set in Provence he can take this only so far, but with the audience as important as the setting, he still slips in some characteristic Russian sounds, adding a level of warmth to the scene.

One issue that the collaboration with Modest had not yet fully come to terms with concerned the terseness of the language in the libretto necessary for the music written in this new style to continue to flow without the tedium of too much information. In the scene that follows, with the lesser characters who announce the arrival of the king, an overly wordy discussion about Iolanta's condition occurs, along with the doubtful need for a new messenger to establish his credentials. Modest remains fairly faithful to the play with this, but in so doing leaves a stream of information that forces the composer into recitative sometimes devoid of accompaniment just to get through it. The orchestral introduction to this works much more effectively, combining military trumpet calls for the approaching soldiers with vestiges of the lullaby just heard. Even King René and the doctor carry on far too long in recitative, leaving what amounts to a musical hole in the opera. Tchaikovsky rescues this somewhat with René's aria about his and his daughter's suffering, although the relatively sparse orchestral writing for this aria may give some hint of the composer's feelings about the misguided king. The doctor also gets an aria to answer his dismissal, and while vocally less interesting than Rene's, orchestrally it becomes more vibrant, with hints of a Moorish flavor; more importantly, it's treated as an extended upward sweep, symbolic of the hope of light that can only come from sacrifice.

Tchaikovsky's music engages the listener dramatically through audible means, such as the distinctions between winds and strings, and the featuring of certain instruments, such as the cello before the lullaby or flutes to represent the garden, but he uses means inaudible to most listeners as well. Darkness and light in a way constitute the central drama of the work, not only the difference between seeing and blindness, but the ability of people to "find the light," as it were. The doctor, with the help of Allah, can see the goal, but René, shrouded in his own sense of suffering and misjudgment, cannot. Iolanta, despite her blindness, sees with her pure heart more than her father does. Musically Tchaikovsky uses keys to bolster these different positions, which most listeners will not consciously hear, but this nevertheless adds a structural dimension worth noting. To some extent this goes back to the eighteenth century when individual keys were thought to have specific significance, and Tchaikovsky uses the key of C most aptly for the representation of light. The long association of that key with light finds its strongest illumination in Haydn's *Creation*, where, near the beginning when God creates light, he does so in the key of C. Tchaikovsky uses other keys for various purposes as well, but none as clearly as C for light.

Both Robert and Vaudémont get their own arias, although Robert's may seem somewhat extraneous as he raves about his intoxication with his beautiful Mathilda, the reason he intends to break off his engagement to Iolanta. Vaudémont follows this with an aria coming much closer to passion, or at least its potential in this case since he has no one specific in mind, but of course it prepares us for the genuine ardor he experiences when he sees the sleeping Iolanta (accompanied by flutes) and then gets to know her; both the orchestral and vocal writing here far surpass Robert's. After Robert leaves, Vaudémont and Iolanta sing their duet, the centerpiece and by far the most substantial part of the opera, taking up almost a full third of the work. It starts with accompanied recitative, with the orchestra favoring winds (especially flutes) for her and strings for him, but as the duet proper proceeds and she begins to understand both light and love at least vaguely, the full orchestra takes over, fusing what had previously been separated, and using touches of C major for light. At the highest point of fusion the harp plays a central part, allowing the role of transcendence the harp so often takes in Tchaikovsky's works, together with orchestral writing at its best.

In the end she endures the painful procedure and gains her sight, which at first confuses her. As the work ends in general rejoicing, the orchestral writing brings together solo flute, harp, violin, and cello in the fully integrated texture.

We can only regret that Tchaikovsky's operatic career ended at this point, since *Iolanta* revealed great potential for possible future endeavors. With *Onegin* he wrote a masterpiece, but not something that gave him the key to how he should continue with the medium. In his approach to *Iolanta* he appeared to find that key, and had he lived long enough to write more operas, they may very well have even surpassed this one.

8

TWO FAIRY-TALE BALLETS

Tchaikovsky may very well have been discouraged by the lukewarm reception of *Swan Lake* when he contemplated writing another ballet, since over a decade passed before he tried his hand at it again. In 1876 he stood very much at the beginning of his career, with only a handful of real achievements under his belt, but by 1888 he had reached a pinnacle, with major successes in every area of composition. More important than the response of audiences was the growth he had gone through as a composer and person in those years, reaching an extraordinarily high level of sophistication both in mastering technique and infusing works with passion. That passion, though, because of the acquired sophistication, did not have to be personal in such a raw way as it did earlier, but he could now step back at least one or two paces, and create great works without having to put himself directly into them. That certainly did not mean later works ceased to be personal, the obvious example being his *Pathétique* Symphony, but he now had more resources on which to draw. In the case of ballet, it meant he could practice the dictum he had espoused much earlier to Nadezhda von Meck, that in contrast to symphonies and opera, ballets could indulge pleasantly in fairy tales and even childlike fantasy, giving relief from the overwhelming burdens of life.

THE SLEEPING BEAUTY

By 1888 ballet itself had also changed profoundly in Russia, and with the reputation that Tchaikovsky now held, he would be an obvious composer to become involved in the new direction that ballet took. Once again Ivan Alexandrovich Vsevolozhsky played a leading role in the transformation, setting about to do this after his appointment by Tsar Alexander III as director of the Imperial Theaters in 1881. He had visions of ballet in St. Petersburg aspiring to a much higher artistic level than had been true in the past, and one large step in his reforms involved getting rid of house composers for ballet. They should be replaced by the best composers available in the country, of which Tchaikovsky would be an obvious choice. As early as 1886 Vsevolozhsky approached Tchaikovsky with ideas for a ballet, possibly with settings from *Salammbô* or *Undine*, and while the latter at first seemed appealing because of his much earlier attempt at an opera on that subject, nothing came of these. Their discussions took a new direction in May 1888 when Vsevolozhsky wrote the following note to Tchaikovsky: "I conceived the idea of writing a libretto on *La belle au bois dormant* after Perrault's tale. I want to do the mise-en-scène in the style of Louis XIV. Here the musical imagination can be carried away, and melodies composed in the spirit of Lully, Bach, Rameau, etc., etc. In the last act indispensably necessary is a quadrille of all of Perrault's tales." When Tchaikovsky finally saw the scenario, he wrote back that he was "charmed, delighted beyond all description. It suits me perfectly and I could ask for nothing better to put to music. One could not better combine for the stage the virtues of this delightful subject, and to you its author, permit me to express my sincere congratulations" (WB 104). They agreed on the terms, and late in 1888 composition began. Unlike the haphazardness of *Swan Lake*, he now not only had a commission but the best possible team with which to join forces, including Vsevolozhsky as the librettist, and Marius Petipa as choreographer.

As the first step, Vsevolozhsky had to write the libretto, and not surprisingly he made some radical changes from Charles Perrault's tale of *The Sleeping Beauty in the Wood*, published in 1695. The story used in the ballet, aside from the nasty fairy Carabosse and a fairly harmless ogre who turns up in the Tom Thumb episode in the final act, is generally filled with sweetness and charm. Not so Perrault's tale: like many fairy tales from bygone centuries, including those by the Brothers Grimm, his would have scared the living daylights out of any child hearing it, and if read as a bedtime story, it would surely leave the hapless child with terrifying nightmares. As we know the story from the ballet, a king and queen celebrate the christening of their infant daughter by inviting guests that include fairies. They inadvertently omit the wicked and ugly fairy Carabosse, who comes anyway, but offended by being slighted, she foretells that the girl will prick her finger on a spindle and will die. The Lilac Fairy, a good fairy, cannot completely undo the curse, but she can make the sleep lengthy instead of permanent, allowing the girl to awaken when a prince finds her and kisses her. At the age of twenty the Princess receives a spindle from Carabosse in disguise, pricks her finger, and falls into a deep sleep. The Lilac Fairy puts the whole castle to sleep so they can attend to her when she awakens, and hides the castle in deep undergrowth. A century later a prince, while hunting, meets the Lilac Fairy, who reveals the image of the sleeping princess to him, and he falls in love with this vision of her. Taken to her, he kisses her, and she awakens along with the household; they fall in love, and get married. The celebration of their marriage includes danced pantomimes from other tales by Perrault. End of story.

The original has obvious similarities, but toward the end it diverges sharply. The Lilac Fairy puts the household to sleep with the exception of the King and Queen and a few others. The prince who awakens her a century later (not with a kiss) comes from a strange family, and his mother, a queen, hails from a family of ogres, who pass their worst attributes on to her (the king marries her not out of love but because she brings wealth). When the Prince awakens the Princess, they marry and they live together for two years before he tells his parents; during that time she bears a daughter (Dawn) and a son (Day). Then they move in with his parents, his father dies, and duty calls him as the new king away to the battlefield, which leaves the realm in his mother's care. Ever the ogre, she commands the steward to roast little Dawn for her supper, but instead the terrified steward serves her a deliciously prepared lamb, while hiding the child with his wife. This is repeated with Day, and later the Princess herself, but as she is a bit tough after a century of sleep, he has difficulty finding the right kind of animal to replace her; he finally succeeds with a doe. One day while walking, the Queen discovers the family she thought she had eaten, and in a rage forces the steward to prepare a cauldron full of snakes and vipers, which everyone will be forced into, including himself. Just before she has them all thrown into the cauldron, her son unexpectedly returns home, and horrified by the sight, demands to know what it means. No one will say, but his mother, in a sudden fit of madness, leaps into the cauldron, where the nasty critters immediately devour her; her son soon consoles himself with his family.

Despite the gruesome possibilities, the story still ends happily, but clearly does not provide suitable material for a ballet. Undoubtedly Tchaikovsky had read Perrault's tale, which even gives some suggestions about instrumentation, for example in the scene after the Princess awakens. The Prince does not have the heart to tell her that she looks like a grandmother since she wears clothes a century out of style, but while dining in the castle, "the violins and oboes played old pieces of music, which were excellent, even though they had not been played for over a hundred years." Possibly from this Vsevolozhsky got his notion of using music that sounds like Lully, Bach, or Rameau, and Tchaikovsky may not have been entirely averse to music with a neoclassical sound, although for him that would probably have been something closer to Mozart. As for the subject matter of the tale, despite the dark ending of his previous ballet, it's unlikely he would have wanted this one to go where Perrault took it. For an evil character, Carabosse provided more than enough material, and dramatically he could create conflict with music distinctly connected to her, in contrast with the rest of the music.

Whereas Tchaikovsky could in a way identify with aspects of *Swan Lake* because of the impossibility of love, giving the whole thing a dark edge, in this case he appears not to have had any such inclination, preferring the happy fantasy. This has not stopped all speculation that the work could have been a type of allegory about life in Russia at the time, although since the scenario came from Vsevolozhsky, imputing any such significance presumably would have fallen on him instead of the composer. At the simplest level the tale could be an allegory about the cycle of life, moving from infancy through youth, love, and marriage, although that does not account for the gap of a century between youth and love. Perrault took a crack at that type of allegory in his moral following the story, extolling the virtues of patience, which modern girls in his time appeared to be lacking. Taking it to the level of politics, the King plays a fairly insignificant role, aside from decreeing that the kingdom be rid of needles or other sharp pin-like objects on the penalty of death, and when peasant girls are found knitting, he condemns them to death. Only the intervention of the Queen and Aurora softens the King to grant clemency. His master of ceremonies/chief steward gets more notice than the King himself, and because of his incompetence in leaving Carabosse off the guest list, bad things happen. These factors could reflect on the King, surrounding himself with incompetence and corruption; Roland John Wiley suggests this may take a poke at Tsar Alexander III, although it's hard to imagine that Vsevolozhsky would have wished to bite the hand that fed him.

Wiley doubts that Tchaikovsky would work on a ballet that lacks any philosophical meaning, but in fairy tales it may be difficult to find much philosophy, aside from Perrault's moral. In his excellent study of the ballets, Wiley makes a very interesting point about Tchaikovsky abandoning the harp and replacing it with a piano in Act 3, first heard in the *pas de quatre* for fairies representing gold, silver, sapphire, and diamonds. Shortly after this, in Aurora's solo adagio, the piano has clearly replaced the more ethereal harp, perhaps suggesting something of an impoverishment in the state of affairs that has been reached, or a drift from the spiritual realm denoted by the harp to something more prosaic. The names given to the two main characters may be of some interest as well. Vsevolozhsky appears to have come up with Aurora (Dawn) for Perrault's nameless princess (who had a child named Dawn), and here the notion of rebirth after a century emerges clearly enough. There seems to be no indication of who named the prince Désiré, but one wonders if that may have been Tchaikovsky, considering that the feminine form of that name had been so central to his life over a decade earlier, with Désirée Artôt, the woman he loved who haunted him in his works for years to come, as chapters 1 and 2 suggested. If there's anything in that, it could be a fascinating sexual twist to now use that name for a male character.

When writing *Swan Lake*, Tchaikovsky appeared to have plowed ahead on his own, after examining other ballet scores, without any input from a choreographer and simply expecting the dancers to comply with his terms. In 1888 he had all the resources of the Maryinsky to back him up, with one of the greatest of all choreographers, Marius Petipa, as one of his collaborators. Much has been made of this new opportunity, including the fact that Petipa designed a plan with details of the dances for Tchaikovsky to use while composing. A close examination of this plan, as Wiley has made, suggests some notable discrepancies, to the point that it appears Tchaikovsky made little use of the plan. He wrote the music for it very quickly, probably before Petipa had completed his plan, and very few meetings between the two of them took place. Since the position of a house ballet composer had just been abandoned, Petipa was still accustomed to regular meetings with the composer, but with a freelance composer such as Tchaikovsky, who spent much of his time abroad, opportunities for that type of meeting had all but vanished. No doubt Tchaikovsky made certain types of adjustment to the music after he had composed it to accommodate some of Petipa's needs, but despite the new working conditions for ballet, he appears to have carried on almost as independently as a decade earlier.

Music for ballet clearly had to be different than other types of music, but for Tchaikovsky it remained crucial to think of the music as an organic entity, carrying the drama in the most important ways, and therefore standing as the essence of the work to which the dancing needed to be accommodated—not the other way round. In *Swan Lake* he had accomplished this among other things with the swan theme that appears in each act, and could be altered in tone to suit the dramatic purposes of the act. Now his musical language had reached a much higher level of sophistication, and this resulted in greater subtlety in *The Sleeping Beauty*, but still working at an audible level. I noted certain Wagnerisms in his first ballet, both in the music and in the scenario, and as unlikely as that may seem for *The Sleeping Beauty*, the same holds true. Certain story parallels would not have been the composer's doing, such as the deep sleep that ends with a kiss from a prince (Brünnhilde and Siegfried in the Ring Cycle), and this may simply result from similarities among the archetypes from which stories emerge.

Musically, though, notice of some basic Wagnerian elements cannot be avoided. Critics at the time, still not accustomed to the new direction of ballet, found his score too symphonic, and to some extent the symphonic character of it had something Wagnerian about it. Of course that did not mean continuous, through-composed music of the type written by Wagner, since that could not have been danced to; the capabilities of dancers had to be kept in mind. The issue concerned the musical telling of the story and realization of the drama, and here Wagnerian techniques at the simplest level could be very useful. For the characters who play crucial roles in the drama, especially Carabosse and the Lilac Fairy, whose powers come into conflict and who influence the outcome, a strong differentiation in the music had to be evident, music that could be identified with the character as well as the tone emanating from her. It should be possible for that music to evoke the presence of the character even if we do not see her on stage, and to accomplish this, Tchaikovsky could use something akin to Wagnerian leitmotifs, in the case of these two fairies in a way distinguishing between good and evil. With the musical sophistication he now possessed, he could use these leitmotifs subtly, not simply hitting the listener over the head with one or the other, but making them more of the musical texture or even combining them if necessary.

Since the first performance of *The Sleeping Beauty* already had first-rate choreography in place, it did not have to be reworked the way *Swan Lake* did, so the ballet we now know looks remarkably like the original. That, of course, does not mean every production will be the same. Using every bit of the score results in a fairly long performance, more than three hours, and few houses will keep it that long. Some trimming can be done without seriously disrupting the drama, such as some of the corps de ballet sections in the prologue, or some of the fairy-tale sequences in the final act. Compared with *Swan Lake* there are fewer extraneous dance numbers, but the last act provides the best opportunity for trimming since the drama in effect ended at the close of Act 2. After the waking of Aurora and the demise of Carabosse, nothing remains but celebration, all completely charming and engaging, but not really essential. Some of the likely cuts include the *pas de quatre* of precious stones, Cinderella and Prince Fortune, and the Sarabande before the Act 3 finale. Cuts in Acts 1 and 2 would seriously disrupt the drama, so these acts normally remain intact. Similarly, the opportunities for spectacular dancing or the charm of some of the fairy-tale enactments in Act 3 are too good to miss, so it would be highly unusual to cut the *pas de deux* for the Bluebird and Princess Florine with its brilliant choreography, or the delightful *pas de caractère* for Puss in Boots and the White Cat as well as Little Red Riding Hood and the Wolf; clearly the *pas de deux* for Aurora and the Prince near the end must stay.

While Petipa's original choreography always remains the backbone of the work, some notable choreographers or dancers have made adjustments, sometimes necessary because of the abilities or status of certain dancers. A well-known version, available on DVD (Canadian Broadcasting Corporation, 1972), has Rudolf Nureyev as Prince Florimund, and he added some of his own choreography for this production staged for the National Ballet of Canada in Toronto, with Veronica Tennant as Aurora. The entire performance runs a mere one hour and twenty-seven minutes, barely half the length of certain others, and one suspects some of the deep cuts in the prologue happened to get Nureyev onto the stage more quickly (his character does not appear until the beginning of Act 2, normally the midway point of the ballet). As wonderfully as Nureyev and Tennant dance, they are almost upstaged in Act 3 by Karen Kain and Frank Augustyn as Princess Florine and the Bluebird, two of the most brilliant young dancers in the world at that time. Celia Franca, the director of the company, presents a delightfully nasty Carabosse.

A very recent production has become fairly well known since it was broadcast live to theaters from the Royal Ballet in London in December 2013 and then as an encore in April 2014, starring Sarah Lamb (from Boston) as Aurora and Steven McRae (an Australian) as Florimund. This production celebrates a landmark event—the opening of the Royal Opera House, Covent Garden, in 1946 after the war (with Margot Fonteyn as Aurora)—and also includes new choreographies. Like Live in HD operas from the Met, this shows similar possibilities for ballet, and hopefully this will catch on even more. An issue in the performance of ballet concerns the amount of pantomime that should be used, and some companies, especially the major Russian ones, keep that to a minimum, not allowing it to get in the way of classical ballet motion—perhaps with the assumption that audiences know the works and too much pantomime may demean them. In reaching out to a larger audience in the cinema, one not as well versed as audiences attending at a major house, those assumptions do not hold, and pantomime may make the difference for some between awareness of what's going on and not knowing. This production by the Royal Ballet uses lots of pantomime, certainly more than would be typical in Russia. For a comparison with a traditional classic Russian production, one can watch the DVD (Kultur, performed in 1982) from the Kirov Ballet (the Soviet-era name for the Maryinsky, originally the Imperial Ballet), with the spectacular dancing of Irina Kolpakova and Sergei Berezhnoi, and in this case a man, Vladimir Lopukhov, as Carabosse, adding even more menace. This one makes a few deletions, but not many.

A few points about the music require special mention (for a detailed study, Wiley's *Tchaikovsky's Ballets* is especially useful). The two most prominent motifs, representing the forces of good and evil, reveal themselves when the characters who embody them make their entries, starting with the Lilac Fairy's motif when she and her entourage dance near the beginning in the Scène dansante, and later with Carabosse, who interrupts the happy christening proceedings in the finale of the prologue. As we would expect, the Lilac Fairy's motif has a smooth legato line, played softly, while Carabosse's is much noisier, punctuated, and angular. When we hear these motifs associated with their characters in the prologue, we immediately recognize them, since we have heard them before—in the ballet's overture. As often happens in overtures, it becomes a musical mini-drama, alerting us from the outset what the forces in the drama will be, and even to some extent how they will interact. The first two bars of the overture musically give us Carabosse, starting with *fortissimo* chords, a punctuating sixteenth-note figure, and the alternating leaps of a tritone. This wildly dramatic material at *allegro vivo* carries on for some time, but finally becomes diffused with offbeat chords that bring it to a halt.

A new section starts *andantino*, quietly, in 6/8 time, on a single note that blossoms into harmony with a flourish in the harp, leading to the *dolce* entry of the Lilac Fairy's motif in wind instruments. This gentleness gradually gives way to *crescendo* as the strings take over, and still carrying this motif, a much louder and triumphant figure encroaches, implying that in the battle of these conflicting forces, the Lilac Fairy will win. Even without knowing the associations with the characters, that will soon become evident, since the musical quality of the motifs leaves no question about the outcome. Those motifs will continue to interact throughout the ballet, carrying forward the dramatic struggle, reaching their peak near the end of Act 2 when the kiss prompted by the Lilac Fairy shatters Carabosse's powers. Other motifs, associated with the Prince or Aurora, also recur at key points, adding further levels of drama and thematic interconnection. Tchaikovsky uses certain instruments for identification purposes as well, such as the flute for the fairy representing a canary who sings, or the extended violin obbligatos for Aurora, so lengthy they seem like sections of a violin concerto. In

Act 3, after all the entertainments have ended, the Lilac Fairy makes a final triumphant appearance, accompanied of course by her now somewhat altered motif, and this can happily bring the work to a close, with no Carabosse to interfere.

THE NUTCRACKER

The Sleeping Beauty had been a moderate success in 1890–1891, enough in the mind of Vsevolozhsky that his collaboration with Petipa and Tchaikovsky should be renewed as soon as possible at the Maryinsky in St. Petersburg. Their planning took a new turn when they considered a double bill—a short ballet and opera on the same program—and Tchaikovsky came up with the idea of *King René's Daughter (Iolanta)* as the one-act work for the opera half. About a decade earlier Tchaikovsky had read E. T. A. Hoffmann's story *Der Nussknacker und der Mausekönig* (The Nutcracker and the Mouse King), a copy of which he owned, but it did not occur to him to do anything with it. Vsevolozhsky also knew the tale, from Alexandre Dumas's French adaptation of the Hoffmann story, *Casse-Noisette*, and he appears to have made the selection, evoking no enthusiasm from Tchaikovsky, who saw the opera as the work of substance—with a ballet tacked on to fill out the program. When this double bill opened in January 1892, the ballet came so late in the evening that neither the critics nor the audience paid a lot of attention to it, dismissing it without much ado. When Tchaikovsky died in 1893 this ballet had more or less fallen out of the repertory, and it would remain on the fringes for a number of decades.

It may have languished in ballet purgatory indefinitely had it not been for an encounter of Willam Christensen, artistic director of the San Francisco Ballet, with some Bay Area Russian immigrants, who suggested in 1944 that he give it a try for a Christmas program he had in mind. The year before he had done a pre-Christmas ballet because the War Memorial Auditorium happened to be available at that time, and now he needed another work. He did not know *The Nutcracker*, but the Russians he consulted told him this one would be ideal because of its Christmas Eve subject matter. Christensen needed to find someone in the United States who actually knew the ballet, and that led him to ex-Maryinsky dancers George Balanchine and Alexandra Danilova, now based in New York, who had experience with it from their student days in St. Petersburg. Not able to reconstruct the choreography in their minds, they suggested he take the scenario and design his own choreography; Balanchine himself would do exactly that when he staged it in New York in 1954.

The performance in San Francisco in 1944 seemed fairly inauspicious, although it clearly delighted the home audience. After Balanchine's New York production a decade later, other cities in the United States and Canada began to take notice, and for some of those it quickly became a Christmas tradition, allowing a Christmas fantasy guaranteed to make viewers happy. Unlike *Swan Lake* and *The Sleeping Beauty*, Petipa's original choreography had not made the journey out of Russia or later the U.S.S.R., so as the popularity of *The Nutcracker* surged not only in major companies but regional ones as well, productions could without impunity set it anywhere the producers liked, including their hometowns. Jennifer Fisher has noted many of these, including ones with kilts in towns with a large Scottish population, a Mexican piñata or cowboys in the American Southwest, the hula in Hawaii, or even hockey in Canada. There has been a Barbie-doll version, political send-ups in the manner of Gilbert and Sullivan, a setting of the story in an *Oliver Twist* type of orphanage, versions with cross-dressing, ones with Duke Ellington arrangements, inner-city settings, the use of gospel choirs ("Sugar Rum Cherry"), and all sorts of others. By now every city and many towns in the United States and Canada do some sort of production in December, many very professionally, others amateurish, and all to sold-out audiences, making it perhaps the strongest secular Christmas tradition we have—as much a part of the season as Christmas trees—all because the San Francisco Ballet put it on in 1944. Along with the *1812 Overture* on the Fourth of July in the United States, Tchaikovsky's ballet has become an integral part of popular culture, not only in North America but also in Europe and Asia. Children of all ages love the work, but any audience will have more than its share of young girls dressed to the nines, many of whom take ballet lessons and probably wish they were on stage, as some of their friends may very well be. One of the charms of this ballet is the fact that it has many parts for children, which can be filled by those enrolled in local dance schools, eager to take a role in this highlight of the year.

While most people cannot help but love the work, some scholarly critics have let loose their more Grinch-like invective on it. Not only do they complain about the lack of drama, but they carp at Tchaikovsky for wasting his time on such a piece of fluff, invoking his lack of enthusiasm for it and writing it off as an ill-fated commission for which he suspended his better judgment when he took it on. It may not be especially dramatic, but that need not bother us any more than it should for certain opera plots, including some of the most loved. *La bohème* stands as perhaps one of the two most appealing of all operas (along with *Carmen*), and its plot has variously been described as a shabby little thriller or as having "chlorotic charm"; recently, an ad in St. John's, Newfoundland, aptly described the plot this way: "Love, despair, poverty INTERMISSION illness, death." Why should we care about these underachieving garret dwellers who can't seem to make up their minds as to whether they're in love or not? Certainly not because of any intelligible drama, which seems all too often to be lacking in opera. We care because Puccini's music makes us care, carrying most of us away on waves of sympathy and emotion that become genuine in the musical telling of the tale. Fortunately, ordinary audiences can exercise better judgment than many critics when it comes to such things, keeping *La bohème* and *The Nutcracker* front and center.

The story that came to Tchaikovsky from Vsevolozhsky and Petipa could have been more dramatic if they had stuck more closely to Hoffmann's original, which, like most fairy tales from the eighteenth and nineteenth centuries, has some fairly gruesome elements. Hoffmann's story lies somewhere between a novella and novel as far as length goes, so of course he can go into more detail about characters and also make his story more elaborate, even having stories within stories. He sets it on Christmas Eve in the home of the medical officer Stahlbaum, not a joyful occasion but in an eerie atmosphere, with the two children Fritz and Marie (Clara in the ballet) cowering in a dark corner. Fritz thinks he sees a small ugly man darting across the vestibule carrying a casket, but this turns out to be their godfather, the Supreme Court justice Drosselmeier, a somewhat frightening figure with a patch over one eye. Aside from his judiciary skills, he's an expert toy maker, and he brings various homemade gifts, including a large nutcracker, in the shape of a soldier. Fritz has something of a mean streak, and grabbing the nutcracker from Marie, he attempts to break an exceptionally hard nut with it, breaking three of its teeth. Marie rescues the nutcracker, goes to sleep, and has dreams much too vivid to be dreams. Mice appear, with the ugly seven-headed mouse king, who extorts marzipan from her with the threat of completely destroying the nutcracker. She complies, but extortion begets more extortion, leading to a battle between the army of mice and Fritz's gingerbread soldiers led by the nutcracker, who fail to win. Only by throwing her slipper to kill the mouse king does the battle end. The next morning Marie awakens as if from a coma, and has an injured arm, from glass shards from the cabinet holding Fritz's soldiers. Instead of feeling relief that she's alive, her mother chastises her for playing with her toys when she should have been in bed.

Drosselmeier has not yet left, and he now has stories to tell, first about Princess Pirlipat, a queen and a mouse queen, a sausage feast, insults, the dismantling of Pirlipat, a prince who may be Drosselmeier's nephew, and a trip to the capital, with much of it couched in fairly gruesome detail. It's never entirely clear if Marie hears Drosselmeier or if she dreams the stories in her state of delirium. The ballet uses much of the story from the first half, but little of the latter part, and in almost all respects it sweetens the story, leaving an idealized Christmas Eve scene with a young girl who lives out her childlike dreams about winning a handsome prince who's transformed from the nutcracker, after she saves him from destruction. Instead of learning moral lessons or suffering the reprimands of adults, she indulges a fantasy that any young girl would love. While Act 1 of the ballet tells a story, almost all of Act 2 becomes a divertissement, celebrating the joining of Clara and the Prince. If we compare that with *The Sleeping Beauty*, the more dramatic earlier ballet also had one act of entertainments, but that constituted one-quarter of the work instead of close to half, as in *The Nutcracker*. The difference may be more a matter of size than anything else.

SAN FRANCISCO, 2007

It's 19 December 2007, and as a longtime resident of San Francisco you have come to the War Memorial Opera House to see the production of *The Nutcracker* that opened three years earlier. This production has attracted much international attention for a number of reasons, including the fact that the ballet gained its new lease on life in this city in 1944, and in a sense belongs here as in no other American city. Prior productions had always struggled with location, both in the first act and the second: Should it be set in Germany, where the story originated, or in Russia, the home of the ballet; and where was this strange, fantasy wonderland of Act 2, with touches of Spain, the Middle East, China, Russia, and the home of the Sugar-Plum Fairy? In designing this production, artistic director and principal choreographer Helgi Tomasson, along with scenographer Michael Yeargan, had an inspired idea: why not set it in San Francisco, which because of 1944 owned it as much as Germany and St. Petersburg.

The inspiration went further, placing it in 1915, a magical year for the city as it rebuilt itself after the devastation of the earthquake and fire of 1906 and put on one of the greatest world's fairs to be held early in the twentieth century, called the Panama-Pacific International Exposition. Panama figured into this in a celebration of the opening of the Panama Canal built by the United States, and San Francisco played a strategic role as the premier West Coast port, now accessible to ships crossing the Atlantic. But the real significance of the fair for the ballet lay in the fantasy world it created, with spectacular architecture conjuring international motifs, not the least of which was the Middle East, but also ancient Rome and others. Over thirty countries had exhibitions at the fair, allowing the country dances of Act 2, of which the fair had many performances, to fit in easily without contrivance. The fair made Act 2 an integral part of San Francisco, and the distinctive architecture of the city, unlike anything else in the United States, could be the backdrop for Act 1, with outdoor scenes, the interior of an elegant home from 1915, and the costumes worn by dancers and supers.

Unlike the overtures for his previous ballets, this one has no hint of impending disquiet, and as the orchestra conducted by Martin West plays it, the closed curtain takes the form of a nickelodeon screen, first of all wishing everyone the compliments of the season. Then a slide show flashes across, with old shots of the bay and cityscapes both residential and commercial, not without some shots of destruction recalling the events of 1906, but focused much more on the return to vibrancy. A brightly colored poster for the fair, called "The Jewel City, San Francisco, 1915," with a panoramic spotlight shining from behind the Palace of Jewels as well as various glass domes and other exotic structures, highlights the vibrancy; next comes one of a young girl sitting with her grandmother in a carriage covered in flowers, connecting the images to the ballet. Both electric and horse-drawn trolleys bring the images to a storefront, now in color, with the sign "Fine clocks—Drosselmeyer" over the window, and the raising of the curtain allows us into Drosselmeyer's shop, where he puts the final touches on the nutcracker soldier he has just made. He appears somewhat eccentric, with a gray moustache, goatee, and patched right eye, but he has a kindly look, in no way frightening to children. He gets ready to leave, but a mother and child entering the shop delay him, giving him a chance to show off some of the toys he has built.

He leaves the shop, taking us onto city streets, a departure from the typical opening of Act 1, scene 1, already in the Stahlbaum's house where Clara, Fritz, other family, and friends decorate the tree. This street scene has a policeman, a woman pushing a baby carriage, a woman selling flowers, the mother and child from the shop, lads carrying a tree, a butcher with his wares, and people bearing gifts, including Drosselmeyer (played by Damian Smith), en route to the Stahlbaum home. Another curtain raise takes us into the sumptuous parlor with its giant Christmas tree still being trimmed. Guests have already arrived, and Clara, played by the fifteen-year-old Elizabeth Powell, now makes her entrance, gliding down the grand staircase. Having someone that young taking the role corresponds with the original in St. Petersburg, with its twelve-year-old Clara, and allows us to share the magic of all that happens through a child's eyes (Powell looks more like twelve than fifteen). It does, though, set up an interesting problem for Act 2, when Clara needs to dance, unlike Act 1, and this can be resolved in various ways, including the dancer playing the Sugar-Plum Fairy joining the Prince in the late *pas de deux*, or, as happens in this production, transforming Clara into a beautiful young woman to project her as a grown-up lover of the Prince. In some, the dancer playing Clara will do all of this if she can be made to look young enough in Act 1, and that works very nicely in the version with Gelsey Kirkland and Mikhail Baryshnikov with the American Ballet Theater, filmed as a DVD in 1977 (Kultur); few women have Kirkland's face, which can capture the wonder of a child as well as the glow of a young woman.

With the house full of adults and children (played by students in the San Francisco Ballet School), the festivities can begin (Fritz makes his entrance sliding down the banister), starting with a march—one of the best-known tunes from the ballet—danced here by the children, who clearly have a good time anticipating the opening of gifts. For this scene Tchaikovsky had written a masquerade for at least six different nationalities, but even before the first production this was dropped, and rightly so considering all the international dances in Act 2. During the next scene, musically a galop, a fast ballroom dance very popular in the nineteenth century, the children open their presents, some of which are toy musical instruments. Tchaikovsky had heard the Toy Symphony, first thought to be by Haydn but now known to be by Mozart's father, Leopold, and he wished to incorporate the sounds of these instruments, such as drums and horns, into the orchestra here, to create the right festive atmosphere. After the rambunctious galop he gives the parents something more sedate, a minuet, an elegant dance for the nobility in the eighteenth century, and here appropriate for the society family and guests. For the third part of this dance scene he borrowed material from a popular French tune, "Bon voyage, cher Dumollet," similar to the tune he had in a collection in his own library.

Drosselmeyer's first gifts, life-sized puppets of a clown and doll, provide some of the only opportunities for ballet in Act 1, and his next one, the nutcracker, will set off the events of the story, but not before he magically transforms it into a life-sized manikin who dances with his dagger. Back in its small size, Clara embraces the nutcracker, now getting to dance in a limited way. That dance eventually becomes wild, at which point Fritz grabs the nutcracker, breaking off an arm as he pulls it violently; as Clara takes it back to heal it, with the help of Drosselmeyer, the gentleness of the dance returns. The evening winds down with the Grossvater (Grandfather) Dance, at first danced by grandparents, and then with all joining in before the guests depart and the family goes to bed. Clara sneaks back and falls asleep with the nutcracker on a divan, and the music now creates a magical atmosphere for her visions, transporting her to dreamland with flutes, piccolo, and harp. The clock strikes twelve, reminiscent of Berlioz's *Symphonie fantastique* just before the witches' Sabbath, and of course strange things now begin to happen. The clown and doll return, Fritz flits by obnoxiously beating on his drum, Drosselmeyer emerges from the ether dressed in black, and setting the nutcracker aside, he transforms the parlor with the life-sized nutcracker and Clara to become part of the dream.

The dream proceeds, with mice coming out of the woodwork that frighten her, and to fight them off, the nutcracker releases Fritz's tin soldiers from the cabinet, lining them up for battle. The music now sounds suitable for a pantomime instead of dancing, throwing in military trumpets for the soldiers and quick passages in the flutes for the scurrying mice. The battle starts, tin soldiers against mice, and the nutcracker and ugly Mouse King (David Arce, suitably masked) cross swords. Instead of throwing her shoe to kill the Mouse King, Clara has the soldiers bring out an oversized mouse trap (in Hoffmann's story Drosselmeier takes credit for inventing it); she lures the Mouse King to look her way, and snags him in the trap, allowing the nutcracker to stab him. The mouse disappears into a hole, but the nutcracker has fallen wounded, so Clara summons Drosselmeyer to repair him, which he does, standing him up and removing his mask. The Prince (Davit Karapetyan) emerges, greets Clara, and recognizes that she saved him; they dance together briefly before leaving, leading into scene 2 and the entry of the King and Queen from the snow forest. This provides a delightful bit of fantasy for San Francisco, where it does not snow, except in nearby Napa Valley on very cold nights. Now real dancing can begin, first with the Snow Queen (Yuan Yuan Tan) and Snow King (Pierre-François Vilanoba), followed by the women of the corps de ballet—to another of the most famous dances (the Waltz of the Snowflakes), with flute passages that create the illusion of falling snow. An interesting touch in this final scene of the act involves the use of a chorus of women joining the orchestra, giving an even more ethereal atmosphere for what will follow. Toward the end of the scene it snows so hard you don't know how the dancers can breathe; it looks more like the Sierras between Truckee and Lake Tahoe during a good winter than San Francisco.

Instead of the traditional Sugarland, wherever that may be, Act 2 begins in one of the glass pavilions of the world's fair, perhaps a butterfly enclosure, in which the youngest members of the San Francisco Ballet School get to perform as butterflies or other brightly colored winged creatures, some of which may be fairies. Amid this happy scene, somewhere beyond the snow forest, the Sugar-Plum Fairy (Vanessa Zahorian) arrives, making an indelible entrance accompanied by a new instrument that Tchaikovsky had only just discovered and did not exist anywhere in Russia. On 15 June 1891 he wrote about it to Pyotr Jurgenson, insisting on secrecy to assure he would be the first to use it:

> I have discovered a new orchestral instrument in Paris, something between a small piano and a Glockenspiel, with a divinely beautiful tone. I want to introduce this instrument into the symphonic poem *The Voyevoda* and the ballet. The instrument is called the Celesta Mustel and costs 1200fr. You can only buy it from the inventor, Mustel, in Paris. I want to ask you to order one of these instruments. . . . Have it sent direct to Petersburg; but no-one there must know about it. I am afraid that Rimsky-Korsakov and Glazunov might hear of it and make use of the new effect before I can. I expect a colossal effect from the new instrument.

Using the celesta for the theme of the Sugar-Plum Fairy's entrance sets her apart in a unique way, with an instrument never before heard in Russia, giving a feeling of magic and certainly achieving the desired effect. Clara and the Prince arrive, and after being greeted by the Sugar-Plum Fairy, the Prince explains what happened to him and how Clara saved him. Drosselmeyer has also come, and he and Clara now sit down to watch the celebration in her honor.

The celebratory divertissement that follows becomes in effect a tour of national pavilions, starting with Spain and a Spanish Dance (called Chocolate if the scene takes place in the traditional Kingdom of Sweets, or Confiturenburg—but not in this production). There will be six dances in the divertissement, four of them representing countries, and while Tchaikovsky could ably write those for the European countries, it became a little trickier for the ones further afield. For Spain he could easily capture the right atmosphere with castanets and Spanish rhythms, but the one that follows, the Arabian Dance (Coffee), presented a different type of challenge. Unlike Béla Bartók a generation later, who studied Arabic music carefully, Tchaikovsky appears to have known nothing from that part of the world, and built his dance from a Georgian lullaby, "Iav, nana" (Sleep, lullaby), apparently taken from the collection *Fifty Years of Russian Music*. In this production two male attendants in Middle Eastern dancing garb carry in a large, equally Middle Eastern–looking steaming lamp, out of which a genie-like belly dancer (Sarah Van Patten) emerges when they rub it. Not only does the music not in any way sound Arabic, but it creates a Hollywood atmosphere not unlike movies such as *The Thief of Bagdad* (1940) or other magic-carpet films from the forties and fifties that avoid anything authentically Arabic or North African in favor of snake-charmers' music with lots of slow oboe solos. Composers for these films, including Max Steiner for early parts of *Casablanca* (1942), may very well have received their inspiration from Tchaikovsky.

Since the music has nothing Arabic about it, aside from an imagined and possibly colonial sound, staging this dance (and the Chinese one to follow) comes with certain risks of being either overtly or subtly offensive, as has often been true in the past. Staging this as an Arabic pavilion at a world's fair to some extent gets the producers off the hook, set in a city only about three hundred miles north of Hollywood in an atmosphere intended to be fanciful. While anachronistic, the dancers perform respectfully and tastefully. The Chinese Dance (Tea) similarly generates a westernized notion of Chinese music, and in this case, since San Francisco has one of the largest Chinese populations of any North American city, the staging can be a combination of an acrobat (Nicolas Blanc) and New Year's parade, intended for the enjoyment of an American audience. Staying with the athletic motif, this production continues not with the Russian Dance but instead the Dance of the Mirlitons (flutes), in which the brilliantly written trio for flutes is danced as the Olympic sport of rhythmic gymnastics, specifically the artistic twirling of long ribbons, by three dancers. For the middle section of the three-part form they hand their ribbons over to Clara, who watches with Drosselmeyer, dance without the ribbons, and then use them again for the returning A section with the flute trio. Now comes the Russian Dance (Trepak), the least controversial, with the composer on completely familiar ground, a fast dance performed in something of a Cossack style by three dancers whose leaps and twirls seem to defy gravity. The section ends with more children and a version of the Old Woman Who Lived in a Shoe, in this case wearing a skirt more like a rotating carnival tent, large enough to enclose lots of children. Once again Tchaikovsky used familiar tunes—in this case French—to build the melodies.

After this deluge of musical confection, some of the most memorable tunes are yet to come, next being the Waltz of the Flowers, for the Sugar-Plum Fairy and her corps de ballets attendants, now presumably in a horticultural pavilion. This offers an opportunity for spectacular dancing by the soloist, as does the following *pas de deux* for the Prince and Clara, which of course cannot be danced by a young Clara. The dream projection takes her to the future, and here she enters a mirrored closet and emerges as an adult ballerina, danced by Maria Kochetkova. Similar mirror transformations to another world or age are familiar from films, such as Jean Cocteau's *Orpheus* (1949) or Julian Rupert's *Phantom of the Opera* (1925), where female characters actually pass through a mirror. After the lightness of previous numbers, the first section of the *pas de deux*, the *Andante maestoso* for both dancers, changes the tone entirely, with an intensity that puts it on a par with Tchaikovsky's most ardent love music. He follows this with a tarantella, a vigorous Italian dance, for the Prince, and then comes the most famous number from the ballet, the Dance of the Sugar-Plum Fairy, of course featuring the celesta; a coda draws the two of them together again. The final waltz and apotheosis bring the entire company back on stage—a type of musical curtain call with each group or soloist briefly featured. To make the ending follow from earlier events, this one has Drosselmeyer transport the sleeping Clara on her divan back to the parlor of her home, where she awakens from a wonderful dream, clasps her nutcracker, and gets a hug from her mother as she finally goes off to bed.

You have seen the work performed by one of the great ballet companies of the world, with first-rate dancers who can perform the national dances, the *pas de deux*, and solo numbers at the highest possible level. While I know this production from the DVD (Opus Arte, 2008), I saw the ballet done live in San Francisco in December of 1987, with my entire family at the War Memorial Opera House, to the delight of my children, aged five and nine at the time. We lived in Berkeley that year, just across the bay from San Francisco, but normally we live in Halifax, Nova Scotia, where, not unlike many cities of its size (population around four hundred thousand), *The Nutcracker* has been performed continuously in Decembers for over a quarter of a century. Unlike the spectacular dancing possible in San Francisco, we embrace something a little more modest, but in no way does that stop the house (the Rebecca Cohn Auditorium, Dalhousie University) from being sold out every night. The musical quality is exceptionally high, provided by Symphony Nova Scotia, but in a regional house such as this, there will be more participation from dance students, and the main roles will be taken by dancers of a different order than those in the larger centers. The Halifax production certainly does not lack innovation, set in a girls' boarding school instead of the Stahlbaum home (all the girls get to go home for Christmas except for Clara, who has her dream left alone with her rag doll), and for some numbers in Act 2 very fine puppetry replaces dancing. Having experienced both types of production, I can confirm that there is no less enthusiasm in the smaller centers, and some of that may come from families and friends seeing the large number of ballet students involved. In fact, watching someone we know on stage, always very well trained, gives a different type of experience, one that draws us more directly into the work, and may even get us closer to the magical world Tchaikovsky has created. For the thousands who see it every December, Tchaikovsky has become something like a favorite uncle before Christmas (a little like Drosselmeyer), enchanting us and ushering us into the season as nothing else can.

9

ABOVE AND BEYOND

From His Death to the Present

A number of composers from the past continue to fascinate us now, remaining very much alive in the repertory—through books and movies about them, through the use of their music as scenes or soundtracks in movies, or for other reasons; Tchaikovsky clearly stands as one of those composers. The two annual events that keep him front and center in North America have been described—the performance of the *1812 Overture* on the Fourth of July, and the recurrence of *The Nutcracker* every December. Aside from that, his symphonies, especially the last three, as well as a number of the symphonic poems, remain mainstays of every professional orchestra, and many amateur ones as well; *Swan Lake* and *The Sleeping Beauty* are produced more than just about any other ballet; *Eugene Onegin* is one of the most performed operas in the entire repertory, and others, including *The Queen of Spades*, *Cherevichki*, and *Iolanta*, have joined the repertory. In the movies a number of biopics exist; some films have exceptional Tchaikovsky scenes that feature performances of his music, and in the case of the recent *Black Swan* (2010), whose lead actress, Natalie Portman, won an Academy Award, the psychological angst in the film relates directly to the contrast of the two swans from *Swan Lake*. While the moviegoing public took notice of that film, ballet lovers have been treated to a "fourth" Tchaikovsky ballet, John Cranko's *Onegin*, which uses excerpts from Tchaikovsky's music, but nothing from the opera of the same name.

RUSSIAN COMPOSERS OF THE TWENTIETH CENTURY

Russia had no strong musical tradition before Tchaikovsky, Mikhail Glinka being the first prominent composer to emerge, but with the possible exception of his opera *Ruslan and Ludmilla*, his star did not shine far beyond Russia. Four of Tchaikovsky's contemporaries, Alexander Borodin, Mily Balakirev, Modest Musorgsky, and Nikolay Rimsky-Korsakov, members of the so-called Mighty Five along with César Cui, went in different directions, shunning the tradition of western European music in favor of the integration of Russian folk music into their works. This may have created traces of hostility between Tchaikovsky and some of them (especially Cui), but by no means did Tchaikovsky's bent toward central Europe exclude a healthy use of Russian folk music; even in his non-programmatic works that element can usually be found. Russian composers of the next generations consequently had different types of models to follow, and a number of the most prominent ones saw Tchaikovsky as the greatest influence on their careers. Of course Russia and later the Soviet Union had numerous composers relatively unknown in the West, from Tchaikovsky's student Sergey Ivanovich Taneyev to Nikolay Myaskovsky, Tikhon Khrennikov, and Edison Denisov, but others have become household names outside of Russia. The most celebrated of these, including (at the risk of sounding like a song by Danny Kaye) Sergey Rachmaninoff, Sergey Prokofiev, Igor Stravinsky, Dmitri Shostakovich, and Dimitri Tiomkin, saw their musical heritage coming from Tchaikovsky, and some honored this with special acts of veneration. Not surprisingly, most of them had difficulty dealing with the restrictive policies and charges of formalism by Soviet authorities, and all but one (Shostakovich) emigrated to western Europe or the United States (although Prokofiev did return in the mid-1930s). Some of their thoughts about Tchaikovsky are in order here (Tiomkin will be saved for the section on biopics).

Of this group of five composers, only Rachmaninoff, because of his date of birth (1873), had actually met Tchaikovsky, although his love for the older composer's music started in his childhood. In his own words, "it happened that just at that time, Tchaikovsky, who later played such a significant part in my musical development, became known and popular in Russia. It was through my sister Elena that I was first introduced to his music, which touched me to the heart. She used to sing 'None but the Lonely Heart,' and this—as well as some other songs . . . pleased me beyond words" (SR 9). He would accompany her, not always with the written score, but with his own improvisations. While studying at the Moscow Conservatory he found in Tchaikovsky's music what he most wished to emulate: something simple, melodious, and richly emotional, resisting the trends of modernism. As an act of homage he wrote a piano arrangement of the *Manfred* Symphony, and in fact studied every score he could get his hands on; some have unjustly criticized him for sounding too much like Tchaikovsky. Rachmaninoff's own teacher, Nikolay Zverev, had in fact studied music theory with Tchaikovsky, leading to a strong friendship between them. Tchaikovsky and Rachmaninoff also became friends, with the older composer giving the younger one useful career advice as well as tangible assistance, for example critiquing his opera *Aleko*. Tchaikovsky liked this opera so much that he made a proposal: "I have just finished an opera in two acts, *Iolanta*, which is not long enough to fill an evening. Would you object if it were performed together with yours?"

"He actually said these words," the younger man recalled in amazement. "'Would I object?' He was fifty-three years old, a famous musician—and I was only a beginner of twenty!" Rachmaninoff emerged as the finest pianist of his generation aside from being an outstanding composer, but the Russian Revolution in 1917 changed everything for a man of his background. He left Russia that year with his wife and two daughters, first spending a year in Finland, and then emigrating to the United States, where he stayed. He remains best known for his three piano concertos, solo piano works, as well as songs, and while he found his own voice as a composer, he may not have developed as he had without Tchaikovsky's influence.

An affinity between Prokofiev and Tchaikovsky may be more difficult to pinpoint, considering Prokofiev's sense of the piano as something more percussive than lyrical or singing, but he nevertheless understood his musical heritage. In his early twenties he knew little of Tchaikovsky's music, but when asked by his teacher Lyadov at the St. Petersburg Conservatory to identify his favorite composers, he answered Tchaikovsky, Wagner, and Grieg. He later dropped Grieg from the list, but never Tchaikovsky.

The noted Russian bass Fyodor Stravinsky sang in the premieres of a few of Tchaikovsky's operas, including *Vakula the Smith, The Maid of*

Orleans, and *The Enchantress*, and as a result he got to know the composer fairly well. By the time he sang the role of Mamirov in *The Enchantress* in 1887, his son Igor, destined to be one of the greatest composers of the twentieth century, had reached the age of five, and much lively discussion about Tchaikovsky in the Stravinsky household ensued, no doubt in full view of the inscribed photograph of Tchaikovsky the composer had given to Fyodor. The young Stravinsky grew up with reverence for Russia's greatest composer, and even had the pleasure of seeing him at the Maryinsky Theater—at a performance of *Ruslan and Ludmilla*—just weeks before Tchaikovsky died. After leaving Russia and settling in Paris, also a casualty of the Revolution, he participated in Sergey Diaghilev's production of *The Sleeping Beauty* in London, orchestrating a few of the numbers that had been cut from the first performance in St. Petersburg. Aside from this participation, Stravinsky wrote an open letter to Diaghilev, lauding the composer, the work, and the glorious fusion of music and dance. Around this time he came up with the idea for his opera *Mavra*, celebrating the three Russian giants closest to his heart: Pushkin, Glinka, and Tchaikovsky.

No composer of Russian origin has gone further than Stravinsky in paying homage to Tchaikovsky, and he did this, not unlike Tchaikovsky's homage to Mozart with *Mozartiana*, with his ballet *Le baiser de la fée* (The fairy's kiss), to commemorate the thirty-fifth anniversary of Tchaikovsky's death in 1928. The idea for the work was to take themes by Tchaikovsky and integrate them into the composition, as well as write new music in the style of Tchaikovsky's ballets, based on the fairy tale "The Ice Maiden" by Hans Christian Andersen. Stravinsky's dedication reads as follows: "I dedicate this ballet to the memory of Peter Tchaikovsky, identifying his Muse with the fairy. The ballet thus becomes an allegory. This Muse similarly branded him with her fatal kiss, whose mysterious imprint made itself felt in all the work of this great artist." Considering how the story unfolds, it's difficult to decipher exactly what he meant by the dedication. A fairy gives an infant a kiss, but instead of joy, this brings the opposite. After growing up, the young man looks forward to marriage, but on his wedding day the Fairy drags him away to the elysian fields of everlasting bliss, hardly what he would have wanted. The kiss appears to have been more a curse than a blessing. Since the dedication made a link between the Fairy and Tchaikovsky's muse, we must assume that this muse brings disappointment, not unlike fate in Tchaikovsky's existence. Perhaps there are even sexual implications, since the recipient of the kiss misses out on the joys of the marriage bed; Stravinsky undoubtedly knew much about Tchaikovsky's own complex sexual life—the lack of it with Désirée and Antonina, and the string of male lovers.

Identifying the pieces by Tchaikovsky used by Stravinsky has proved to be something of a puzzle for those who have seriously made an attempt. Just over a dozen have been confirmed, all of them piano pieces or songs, the first being the song "Berceuse de la tempête" (Op. 54, No. 10). Unlike this one, which proves easy enough to identify despite the changes to the harmony, in most cases the melodies sound Tchaikovsky-like, but resist any clear recognition, and in the end the work sounds more like Stravinsky than Tchaikovsky. Perhaps in transforming the music in this way, making the music his own instead of a mere arrangement, he paid the ultimate compliment to his idol, in a sense fusing his own musical thoughts with Tchaikovsky's, bringing Tchaikovsky to life for a generation already far removed, listening with twentieth-century ears.

When contemplating why he loved Tchaikovsky's music as much as he did, Shostakovich had difficulty putting this into words, but he did not hesitate to claim that "there is not a single Russian composer of the latter 19th or early 20th centuries who is not indebted in some measure to Peter Tchaikovsky." He compared him to Chekhov as part of the Russian national consciousness, but carefully avoided taking the comparison too far, especially resisting labeling their works as an "elegiac glorification of the Russian twilight of the latter 19th century." While they both took a keen interest in the Russian landscape, this did not lead to sentimentality, but instead unlocked something vital about the Russian people. He especially wished to clear up the misconception about pessimism in Tchaikovsky's music, which was not any more despondent than the works of the Greek tragedians. Instead of succumbing to fatalism, he saw the works as a struggle with fate and a striving to overcome, although with some works such as the Sixth Symphony, this may be a nod to Soviet expectations. As a composer, though, he claimed that whenever he set out to write a new work his thoughts inevitably turned to the approaches used by Tchaikovsky. As a practical example of that, he referred to Tchaikovsky's orchestration, which did not happen after the composition of a short score but instead took place as an integral part of the composition itself. Orchestration then was not an added component, but the sounds of the instruments or their combinations played a vital role in shaping the work. We need to take voices such as Shostakovich's seriously when addressing the issue of Tchaikovsky's place in the modern world. Along with defining something about the spirit of the Russian people, Shostakovich felt more personally that "without Tchaikovsky we could not endure our sorrows" (SH 1–4).

BIOPICS

Any type of biographical work about Tchaikovsky has certain risks associated with it, and this proves especially true of biopics, which cannot go into as much detail as a print biography to clarify some of the issues. In the case of Tchaikovsky, numerous issues can be found, but at least three major ones stand out: 1) how will his homosexuality by treated, 2) how did he die, and 3) what caused the correspondence with Nadezhda von Meck to end. The various film biographies of Tchaikovsky could not be more different in their treatments of these, and since they all indulge in greater or lesser amounts of fiction, the more fictionalized ones almost come as a relief, since the viewer has less need to worry about separating fact from fantasy. Aside from an early and relatively unknown one made in Russia in 1947, *Song of My Heart*, the first of the prominent ones, *Tchaikovsky*, from 1970, also from Russia, stands as an act of homage by a notable Russian composer who made his career in the West, Dimitri Tiomkin. A graduate of the same conservatory as Tchaikovsky, Tiomkin emigrated to the United States in 1925, where he had a brilliant career as a film composer, scoring a number of Alfred Hitchcock's films (*Shadow of a Doubt*, *I Confess*, and *Dial M for Murder*), as well as numerous ones by other leading directors. He returned to the Soviet Union to work on *Tchaikovsky*, a film he not only adapted and conducted the music for but also served on as producer and executive producer; although directed by Igor Talankin, clearly this was his baby. With rich cinematography by Margarita Pilikhina and superb acting by Innokenti Smoktunovsky in the leading role—who treated the composer as shy, modest, and often unsure of himself—it received the Academy Award for best foreign film in 1971.

For two of the issues noted above, this film avoids them completely. Nowhere in it does even a hint of homosexuality arise. With the absence, it implies a tacit assumption that he was not a homosexual, and this leaves us baffled as to why he suddenly severs the tie with his wife. Similarly, about his death, of which various theories abound, including contracting cholera from mistakenly drinking unpurified water, committing suicide by intentionally drinking that water, or an elaborate and highly unlikely plot of enforced protection of its reputation by the School of Jurisprudence (where he received all of his non-musical education) against being tarred as a gay institution, no opinion comes forward here. Only on the issue of why the correspondence with Mrs. von Meck ended after thirteen years does this film take a stand, laying the blame on Wladislaw Pachulsky, his former student and her house violinist and confidant, as his revenge for Tchaikovsky's saying disparaging things about his own compositions. Tchaikovsky did not encourage him as a composer, but it's far too easy to blame the end of the correspondence on the conniving of an intermediary rather than on the possibility of her financial or mental collapse, or on the prospect that the composer lost interest after he became financially secure. Making Pachulsky the villain proves every bit as fictitious as denying Tchaikovsky's homosexuality.

These details, coming in good measure from director and screenwriter Talankin, need not trouble us as part of an otherwise fine film. Because of Tiomkin's major role in the production, his efforts should attract more attention, and in fact his treatment of the music stands as one of the main features of the film. As one of the finest film composers of the twentieth century, also experienced at adapting the music of others, he had the skills to bring something to this as no one else could, and in so doing he paid tribute to the composer he loved so completely. The film almost exclusively uses music by Tchaikovsky, but not necessarily as Tchaikovsky wrote it. Instead of simply adding music at the biographically appropriate places to do so, he changed it in ways that often allow the music to work like film music, informing us musically of significant ideas or emotions. This could be done with distortion to add an element of menace, for example the distressing tangle of music in the head of Tchaikovsky the child at the beginning, or the progressive distortion of the waltz from Act 2 of *Eugene Onegin* to represent the disintegration of his marriage. Tiomkin had used distortion brilliantly in

Hitchcock's *Shadow of a Doubt*, making the waltz from *The Merry Widow* impossible to dance, and giving clues to the identification of Uncle Charlie as the murderer of wealthy widows (I have written about this at length in my book *Hitchcock's Ear*). Numerous of Tiomkin's other distortions and tactical changes have been itemized by Christopher Palmer in his book *Dimitri Tiomkin: A Portrait*. It should not surprise us that in a film tribute to a great composer by a fellow composer, the treatment of the music should take on a special life of its own.

In both opera and film not everyone—especially critics—gets what's going on. Some critics have objected to Ken Russell's biopic of Tchaikovsky, *The Music Lovers*, because Russell plays havoc with the facts; most Mozart scholars objected to *Amadeus* by Peter Shaffer and Milos Forman for the same reason. At the end of one of the best of all opera cartoons, *What's Opera, Doc?*, a dying Bugs Bunny revives sufficiently to give this aside to the audience: "Well, what did you expect in an opera—a happy ending?" It appears that some of us need a similar type of prompting about a film by Ken Russell, director of *Mahler*, *Lisztomania*, and *Salome's Last Dance*, among others: Well, what did you expect, a real biography? Russell loves hyperbole, outrageous extremes, and phantasmagoria, and he's very good at it. *The Music Lovers* came out in the same year as Tiomkin's *Tchaikovsky*, 1970, and unlike that film, Russell made no pretense of historical accuracy, opting for his own peculiar agenda, as Shaffer/Forman did with *Amadeus*. In extreme contrast to the sexless composer in *Tchaikovsky*, almost everyone seethes with overcharged libidos in *The Music Lovers*, certainly Tchaikovsky (Richard Chamberlain), erupting with homoerotic desire, and even Nadezhda von Meck. While some have panned Russell's overblown portrayal of Tchaikovsky's homosexuality, he probably got closer to the truth than Talankin did, and for someone not interested in facts, he comes up with more plausible explanations of the marriage breakup and death.

The title scrupulously avoids the name Tchaikovsky, and that appears to be strategic, since this film is as much or more about Antonina Milyukova, the composer's wife, played ravishingly by Glenda Jackson; just as *Eugene Onegin* should have been titled *Tatiana*, this film could have been called *Nina*. Jackson appears in the earliest shots in crowd scenes, she steals the show in her relationship with Tchaikovsky, and she dominates the end of the film as she goes mad; the final image we see has her looking through asylum bars. Throughout she is so sexually overcharged that Tchaikovsky can do nothing but recoil in abhorrent revulsion when she comes on to him, especially on the train back to Moscow after their honeymoon when she strips naked, leaving absolutely nothing to the imagination. No one could pull this off the way Jackson does, and if we weren't sure the film was about her before this point, this clinches it. It appears that Russell had less interest in the composer and his music than in the bizarre relationship between a gay man trying to project normalcy in the late nineteenth century and a sensual woman who allows him no such opportunity. After the breakdown of the marriage, he returns to his former way of life while she descends further into madness, with her mother serving as her madam, procuring men before the final institutionalized collapse. As a filmmaker Russell indulges in a certain type of genre, which is not for everyone. Tchaikovsky for him provided a means to an end, offensive perhaps to Tchaikovsky scholars, but if we watch it looking for biography, we have missed the point.

After 1970 Tchaikovsky ceased to inhabit the large screen of cinema, reduced to the miniaturized screen of television—especially the BBC. One of these pieces appeared in 1997, part of a series, in this case titled *Great Composers: Tchaikovsky*, directed by Simon Broughton with narration by Kenneth Branagh. Unlike most others, this one is a documentary, with lots of interviews of prominent musicians and musicologists, including the scholars Alexander Poznansky, David Brown, and Elkhonon Yoffe, and the musicians Yuri Temirkanov (conductor), Mikhail Rudy (pianist), Evgeny Kissin (pianist), and Graham Vick (conductor). It even has interviews with a tram driver from St. Petersburg who clearly knows her Tchaikovsky, and she actually sings some familiar passages; unfortunately on the readily accessible YouTube version none of the Russian commentary has been given subtitles in English. Near the beginning Poznansky indignantly declares that "it's time we change our perception of Tchaikovsky from gay, mad Russian and set the record straight," no doubt reacting to the likes of Ken Russell. He does not wish to take homosexuality out of the equation, later assuring us that we "need to understand his homosexuality to understand *Romeo and Juliet*," and probably other works as well, but the rhetoric simply needs to be toned down. Rudy points out that he knew nothing of

Tchaikovsky's homosexuality until he attended the Moscow Conservatory, where at most this was treated as a "shameful secret," an interesting commentary on the suppression of this subject during the Soviet era. This one-hour documentary gives more about the music than the man, with Brown explaining facets such as the descending fate motif, along with other commentary about the music performed by the St. Petersburg Philharmonic under the baton of Temirkanov. Despite the short length, it provides a very satisfying introduction of the composer to the general listener.

Another BBC program aired in 2007, this time in two parts, called *Tchaikovsky: A Personal Exploration by Charles Hazlewood*. To make this program, Hazlewood traveled to Russia to visit sites and conduct the Maryinsky Young Philharmonic performing various chestnuts from the composer's output. The program gives a curious mixture of Hazlewood talking, interviewing, being seen as he visits important locations, and conducting—all of this interspersed with acted scenes from Tchaikovsky's life. It's not always clear if it's about Tchaikovsky or Hazlewood, especially with all the close-ups of his conducting, producing the appropriate facial expressions of a man with a deep understanding of his subject. While lacking the panache of Ken Russell's film, this one takes the issue of homosexuality even further, actually showing Tchaikovsky (played by Ed Stoppard) getting it on with a friend in the bushes on a city street, and it also has lots of focus on his gay lovers such as Eduard Zak, Yosif Kotek, and others. At no point do we hear anything of the existence of Désirée Artôt. The actor playing Nikolay Rubinstein makes him look much older than Tchaikovsky (in fact, the age difference was five years), and various other inaccuracies creep in. Unless one happens to be a devoted fan of Hazlewood, this one, available on a 2008 DVD, does not represent the most likely choice for getting acquainted with Tchaikovsky and his music.

TCHAIKOVSKY AS FILM MUSIC

Literally hundreds of movies use music by Tchaikovsky, often very intelligibly, but my focus will be on five from 1940 to 2010 that treat this in special ways, often going beyond the music itself to scenes of actual performances that play a role in our understanding of the film or part of it. The first of these, and undoubtedly the best known, comes from none other than Walt Disney, his 1940 classic *Fantasia*. Unlike many other animated films, this one puts the music first, with eight sections each based on a well-known musical work (or a part thereof), with the music performed by the Philadelphia Orchestra, visible in silhouette or muted light between numbers. The conductor, Leopold Stokowski, gets to meet Mickey Mouse—the star of some of the numbers—at one point, and he's also caricatured in Musorgsky's *Night on Bald Mountain* with the "Chernabog" devil striking a pose not unlike Stokowski while conducting. Sandwiched between the opening Toccata and Fugue in D Minor by J. S. Bach and Paul Dukas's *The Sorcerer's Apprentice*, where Mickey plays the apprentice, comes Tchaikovsky's *The Nutcracker Suite*, a selection of dances from the ballet, scrambled in this case from the usual order, with the opening overture and march omitted. The six dances used, the Sugar-Plum Fairy, Chinese, Mirlitons, Arabian, Russian, and Waltz of the Flowers (in this order), could not be more familiar, and instead of animations of the nutcracker or other figures from the ballet, Disney and his colleagues use flowers, plants, leaves, and a few fairies thrown in at the beginning and end spreading pixie dust for good measure.

The different plants become animated dancers, and some of these are delightful, such as the thistles as Cossacks in the Russian Dance along with orchids as peasant girls. Another one, presumably intended to be cute in a similar way, raises a problem for us in the twenty-first century, and probably should have in 1940 as well. In the booklet accompanying the Deluxe Commemorative Edition celebrating a half century since the film appeared, the description tells us that the first dance "gives way to the oriental humor of the 'Chinese Dance', performed by a group of mushrooms, constantly interrupted by the smallest of the lot who, no matter how hard he tries, cannot keep in step." The dancing mushrooms become Casper-the-Ghost-like figures, with excessively slanted eyes to ensure they're recognized as Chinese, wearing red traditional Chinese hats. Even in the ballet, as noted in chapter 8, this dance can raise production issues of political correctness if not worse since the music has nothing actually Chinese about it, but this animation goes all the way, not only indulging in stereotypes familiar from American movies, but portraying them as fungi, or somehow parasitic. Others have also written about this, including the red hats, which usually belong to poisonous mushrooms. In 1940, North Americans tended to regard the Chinese not as normal people, but as a source of cheap labor for building railroads, especially on the West Coast, where this film originated. Whether or not any of this was intended at the time, it has left an unfortunate legacy of which we need to be aware.

A stunning use of Tchaikovsky turns up in one of Alfred Hitchcock's later films, *Torn Curtain* (1966), a work plagued with problems that I discuss at length in my book *Hitchcock's Ear*. In this thriller, set mostly in East Germany during the Cold War, an American scientist (Paul Newman) appears to defect but in fact has come to pick the brain of a Leipzig physicist who has solved the riddle of creating a bomb to make all others obsolete, which has eluded the Americans. After he gets the solution, he and his fiancée (Julie Andrews) must escape, and the elaborate scheme for this has them attending a ballet in East Berlin, after which they will be hidden with the props on a ship sailing for Sweden, which the Czech ballet company will visit as its next tour stop. An actual ballet performance at a theater would need to take place, and for this Hitchcock wanted to use Ravel's *Daphnis et Chloé*, but that work not being available, his production designer Hein Heckroth told him about a new possibility that Stanley Wilson had found, Tchaikovsky's *Francesca da Rimini*, not a ballet but a symphonic poem that had been choreographed a number of times in the past. Hitchcock needed less than five minutes, so they would have to start from scratch with their own choreography. On 22 October 1965 Heckroth wrote this to Hitchcock: "For our purpose, I propose to compress it to a short love scene, the duel and the end of the two lovers. After their death Malatesta and his evil court take the scene, which is the inferno, as indicated in the music. I will start to work with the choreographer [Michael Panaieff] on this basis on Monday if this is in accordance with you." Hitchcock agreed.

The programme comes from canto 5 of *The Inferno* by Dante, where Dante enters the second circle of hell's abyss, filled with howls and despair. Dante approaches Francesca and Paolo, and asks them to tell him how they came here. She tells the sad tale, of how she was married off to a grotesque man but fell in love with his brother Paolo. They kissed after reading the story of Lancelot, and at that moment her husband entered, attempted to kill his brother, but stabbed Francesca, who stood between them; he then finished off Paolo as well. Hitchcock needed only a fragment of Tchaikovsky's twenty-four minutes of music, and the parts used come from fairly near the end of the work, adapted as described by Heckroth. Francesca would be danced by Tamara Toumanova, a Russian-born ballerina who lived and worked in the United States.

As often happens in Hitchcock's films, the borrowed music and in this case the story that goes along with it—danced as an actual performance—directly serve the drama of the film. Dante's narrative unfolds in the second level of hell, and considering the state of the Cold War in the mid-1960s, Western filmgoers would be inclined to place East Germany with its harshly repressive authoritarian rule in a similar range. More specifically, Francesca and Paolo have been carrying on in an illicit way, and the Americans played by Newman and Andrews do the same, now in urgent need of escaping the authorities. Their plan does not work as it should when the prima ballerina recognizes Newman from the stage, and she alerts the police, who flood into the theater; he realizes they're surrounded when a couple of policemen pop up from the orchestra pit trying to spot him. Since the flames of hell are represented on the stage, the audience has the inferno on its mind, so when Newman stands and shouts, "Fire" (sounding enough like the German *Feuer* to have the right effect), members of the audience panic en masse and rush for the exits. In one of Hitchcock's best sequences of shots in the film, Newman and Andrews come up against a tightly packed flow of humanity as the crowd surges for the exits while they attempt to reach the stage door, this flow offering another representation of hell on earth.

When Newman shouts, the ballet stops, but until that point the music plays an interesting role in both the ballet and the drama developing in the theater. Until Toumanova recognizes him, with her sharp glare heightened by the camera, the visual focus has been on the ballet with its vivid colors, simulated fire, and Toumanova's pirouettes. When she becomes involved in the other drama, alerting the police to his presence, the camera shifts to the house, showing police milling about and their quarry squirming. While this happens, the music does not stop, but Tchaikovsky's music now accompanies the escape drama, and as it builds to a climax, the viewer has the feeling this music belongs to the house drama, not the ballet. Even though Hitchcock initially wanted *Daphnis et Chloé*, he ended up with music and a ballet that could not have been more apt, bridging the ballet and the film's drama perfectly. For four and a half minutes Tchaikovsky takes over the film, and gives the drama an intensity it would not have otherwise had.

A Tchaikovsky scene turned up in a film about three decades later with similar implications for the film, *The Talented Mr. Ripley*, directed by Anthony Minghella. A wealthy shipyard owner in New York sends a pianist he just met, Tom Ripley (Matt Damon), to Italy to find his dissolute son Dickie (Jude Law), but while in Italy Tom comes over to Dickie's side, lying about his impoverished background and living the good life. Tom falls in love with Dickie, and while in San Remo, out on a small rented boat, they quarrel. In duel-like fashion, Tom strikes his friend with a large oar, finishing him off and then sinking the boat. A few months later in Rome Tom runs into Meredith (Cate Blanchett), whom he met when entering Italy, and she invites Tom, who has now assumed Dickie's identity, to join her at the opera. We expect it to be an Italian opera in Rome, but not so: we see them at *Eugene Onegin*; the excerpt prepared for the film starts at the end of Lensky's aria in Act 2, and continues into the duel in which Eugene shoots Lensky. The parallel duel scenes in the film and opera leap out at us, but more to the point, we have a character in the film who lives a dissipated life and becomes bored with his friend; this parallels Eugene's response to Lensky, getting his little revenge by preventing Olga from dancing with Lensky at Tatiana's name day celebration. In *The Talented Mr. Ripley*, with Dickie dead, Tom takes over his identity as completely as possible, now living the dissolute life. As the film continues, and one murder leads to another, the connection with *Onegin* ends, but when the opera scene occurs at the center of the film, it makes perfect sense to use Tchaikovsky's opera.

A film made around the same time, Bernard Rose's *Anna Karenina* (1997), starring Sophie Marceau, could not be more packed with music by Tchaikovsky, not surprising for a realization of a novel by Leo Tolstoy, a writer who knew Tchaikovsky and admired his music. No film, though, places as much focus on Tchaikovsky as Darren Aronofsky's *Black Swan* (2010), about the distressed life of a young ballerina, Nina Sayers (Natalie Portman), who wins the leading role in a new production of *Swan Lake* in New York (Portman won big awards for the role, including an Oscar, Golden Globe, and SAG, but controversy has dogged her regarding how much of it she actually danced). The music of *Swan Lake* of course dominates the film, not only the rehearsal and

performance scenes, but also as film music, catching the right atmosphere for the mental transformation that Nina goes through. Much of
that music has been adapted by Clint Mansell and Matt Dunkley to
sound even more tormented than Tchaikovsky's, often slipping into
something as precarious as Nina's fragile mental condition. She must
work closely with the French director of the production, Thomas Leroy
(Vincent Cassel), who in some ways becomes a Rothbart-like figure,
bullying her sexually and otherwise into being a dancer with feeling. He
has his black swan as well, Lily (Mila Kunis), whom he seems to prefer
over Nina, and uses to get what he hopes for from Nina as a dancer; Lily
more than once offers to dance the black swan, which Thomas doubts
Nina can handle.

Like Tchaikovsky's swan, moving from the ecstasy of love and the
chance of salvation to utter despair and suicide, Nina finds her ecstasy
in winning the most coveted role in the world, but as she tries to live up
to the challenge of dance, her mind progressively disintegrates as she
sees dark visions, and cannot distinguish these visions from reality. Near
the end she imagines she has murdered her rival for the role, Lily, but
instead of stabbing Lily with a large shard of a broken mirror, she has
stabbed herself, and dies at the end of the first performance with a
growing bloodstain on her abdomen. Mirrors, of course, have often
been used symbolically in literature and film, so not surprisingly here
the shard proves to be her undoing. Earlier on more than one occasion
she has looked into mirrors to see her doppelganger, moving independently from herself, heightening the division between illusion and reality. That this confusion, mixed with her quest for perfection but impossibility of coping, should do her in somehow seems apt. Her own death
becomes as necessary as the death of the character she plays, and the
music from near the end of Act 4 carries her to her demise, as she
believes she has reached perfection.

Her relationship with her mother, not unlike that of Erika and her
mother in Michael Haneke's film *La Pianiste*, based on Elfriede Jeli-
nek's *Die Klavierspielerin* (The piano teacher), also gets special treatment, in fact with links to Tchaikovsky's music. The music for the film
starts with the introduction to *Swan Lake*, which, as described in chapter 4, falls into three parts, the first beautiful but melancholy, the second wildly destructive, and the third attempting to return to the beauty
of the first part without success. This treatment of form, well known

from Mozart and Schubert, serves a dramatic function, moving the nostalgia of a beautiful past through a dismantling and destruction of that to a futile attempt to return to it. Visually the film starts with a dream sequence, of Nina's dancing encroached on by a menacing male figure, and then moves to Nina with her mother who fauns over her and consoles her. This relationship goes well for a time, but eventually it disintegrates as Nina can no longer tolerate her mother's overbearing control, and collapses completely when Nina thinks she has brought Lily to her bedroom for a night of unrestrained sex (the drug given by Lily to Nina helps the illusion along). Mother eventually tries to patch things up between them, but only makes matters worse by not waking Nina in time to get to the first performance, believing the role will kill her. Mother may be right, but the damage proves irreconcilable, as the relationship goes the way of Tchaikovsky's musical introduction. The film may have flaws, including the impossibility of Portman with a limited amount of training dancing as much as some have claimed (her ballet body double Sarah Lane called the filmic impression of Portman actually doing all of the dancing an insult to professional dancers), but it nevertheless brought both ballet and Tchaikovsky to the screen in a most prominent way a decade into the twenty-first century.

A "NEW" BALLET

It seemed regrettable to John Cranko, the South African dancer and choreographer, that the world had only three ballets by Tchaikovsky, the greatest of the nineteenth-century ballet composers, and he decided to do something about that. During the 1950s, while a choreographer at the Sadler's Wells Ballet, he unsuccessfully proposed the idea of a ballet version of *Onegin*, using music by Tchaikovsky but not music from the opera. In 1961 he became the artistic director of the Stuttgart Ballet, and the German company gave his idea a much warmer reception than the British one had. To follow through with this he first needed a musical score by Tchaikovsky that audiences would recognize as being by that composer but would not otherwise be familiar with, so he engaged the German composer/conductor Kurt-Heinz Stolze to prepare something that would satisfy those conditions. To achieve this, Stolze took a number of Tchaikovsky's piano works, especially *The Sea-*

sons, Op. 37a, known to very few aside from Russians who play the piano, sections from the opera *Cherevichki*, also little known in the early 1960s, and portions from a couple of the symphonic poems (*Romeo and Juliet* and *Francesca da Rimini*)—not the well-known themes, but more the connecting passages between these. Anything from the piano pieces would of course have to be orchestrated in a style similar to Tchaikovsky's, for example with alternating flutes, clarinets, and oboes, and the already orchestrated works would also need some revision to make them suitable for a pit orchestra. In the end Stolze achieved exactly what Cranko wanted, with a score that sounds like Tchaikovsky and that few listeners will recognize, and beyond that, a score that seems to hang together as a continuous work instead of a series of fragments.

The ballet premiered in Stuttgart in 1965 with Cranko's choreography, and soon went through a major revision in 1967. Since then it has been performed in many other countries by major companies, although surprisingly it did not get to the United States until 1994 (in Boston). When the San Francisco Ballet finally did it in 2012, they imported the production from the National Ballet of Canada in Toronto; I saw this production at the War Memorial Opera House in San Francisco on 28 March 2013, in fact at an extra performance put on after the regular run because of audience demand.

Cranko took the story from Pushkin's original verse novel as well as Tchaikovsky's opera, but presenting this as a ballet without words created some obvious challenges. The first and most crucial was how to stage the letter-writing scene, this most critical part of the opera, if words cannot be used. In the opera Tatiana can sing while she sits and writes, but watching a dancer sitting and writing would hardly do. Cranko solved this by giving Tatiana and Onegin a *pas de deux* in place of her writing, to be perceived by the audience as a flight of her imagination— her illusion of how good things could be between them. Another *pas de deux* comes in the third act before she rejects him, tearing up his letter as he did with hers earlier, balancing her ecstasy in Act 1 with the appropriate dose of moral realism. Clearly in a ballet, music needed to be provided for corps de ballet dance scenes, and most of this could come from *Cherevichki*, an opera rich with dance scenes, as noted in chapter 7. The result has been as it were a fourth ballet by Tchaikovsky, not on the same level as *Swan Lake*, *The Sleeping Beauty*, or *The*

Nutcracker, but still a ballet that in an engaging way has allowed Tchaikovsky to live beyond the grave, giving us something new and enduring over half a century after his death. We need not worry about Tchaikovsky's music disappearing from the repertory any time soon, and with him also living in cinema as well as a new ballet, his future as one of the most loved of all composers appears to be secure.

GLOSSARY

Absolute music. Music that has no programmatic or topical meaning beyond the music itself; it can also be referred to as pure music.

Aria. An extended vocal piece, usually melodic in character with an orchestral accompaniment, and sometimes in a three-part (ABA) form. It can be used in operas, oratorios, or other larger vocal compositions, or it can be self-standing.

Arioso. A short aria, for singer and orchestra, with potential for great emotional depth despite the short length.

Cadenza. A section typically late in a concerto movement in which the solo instrument, playing by itself, can improvise its own material, prompted by music from that movement, and often with virtuosic flourishes.

Canzonetta. A light vocal piece originating in the sixteenth century. If used in instrumental works it implies something with a carefree vocal flavor.

Chromatic. Derived from the chromatic or stepwise scale. Chord progressions can be described as chromatic if they deviate from the usual diatonic progressions by moving in a stepwise manner.

Corps de ballet. In Tchaikovsky's time a dance performed by an even number of dancers, usually all doing the same step at the same time in perfect symmetry. Early in the twentieth century that became less rigid, as different ranks could do different steps.

Counterpoint. The interaction of two or more independent lines. The emphasis is on their horizontal motion, but the lines also align harmonically, although not always. J. S. Bach was the great master of counterpoint, with such pieces as two- and three-part inventions and highly complex fugues, typically with four lines.

Da capo aria. An aria with a three-part form (ABA) in which B uses material contrasting to A, and the return of A will not be written out (but with the expectation of alteration through ornamentation).

Deceptive cadence. A cadence that progresses from V (dominant) to vi (submediant) instead of the expected V to I (tonic).

Diatonic. Based on major or minor scales; it can also refer to harmonic progressions that do not deviate from steps between chords that can be found in these scales.

Diminution. The statement of a theme in uniformly shorter note values. For example, if the original statement had been in quarter notes, its diminution will be in eighth notes.

Divisi. Divided, meaning in orchestral writing that instruments normally playing a line together will divide into two or more lines.

Dominant (pedal). Next to the tonic (home chord or key), the most important and strongest point of departure or arrival in a harmonic progression. In major or minor scales this is a fifth above the tonic, and its importance as a destination applies to both harmonic progressions and the modulation of keys. As a key destination it needs to be prepared by its own dominant, allowing it to be felt as *in* the dominant key and not simply *on* it. A dominant pedal extends the dominant with a fixed bass line a fifth above the tonic.

Dynamics. The level of loudness or softness of the volume.

Enharmonic. The same notes with different spellings, such as A sharp and B flat.

Fugue, fugato. A highly developed procedure of imitative counterpoint, in which the theme is stated successively in all voices and undergoes an elaborate expansion or development. It may have more than one theme, and may comprise an entire composition. "Fugato" refers to a passage or section within a larger composition that behaves in a fugue-like way.

Group. The term I prefer in discussions of sonata form to distinguish the two sections of the exposition that encompass the two primary key areas. The first group will be in the tonic key, and the second group in the dominant (or relative major if the work is in a minor key). Some older definitions use the word "theme" instead of "group," but this adds confusion since the group may have more than one theme.

Harmonics. In string playing harmonics are produced by touching the string lightly above the note being stopped. This alters the vibration of the string and produces a frequency higher than the stopped note, and that frequency depends on the ratio by which the light touch divides the string. When the composer desires this, the mark ° is typically placed above the note, and this allows notes much higher than those possible from normal stops.

Leitmotif. A musical fragment that takes on dramatic significance, possibly representing a person, object, or emotion. When it recurs in the course of an opera, as happens typically in Wagner's, it reminds the listener of the association. This can become much more complex when the fragment is developed motivically, and can interact with other leitmotifs.

Major, minor. The two most commonly used scales, or musical building blocks, during the eighteenth and much of the nineteenth centuries. The major scale (do, re, mi, fa, sol, la, ti; also known by the names tonic, supertonic, mediant, subdominant, dominant, submediant, leading tone) has seven notes moving upward by these intervals: whole step, whole step, half step, whole step, whole step, whole step (followed by a half step back to the tonic). The minor scale has different harmonic and melodic forms, but the constants are the fact that the mediant (third) and submediant (sixth) are a half step lower than in the major scale.

Meter. With the use of bar lines the number of pulses within the bar defines the meter. The most common are two (2/4), three (3/4), four (4/4 or C for common time), and six (6/8), but many others are possible, such as 9/8 and 5/4 (used by Tchaikovsky in the second movement of the Sixth Symphony). In each case there will be an alternation of strong and weak beats, with the strongest coming on the first beat. Movements or pieces do not have to retain the same meter throughout, and composers can temporarily change the meter by putting accents on normally weak beats.

Modulation. The means by which key changes occur, which can happen swiftly or be drawn out over a more extended period. Some modulations are fundamental to form, such as the move to the dominant in the exposition of sonata form, and the return to the tonic for the recapitulation. Some modulations can generate considerable tension, especially with changes to unexpected keys.

Motif, motivic. A motif is a recognizable musical passage shorter than a theme, usually only a few notes, which can be used in a motivic manner to generate development.

Neoclassicism. A trend generally associated with Stravinsky and Prokofiev of using models from eighteenth-century music, sometimes identifiable compositions but more commonly for the purpose of putting expressive constraints on the music, by means of motivic clarity and formal symmetry.

Obbligato. A passage that features a solo instrument in an orchestral texture.

Orchestration. The ways of combining instruments in orchestral writing in order to generate different sound textures in the orchestral palette. Unlike instrumentation, which simply refers to the instruments used, orchestration concerns the nature and quality of sounds that varying combinations produce. Some composers start with a short score, adding orchestration later, but not Tchaikovsky, who considered this a fundamental part of composition.

Pas d'action. A dance for a dramatic scene.

Pas d'amour. A dance for a love scene.

Pas de deux. *Pas* is literally "step" in French. The number in French indicates the number of dancers. A grand *pas de deux* is typically the climax of the ballet, for the ballerina and her partner, and may consist of solo dances as well as the two of them together.

Patter. A passage in a song or light aria with rapid repetition, and usually with a comical association.

Phrase. A unit of musical syntax, comparable to a sentence in spoken language, which acts as a unit in the construction of larger musical periods or paragraphs.

Point (en pointe). A dancer is on point when she stands or dances on the tips of her toes, made possible by special blocked shoes with room allowing her to pad her toes.

Recitative. In any large vocal work there can be various kinds of recitative, ranging from secco (dry) to get through dialogue quickly, to accompanied, with musical content that allows it to convey deep emotions (with full orchestral accompaniment). Tchaikovsky generally only used the latter.

Relative major. For works in minor keys the relative major key has the same number of sharps or flats as the home minor key, and is a minor third above.

Rhythm. The pattern of movement in time. Calibrations of this normally involve whole notes, half notes, quarter notes, eighth notes, sixteenth notes, and thirty-second notes, each of these being half the length of the previous one, and they can be extended by half the length again by adding a dot after the note. Other patterns can be added—for example, by groupings of three to make triplets. Rhythmic patterns can have topical associations, such as with life-affirming dances or folk music.

Scherzo. Joke (in Italian). A piece or movement with a light, often humorous, character.

Semitone. A melodic interval of a half step. Most scales involve combinations of semitones and whole steps, although the chromatic scale consists of semitones only.

Sonata form. A form or musical procedure that originated in the eighteenth century and became the norm for first movements of instrumental works (not to be confused with sonata, which simply denotes a type of instrumental composition). The three basic sections include an exposition, where themes are introduced, which itself has two sections or groups—the first in the tonic and the second in the dominant (or relative major for works in minor keys); a development, in which the themes can interact amid key changes that at times can be rapid; and a recapitulation back in the home key, where the themes recur but usually have been altered in some way. This format allowed a dramatic approach not unlike works for the stage, where the first section introduces the protagonists, the second sees them in dramatic interaction or conflict, and the third attempts some sort of resolution, which may or may not be successful. Movements in sonata form may begin with an introduction, usually slow in contrast to the faster tempo of what follows, and end with a coda. The term "form" is in many ways inappropriate, since this is not a procedure that needs to be followed rigorously, and in fact can become more dramatic when it deviates from the expected outline.

Sonatina. With the characteristics of a sonata but on a smaller scale, most often used in piano pieces.

Suite. A type of composition originating in the seventeenth century made up of dance movements, such as the allemande, courante, sarabande, and gigue. Even though each dance has a distinctive character, the combination of these in a suite will have some element of unity.

Syncopation. Instead of writing notes on the beats of the bar, composers create syncopation by placing notes in a continuous pattern on the offbeats, thereby generating an element of instability. This became fundamental to jazz in the twentieth century, but composers earlier often used syncopation for contrast with more stable material.

Theme. A passage usually at least a phrase in length with definable melodic material that gives the movement or piece distinctive character. Since form in music depends on the engagement of the memory, themes help to define the strong points in a formal structure, such as the return of the opening theme corresponding with the return of the home key to mark the beginning of the recapitulation in sonata form.

Timbre. Tone color, texture, or quality.

Tonic. In both harmonic and tonal progressions the tonic gives the home harmony or tonality. Pieces or movements usually start and end in the tonic, but not all nineteenth-century composers adhered to that.

Transcription. The adaptation of a composition for an instrument or instruments other than the original one(s). Liszt especially favored this type of adaptation—for example, setting songs by Schubert for piano alone, with added virtuosity.

Transposition. Rewriting (or performing) music in a key other than the original one. A singer with a baritone voice wishing to sing something written for a tenor will transpose to a lower key.

Triad. The combination of the three notes that make up a chord in its most basic form, these tones being the first, third, and fifth degrees of the scale. Triads form the building blocks of harmony, and can be in root position (with the first degree as the lowest note), first inversion (built on the third), and second inversion (with the fifth as bass). More complex chords, such as sevenths and ninths, still contain triads, and then build up in increments of thirds. A triad can be major (major third

+ minor third, from bottom to top), minor (minor third + major third), or diminished (minor third + minor third).

Tritone. Also known as an augmented fourth (or diminished fifth), making the interval a semitone higher than a perfect fourth (or a semitone lower than a perfect fifth). In the Middle Ages composers avoided this interval because of its unnatural and somewhat dissonant character, even referring to it as the *diabolus in musica* (the devil in music). Because of that, the association can at times be implied in more recent music.

Tutti. All: in a concerto this indicates the ensemble as opposed to the solo.

SELECTED READING

Abraham, Gerald, ed. *The Music of Tchaikovsky*. New York: W. W. Norton, 1946.

Bowen, Catherine Drinker, and Barbara von Meck. *"Beloved Friend": The Story of Tchaikowsky and Nadejda von Meck*. New York: Random House, 1937. An older source of the letters, but still useful.

Brown, David. *Tchaikovsky*. Vol. 1, *The Early Years, 1840–1874*. New York: W. W. Norton, 1978.

———. *Tchaikovsky*. Vol. 2, *The Crisis Years, 1874–1878*. New York: W. W. Norton, 1983.

———. *Tchaikovsky*. Vol. 3, *The Years of Wandering, 1878–1885*. London: Victor Gollancz, 1986.

———. *Tchaikovsky*. Vol. 4, *The Final Years, 1885–1893*. New York: W. W. Norton, 1991. These four volumes comprise the most comprehensive biography in English, and put forward a high level of scholarship.

———. *Tchaikovsky Remembered*. London: Faber and Faber, 1993.

———. *Tchaikovsky: The Man and His Music*. New York: Pegasus Books, 2007.

Chasins, Abram. *The Van Cliburn Legend*. New York: Doubleday, 1959. An excellent account of Cliburn's experiences performing in the Tchaikovsky Competition, from the time.

The Collected Tales of Nikolai Gogol. Translated by Richard Pevear and Larissa Volokhonsky. New York: Vintage Books, 1999.

The Diaries of Tchaikovsky. Translated by Wladimir Lakond. New York: W. W. Norton, 1945.

Evans, Edwin. *Tchaikovsky*. London: J. M. Dent and Sons, 1902. An older English biography closer to the composer's time.

Fisher, Jennifer. *"The Nutcracker*: A Cultural Icon." In *The Cambridge Companion to Ballet*, edited by Marian Kant, 246–255. Cambridge: Cambridge University Press, 2007. Fisher describes the scope of the performance tradition.

Fleming-Markarian, Margaret. *Symbolism in Nineteenth-Century Ballet: Giselle, Coppélia, Sleeping Beauty and Swan Lake*. Oxford and New York: Peter Lang, 2012.

Garafola, Lynn. "Russian Ballet in the Age of Petipa." In *The Cambridge Companion to Ballet*, 151–163. Places Petipa in the context of his time.

Garden, Edward. *Tchaikovsky*. London: Dent, 1973. Another fine biography.

Garden, Edward, and Nigel Gotteri, eds. *"To My Best Friend": Correspondence between Tchaikovsky and Nadezhda von Meck, 1876–1878*. Translated by Gallina von Meck. Oxford: Clarendon Press, 1993. An excellent scholarly translation—a pity it's the only volume of the intended three.

Hertz, Henrik. *King René's Daughter.* Translated by Theodore Martin. London: Wm. S. Orr, 1850.

Hoffmann, E. T. A. *Nutcracker and Mouse King.* Translated by Joachim Neugroschel. New York: Penguin Books, 2007.

Holden, Anthony. *Tchaikovsky.* London: Transworld, 1995. A very readable biography.

Hurley, Thérèse. "Opening the Door to a Fairy-Tale World: Tchaikovsky's Ballets." In *The Cambridge Companion to Ballet,* 164–174.

Jackson, Timothy L. *Tchaikovsky: Symphony No. 6 (Pathétique).* Cambridge: Cambridge University Press, 1999.

Kearney, Leslie, ed. *Tchaikovsky and His World.* Princeton: Princeton University Press, 1998. An important collection of essays, prepared in conjunction with the summer series at Bard College. It includes letters about his homosexuality not previously published in English.

Kersley, Leo, and Janet Sinclair. *A Dictionary of Dance Terms.* London: Adam and Charles Black, 1977.

Koegler, Horst. *The Concise Oxford Dictionary of Ballet.* Second edition. London: Oxford University Press, 1982.

Morton, Lawrence. "Stravinsky and Tchaikovsky: *Le Baiser de la fée.*" In *Stravinsky: A New Appraisal of His Work,* edited by Paul Henry Lang, 47–60. New York: W. W. Norton, 1963. Has useful information, but Morton does not disguise his disdain for Tchaikovsky.

Orlova, Aleksandra. *Tchaikovsky: A Self-Portrait.* Oxford: Oxford University Press, 1990.

Palmer, Christopher. *Dimitri Tiomkin: A Portrait.* London: T. E. Books, 1984.

Perrault, Charles. *The Complete Fairy Tales.* Translated by Christopher Betts. Oxford: Oxford University Press, 2009.

Poznansky, Alexander. *Tchaikovsky's Last Days: A Documentary Study.* Oxford: Clarendon Press, 1996. A collection of documents.

———. *Tchaikovsky: The Quest for the Inner Man.* New York: Schirmer Books, 1991. A psychological probing into the composer's mind.

———. *Tchaikovsky through Others' Eyes.* Bloomington: Indiana University Press, 1999.

Pushkin, Alexander. *Eugene Onegin.* Translated by Charles Johnston. London: Penguin Books, 1977.

———. *The Queen of Spades and Other Stories.* Translated by Rosemary Edmonds. London: Penguin Books, 1962.

Robinson, Harlow. *Sergei Prokofiev: A Biography.* New York: Paragon House, 1987.

Russian Masters 1: Glinka, Borodin, Balakirev, Musorgsky, Tchaikovsky. The New Grove, edited by Stanley Sadie. New York: W. W. Norton, 1986.

Schmidgall, Gary. *Literature as Opera.* Oxford: Oxford University Press, 1977. Has an interesting chapter on the differences between Pushkin's and Tchaikovsky's *Eugene Onegin.*

Schroeder, David. *Hitchcock's Ear: Music and the Director's Art.* London and New York: Continuum, 2012.

Seroff, Victor I. *Rachmaninoff.* New York: Simon and Schuster, 1950.

Shostakovich, Dimitri, et al. *Russian Symphony: Thoughts about Tchaikovsky.* Freeport, NY: Books for Libraries Press, 1947. A collection of essays, with a useful although short introduction by Shostakovich.

Stanislavski, Constantin, and Pavel Rumyantsev. *Stanislavski on Opera.* Translated and edited by Elizabeth Reynolds Hapgood. New York: Theatre Arts Books, 1975. An important study of how to direct *Eugene Onegin* by one of the greatest of all dramaturges.

Tchaikovsky, Modeste. *The Life and Letters of Peter Ilich Tchaikovsky.* Translated by Rosa Newmarch. 2 vols. New York: Vienna House, 1973. Gives the composer's life from the perspective of his brother, with much omitted that he considered unsuitable.

Tchaikovsky, Piotr Ilyich. *Letters to His Family: An Autobiography.* Translated by Galina von Meck. New York: Stein and Day, 1981. A good collection of letters.

Volkov, Solomon. *Balanchine's Tchaikovsky: Interviews with George Balanchine.* New York: Simon and Schuster, 1985.

Warrack, John. *Tchaikovsky.* London: Penguin, 1973. Another highly readable biography.

————. *Tchaikovsky's Ballet Music*. Seattle: University of Washington Press, 1979. A short but perceptive study of the ballets.

————. *Tchaikovsky: Symphonies and Concertos*. London: BBC, 1974. In the same series as the item above.

Wiley, Roland John. *A Century of Russian Ballet: Documents and Eyewitness Accounts, 1810–1910*. Oxford: Clarendon Press, 1990.

————. *Tchaikovsky*. Oxford University Press, 2009. An excellent biography, with some of the most up-to-date research, and perceptive discussions of the music.

————. *Tchaikovsky's Ballets*. Oxford: Clarendon Press, 1985. A comprehensive and indispensible study of the ballets.

Yoffe, Elkhonon. *Tchaikovsky in America: The Composer's Visit in 1891*. New York: Oxford University Press, 1986.

Zajaczkowski, Henry. *An Introduction to Tchaikovsky's Operas*. Westport: Praeger, 2005. A useful study, with relatively short chapters on all the operas.

SELECTED LISTENING

DVDS

Anna Karenina. Directed by Bernard Rose. Burbank, CA: Warner Home Video, 2011.

Black Swan. Directed by Darren Aronofsky. Beverly Hills, CA: Twentieth Century Fox, 2010.

Cherevichki [The Royal Opera, Covent Garden]. Directed by Francesca Zambello. London: Opus Arte, 2010.

The Enchantress [Nizhegorodsky State Academic Theatre of Opera and Ballet]. Pleasantville, NY: Video Artists International, 2010.

Eugene Onegin [Metropolitan Opera]. Directed by Fiona Shaw. Berlin: Deutsche Grammophon, 2014.

Fantasia [remastered]. Directed by Walt Disney. Burbank, CA: Buena Vista Pictures, 1990.

Iolanta [The Bolshoi Opera]. Directed by Oleg Moralev. Pleasantville, NY: Video Artists International, 2010.

The Maid of Orleans [The Bolshoi Opera]. Directed by Boris Pokrovsky. West Long Branch, NJ: Kultur, 1993.

Mazeppa [Kirov Opera and Ballet]. Directed by Irina Molostova. London: Decca Music Group, 2004.

The Music Lovers. Directed by Ken Russell. Beverly Hills, CA: Twentieth Century Fox, 2011.

The Queen of Spades [The Bolshoi Opera]. West Long Branch, NJ: Kultur, n.d.

San Francisco Ballet Nutcracker. Directed by Matthew Diamond. London: Opus Arte, 2008.

The Sleeping Beauty [The Kirov Ballet]. Directed by Elena Macheret. West Long Branch, NJ: Kultur, n.d.

The Sleeping Beauty [National Ballet of Canada]. Directed by Normal Campbell. Pleasantville, NY: Video Artists International, 2004.

Swan Lake [Margot Fonteyn and Rudolf Nureyev]. Directed by Truck Branss. Hamburg: Deutsche Grammophon, 2005.

Swan Lake [Mariinsky Theatre]. Directed by Ross MacGibbon. London: Decca, 2007.

The Talented Mr. Ripley. Directed by Anthony Minghella. Hollywood: Paramount Pictures, 1999.

Tchaikovsky. Directed by Igor Talankin. New York: Kino International Release, 1985.

Tchaikovsky: The Tragic Life of a Musical Genius. Directed by Matthew Whiteman. London: BBC, 2008.

Van Cliburn in Moscow. Volume 1 [Beethoven, Piano Concerto No. 5; Tchaikovsky, Piano Concerto No. 1]. Pleasantville, NY: Video Artists International, 2008.

CDS

Complete Concertos. Werner Haas, piano; Orchestre National de l'Opéra de Monte-Carlo, conducted by Eliahu Inbal. Salvatore Accardo, violin; BBC Symphony Orchestra, conducted by Sir Colin Davis. Maurice Gendron, cello; Wiener Symphoniker, conducted by Christoph von Dohnányi. Philips, 2003. 475 256-2. Includes everything.

Complete Piano Works [solo]. Viktoria Postnikova. Warner Classics & Jazz, 2008. 2564 69675-1. On seven CDs, with everything included.

Complete Suites for Orchestra. New Philharmonia Orchestra, conducted by Antal Dorati. Philips, 1996. 454 253-2.

In the Silence of Night [songs]. Irina Mishura, mezzo-soprano; Valéry Ryvkin, piano. VAI Audio, 1996. VAIA 2003. Only a sampling of the songs.

The Oprichnik. Orchestra e Coro del Teatro Lirico di Cagliari, conducted by Gennady Rozhdestvensky. Brilliant Classics, 2003. 94390. This opera is not available on DVD.

Orchestral Works [symphonic poems]. Detroit Symphony Orchestra and National Symphony Orchestra, conducted by Antal Dorati. London, 1994. 443 003-2. Does not include symphonies.

Piano Concerto No. 1. Vladimir Horowitz; NBC Symphony Orchestra, conducted by Arturo Toscanini. RCA Victor, 1992 (recorded in 1943). 60321-2-RG. A historic performance by one of the great pianists.

Piano Concerto No. 1; Symphony No. 4. Vladimir Ashkenazy; London Symphony Orchestra, conducted by Lorin Maazel. Decca, 2011. 478 3367. First-rate solo performance.

Souvenir de Florence, Op. 70; Serenade in C, Op. 48. Irish Chamber Orchestra, conducted by Fionuala Hunt. Black Box, 1999.

The String Quartets. St. Petersburg String Quartet. Sony, 1993. SM2K 57 654.

Symphonies 1–6; "Manfred" Symphony; Romeo and Juliet; Francesca da Rimini. London Philharmonic Orchestra, conducted by Mstislav Rostropovich. EMI, 1995. 50999 5 14493 2 7.

Trio for Piano, Violin and Violoncello in A Minor, Op. 50. Yefim Bronfman, piano; Cho-Liang Lin, violin; Gary Hoffman, cello. Sony, 1994. SK 53269.

Violin Concerto. Nathan Milstein; Wiener Philharmoniker, conducted by Claudio Abbado. Deutsche Grammophon, 1973. 00289 477 5914. A fine performance by a great violinist.

INDEX

Actors Studio, 88
Allegri, Gregorio, 54; *Miserere*, 54
Anantawan, Adrian, 121–122
Aronofsky, Darren, 190
Artôt, Désirée, 4–5, 7, 10, 20–22, 27–29, 30, 31, 159, 181, 186
audience, xvii, 5, 11–12, 24, 40, 62, 73, 105, 112, 117, 142, 152, 162, 166, 189
Auer, Leopold, 35, 48
Auschwitz, 46
autobiographical, 4, 12, 17, 129, 131

Bach, Johann Sebastian, 21, 40, 50, 156, 158, 187
Balakirev, Mily Alexeyevich, 1, 6–8, 123, 178
balalaika, 53
Balanchine, George, 164–165
Bartók, Béla, 45, 172
Batyushkov, Konstantin Nikolayevich, 5
Beaumarchais, Caron de, 137; *The Barber of Seville*, 137; *The Marriage of Figaro*, 137
Beczala, Piotr, 89
Beethoven, Ludwig van, viii, 4, 25–26, 28, 40, 41–42, 43–45, 49, 51, 105, 106–107, 111, 116, 122, 123, 126, 127, 131; *Diabelli Variations*, 51; *Fidelio*, 43; Piano Concerto No. 4, 26; Piano Sonata, op. 13 (*Pathétique*), 127; Piano Sonata, op. 101, 116, 126; String

Quartet, op. 132, 44–45; String Quartet, op. 135, 44; Symphony No. 3 (Eroica), 26, 126; Symphony No. 5, 25–26, 107, 116, 126, 131; Symphony No. 6 (Pastoral), 4, 105; Symphony No. 9, 123, 127
Begichev, Vladimir Petrovich, 61
Bellini, Vincenzo, 43
Berg, Alban, 22; *Chamber Concerto*, 22; *Lyric Suite*, 22
Berlioz, Hector, 4, 40, 43, 105, 111, 125, 127, 130, 170; *Symphonie fantastique*, 125, 130, 170
Bizet, Georges, 128, 140, 151; *Carmen*, 128–129, 140
Black Swan, 177, 190–192
Bolshoy, 60, 141
Borge, Victor, 25
Borodin, Alexander Porfir'yevich, 1, 45, 178
Boston, 12–15, 20, 193
Boston Pops Orchestra, 12
Brahms, Johannes, 40, 44–45, 105
British Broadcasting Corporation (BBC), 65, 141, 185–186
Broughton, Simon, 185
Brown, David, xx, 20, 22, 185
Bülow, Hans von, 20
Buketoff, Igor, 13, 14
Byron, George Gordon, Lord, 4, 11; *Manfred*, 11

ABOUT THE AUTHOR

David Schroeder is professor emeritus at Dalhousie University in Halifax, Canada, and he holds a PhD from Cambridge University. He has given frequent pre-concert talks, including for the Mostly Mozart series at Lincoln Center in New York, and has been interviewed by CBC, BBC, NPR, and numerous newspapers. His other books include *Mozart in Revolt*; *Haydn and the Enlightenment*; *Cinema's Illusions, Opera's Allure*; *Our Schubert: His Enduring Legacy*; and *Hitchcock's Ear: Music and the Director's Art*. His latest book is *Experiencing Mozart: A Listener's Companion*.

CPSIA information can be obtained at www.ICGtesting.com
Printed in the USA
BVOW03*1647020215

385796BV00002B/2/P

9 781442 232990